Welfare for Autocrats

Welfare for Autocrats

How Social Assistance in China Cares for its Rulers

JENNIFER PAN

OXFORD
UNIVERSITY PRESS

OXFORD
UNIVERSITY PRESS

Oxford University Press is a department of the University of Oxford. It furthers
the University's objective of excellence in research, scholarship, and education
by publishing worldwide. Oxford is a registered trade mark of Oxford University
Press in the UK and in certain other countries.

Published in the United States of America by Oxford University Press
198 Madison Avenue, New York, NY 10016, United States of America.

© Oxford University Press 2020

Library of Congress Control Number: 2020932174

ISBN 978-0-19-008743-2 (paperback)
ISBN 978-0-19-008742-5 (hardcover)

3 5 7 9 8 6 4 2

Paperback printed by Marquis, Canada
Hardback printed by Bridgeport National Bindery, Inc., United States of America

to my family

Welfare for Autocrats

What are the costs of the Chinese regime's fixation on quelling dissent in the name of political order, or "stability"? In *Welfare for Autocrats*, Jennifer Pan shows that China has reshaped its major social assistance program, Dibao, around this pre-occupation, turning an effort to alleviate poverty into a tool of surveillance and repression. This distortion of Dibao damages perceptions of government competence and legitimacy and can trigger unrest among those denied benefits. Pan traces how China's approach to enforcing order transformed at the turn of the 21st century and identifies a phenomenon she calls seepage whereby one policy—in this case, quelling dissent—alters the allocation of resources and goals of unrelated areas of government. Using novel data sets and a variety of methodologies, *Welfare for Autocrats* challenges the view that concessions and repression are distinct strategies and departs from the assumption that all tools of repression were originally designed as such. Pan reaches the startling conclusion that China's preoccupation with order not only comes at great human cost but in the case of Dibao may well backfire.

Contents

List of Figures

List of Tables

Acknowledgments

I began the research that launched this book in 2011, and I made my final edits in 2019. I could not have made this journey without the support of many, many people.

To Elizabeth Perry, my dissertation committee chair, thank you for giving me the courage to pursue my passions. It is a rare gift to receive guidance that is invaluable and influential, but given in a way that allowed me ample room to pursue my own interests and approach. This book would not exist if not for you.

To Gary King, my mentor and teacher, thank you for your generosity in every sense of the word. I have learned (and continue to learn) an extraordinary amount from you, and in the process I discovered the joy of research and discovery. Your belief in me inspired me to address larger questions than I would otherwise have dared.

To my many colleagues in graduate school at Harvard University, thank you for your ideas, questions, and insights for my dissertation, which grew into this book. Thanks to my dissertation committee—Elizabeth Perry, Gary King, Jorge Dominguez, and Peter Hall—for bringing your fierce intellects and diverse perspectives to bear on my project. To my dissertation reading group— Molly Roberts, Shelby Grossman, Amanda Pinkston, Chiara Superti, and Vanessa Williamson—thank you for reading more versions of this book than I can fathom. Your friendship and support sustained me through many challenges. To my CGIS office mates, thank you for being the best sounding boards.

To the incredible and tireless research assistants at Boston University, Fudan University, Harvard University, Stanford University, Wuhan University, Xi'an Jiaotong University, Zhejiang University, and Zhengzhou University, thank you for your work on this project over the years. To my Chinese colleagues and friends, thank you for helping me build such a great research team, and for all of the other introductions, insights, and assistance along the way. A special thanks to Tianguang Meng for his support. To the wonderful librarians at Harvard and Stanford, Nancy Hearst and Zhaohui Xue, thank you for your responsiveness and help on my many requests. I am solely responsible for all mistakes of fact, interpretation, or analysis in this work.

To my colleagues across Stanford, thank you for making me feel welcome and well supported. To my colleagues in the Department of Communication, thank you for your camaraderie and suggestions at the faculty dinner and other points along the way. To Jean Oi, Andy Walder, and the other participants of the China Social Science Workshop, thank you for pushing me to get to the bottom of what is going on. To the communities at CASBS and IRiSS, many thanks for your support and suggestions.

To all those who have read this book or its various incarnations all the way through, I am deeply grateful. To Dorothy Solinger, I am incredibly appreciative of your generosity in engaging with my work. Your scholarship on Dibao and China have been invaluable, and I am in awe of your tireless energy. To Mark Frazier, Steve Levitsky, Prerna Singh, and Jeremy Wallace, thank you for your insights and advice at my early book workshop. To Ben Read, thank you for sharing your deep understanding of urban China and its neighborhoods with me. I am also deeply indebted to my Chinese politics reading group for your ideas, insights, and inspiration.

Many thanks to those who have provided comments and suggestions at different stages of this project—Melani Cammett, Amy Catalinac, Jidong Chen, Sheena Chestnut-Greitens, Greg Distelhosrt, Martin Dimitrov, Mary Gallagher, Yue Hou, Haifeng Huang, Nahomi Ichino, Torben Iversen, Iain Johnston, Horacio Larreguy, Ya-Wen Lei, Peter Lorentzen, John Marshall, Dan Mattingly, Gwyneth McClendon, Noah Nathan, Kevin O'Brien, Susan Pharr, James Robinson, Arthur Spirling, Brandon Stewart, Rory Truex, Yuhua Wang, Yanhui Wu, Chen Xi, Yiqing Xu, David Yang, and Daniel Ziblatt—as well as participants at the Comparative Politics Workshop at Harvard, Berkeley Comparative Colloquium, Authoritarian Practices Beyond National Regimes workshop at the University of Amsterdam, and Understanding the Demand for Democracy workshop at the University of Munich Center for Advanced Studies. For those I have forgotten to include, it is not from lack of appreciation but my forgetfulness.

To my editorial and production teams, thank you for shepherding this book to publication. Many thanks to all the reviewers for your honest reactions and helpful suggestions.

I want to acknowledge all of the institutions and organizations whose funding made this research possible. I am grateful for the support of the Ash Center for Democratic Governance and Innovation, the Harvard Academy for International and Area Studies, and the Institute for Quantitative Social Science. My fieldwork in China, conducted over the course of three years, was funded by a National Science Foundation Doctoral Dissertation Research Improvement

Grant (SES-1226681), the Desmond and Whitney Shum Fellowship from the Fairbank Center for Chinese Studies, the Real Estate Academic Initiative at Harvard University, the Samuel P. Huntington Doctoral Dissertation Fellowship, and the Samuels Family Research Fellowship from the Weatherhead Center for International Affairs, as well as funding from the Harvard University Asia Center.

To my former colleagues at McKinsey, Clinton Foundation, and the Chinese Center for HIV/AIDS, thank you for giving me the opportunity to learn and to grow. To the NYO BA class of 2005, you are the most diverse and impressive group of people I know: thank you for inspiring me with your vision, passion, and fearlessness and for supporting me in the rather unorthodox transition from professional services to academia. My life is much richer (in all but the monetary sense) for it. To my classmates and teachers at CHS and Princeton, thank you for expanding my world and helping me take the first steps of the journey that I am on today.

My final acknowledgment is for my incredible family, to whom this book is dedicated. Your boundless love, patience, and support is what makes everything possible. First and foremost, thanks to my husband, Jared Chung, for being my partner in all things, for urging me to think big, and for making the sacrifices big and small that allow me to pursue my passion. Thanks to my in-laws for your continual encouragement and enthusiasm. Finally, I am profoundly thankful to my parents, Liu Xiangping and Pan Youfang, and my grandmother, Li Huaian, who have given so much of themselves so I can be where I am and who I am today. 谢谢您们为我做的一切.

I

Introduction

Mr. and Mrs. Wang are street vendors, selling mops, wash basins, clay pots, and a mixed assortment of household items not far from their apartment, where they live with their nine-year-old son in a city on China's eastern seaboard.[1] After a serious injury in late 2011 rendered Mr. Wang unable to work, the family's income plummeted. Mrs. Wang turned to the Dibao program. *Dibao* is the common term for China's Minimum Livelihood Guarantee Scheme (最低生活保障), a social assistance program providing unconditional cash transfers to households below a certain income. Much to her dismay, local administrators in her neighborhood[2] told Mrs. Wang that her family had no chance of obtaining the benefit and that she need not even apply. They cited as reasons for their refusal the fact that she could increase her income by finding a second or third job, by borrowing from relatives, or by selling family assets.

A 10-minute walk away in a similar neighborhood, Mr. Li recently qualified for Dibao. Mr. Li's neighborhood administrators proactively helped him obtain Dibao, and his family receives several hundred yuan a month from the program as well as housing subsidies, free health exams, reduced utilities costs, and other intermittent cash and in-kind benefits throughout the year. These benefits are very helpful for Mr. Li, his wife, and their teenage son. Mr. Li is in his 40s, and he is in good health in spite of a small injury to his left elbow. He is not currently employed.

The Wang family and the Li family both face severe financial difficulties. The adults in both families rely on part-time and seasonal jobs that do not provide health or other benefits, and both families have school-aged children they must support. What accounts for their differential treatment? The reasons

---

1. All interviewees directly referenced in this book are given pseudonyms to protect their identities (Ang 2016; Oi 1999; Shirk 1993; Tsai 2007).

2. 社区, which I have translated as *neighborhood*, could also be translated as *community*. Neighborhoods are the urban equivalent of China's rural villages, roughly similar in population and having similar jurisdiction.

neighborhood administrators referenced in rejecting Mrs. Wang were economic, but the Wang family has lower income and lower likelihood of potential access to income than the Li family because Mrs. Wang is its only potential worker, while in the Li family both Mr. and Mrs. Li could work. Neither the economic conditions of the household nor the financial constraints of local governments explain this difference in distribution. The two families reside in the same district of the same city, and although neighborhood administrators directed them differently, the two families sought funds from the same pool. The next explanation that comes to mind is corruption, that somehow because of corruption at the point of welfare distribution, one family ended up with benefits while the other did not. However, the two households have similar social ties within their neighborhoods, and neither household has relatives or long-standing acquaintances among neighborhood administrators or upper-level government officials. While corruption and so-called *favor Dibao* was a highly publicized problem of the Dibao program during the late 2000s, the central regime adopted measures in the early 2010s to standardize the program and reduce the discretion of front-line workers. I found no evidence that program administrators distributed Dibao funds to the Li household as a favor or reward, or as a result of some dyadic exchange. The one notable difference between the two families is that Mr. Li was recently released from prison. Could this account for the Lis obtaining Dibao? And if so, why?

I had come to China to examine differences in social welfare benefits between regions. It was the end of the Hu Jintao era, when social policies had expanded in a variety of areas (Brown, de Brauw, and Yang 2009; Huang 2014, 2015; Lin, Liu, and Chen 2009; Wang 2004). Dibao was China's only non-regressive social welfare program, and the largest unconditional cash transfer program in the world (Gao and Riskin 2009). Unlike conditional cash transfer programs—such as Bolsa Família in Brazil and Oportunidades in Mexico—unconditional cash transfer programs allow recipients to use transferred funds without constraining consumption choices. Research on unconditional cash transfer programs has shown their positive effects on education and income in countries outside of China (Aizer et al. 2016; Baird et al. 2014; Baird, McIntosh, and Özler 2011; Haushofer and Shapiro 2016; Hulme, Hanlon, and Barrientos 2012; Milligan and Stabile 2011). What were the impacts of such a program in China? In Beijing, the policymakers I interviewed emphasized that Dibao was intended to act as a social safety net of last resort for the poor, and in particular for poor people such as the elderly, disabled, and ill who could not participate in the labor market. However, when I made my way down to neighborhoods to talk to front-line Dibao administrators and Dibao recipients, patterns of Dibao distribution did not always match this description. While I saw that many Dibao recipients were unable to work, other Dibao recipients appeared healthy and able-bodied. More puzzling, in the same city and even in the same district within the same city, people who appeared to face the same economic and physical circumstances had differential access to Dibao. What explained these differences in distribution if not fiscal constraints, clientelism, or corruption?

The answer, I came to realize, lies in the recognition that there are two logics governing the distribution of Dibao in urban China. The first logic is exactly what policymakers had emphasized. Dibao is a safety net of last resort, primarily oriented toward those who are destitute and unable to work. The Wang family failed to obtain Dibao because of this logic. In encouraging Mrs. Wang to seek additional employment and Mr. Wang to risk his health with a job that might worsen his injury, neighborhood administrators were concerned with limiting the distribution of Dibao benefits to households whose members could not participate at all in the labor market.

The second logic of Dibao distribution is to preempt threats to political order, and this logic explains the provision of Dibao to households with able-bodied individuals such as Mr. Li. Mr. Li was recently released from prison, where guards injured his left elbow while subduing him. Mr. Li is classified as belonging to the *targeted population*, individuals designated as *potential* threats to the Chinese Communist Party (CCP). Targeted populations encompass individuals whom the regime has insufficient evidence to prosecute but who are placed under intensive surveillance and control so the regime can prevent them from committing "crimes" such as protesting and petitioning in the future. Because of his injury, Mr. Li wanted to petition the government for compensation. Targeted populations are subjected to re-education, and when Mr. Li's block captain, who was a member of his re-education committee, learned of Mr. Li's plan, she informed neighborhood administrators, who in turn informed local police. Neighborhood administrators immediately helped Mr. Li obtain Dibao to "stabilize his mental state" (让他的思想情绪稳定下来) and began to monitor him more closely, which was made easier by the distribution of Dibao because the program requires beneficiaries to provide regular updates on their activities, financial and otherwise, and to open their homes to regular visits from state representatives. In eagerly providing Dibao to the Li family, neighborhood administrators were primarily concerned with public security and political order, or what the Chinese regime calls "stability."

The first logic, of limiting Dibao to the poor who cannot work, is clearly spelled out in policy documents about the Dibao program. For example, the State Council "Interim Measures for Social Assistance" (2014) requires members of Dibao households who are able-bodied to work and gives local governments the authority to reduce or revoke Dibao if recipients fail to work. What is not stated in this policy document is that by working, Dibao recipients may lose their eligibility because the program is means-tested—only households with per capita income below a certain level are eligible. This central-level policy, as well as local policies with even more stringent limitations preventing anyone capable of work from receiving Dibao, influence how front-line workers turn away people who could potentially work from applying for Dibao.

The second logic, of prioritizing Dibao to individuals to preempt disorder, is not spelled out in the main policy documents focused on the Dibao program. Instead, this logic influences the distribution of Dibao benefits through a process I call *seepage*. Seepage occurs when a goal or priority of the regime impacts an unrelated policy, not by changing the core facets of that policy but by changing how resources associated with that policy are allocated. In this case, the goal is political order; the impacted policy is Dibao. The pursuit of political order seeps into Dibao because China's strategy for enforcing political order—the *Comprehensive Management of Public Security*—requires all resources of the regime to be available for maintaining order. The Dibao policy is not changed, and core tenets of the policy are not violated. Policing policies and programs of the domestic security apparatus emphasize how people who can potentially threaten order must receive Dibao if they are eligible based on income. As a result, local administrators go out of their way to ensure that these individuals receive Dibao. Dibao becomes a tool for preserving political power, caring not for the people but instead for China's rulers.

However, many Dibao policymakers and administrators I encountered during my fieldwork genuinely want to improve the lives of the country's poor. In their minds, the logic of limiting Dibao to the poor who cannot work is the only logic of provision. The prioritization of Dibao for targeted populations, individuals undergoing re-education, and other populations the CCP seeks to control is not what comes to mind when Dibao specialists are prompted to think of the Dibao program. Similarly, administrators of the Dibao program at the neighborhood level, who in one breath turn away a Dibao applicant for having the ability to work and in the next breath go out of their way to help a targeted person obtain Dibao, do not see two separate and contradictory logics of distribution. When these front-line workers think of the Dibao program, they think: We must limit benefits to poor households that lack the capacity to participate in the labor market. When these administrators think about targeted populations, they think: We must use all resources at our disposal to manage and control these individuals. Dibao happens to be one of these resources.

The distribution of Dibao to preempt disorder requires grassroots surveillance and often relies on heuristics to identify individuals to target. When individuals are identified, the provision of Dibao benefits supports repression—what

I call *repressive assistance*—by facilitating repeated interactions as well as relationships of dependence and obligation that constrain the autonomy of targeted persons.

Even as targeted individuals are repressed and controlled through the distribution of benefits, the fact that the two logics of benefit distribution are somewhat contradictory generates new forms of protest from those who feel they are entitled to receive Dibao but are denied access. When Dibao is distributed to preempt disorder, those who are denied benefits can see that some who appear able-bodied are given benefits. Those who want to obtain Dibao but are turned away see inequity and unfairness. Their protests are typically small in scale and localized, and local administrators make use of the complexity of Dibao policies, their information advantage over residents, and threats of coercion to defuse protesters. However, demobilized residents are often left disillusioned, embittered, and resentful. The distribution of Dibao to preempt disorder is associated with lower assessments of government capabilities in providing welfare and serving the needs of citizens, as well as lower levels of satisfaction with local governments and political trust.

1.1 Political Order and "Stability"

Much of our thinking on political order is influenced by Samuel Huntington's seminal book *Political Order in Changing Societies*. In this work, Huntington describes political order as the ability of governments to effectively exert authority and to control the governed. The underlying world view is a Hobbesian one of unrelenting competition among individuals, groups, classes, and interests. These social conflicts generate disorder—instability, violence, conflict. And conflicts are particularly intense during the process of modernization, characterized by economic development, urbanization, increases in literacy and education, rising aspirations and expectations, and growing political participation. *Political Order in Changing Societies* argues that strong and adaptable institutions are essential for establishing political order, which must be supplied if countries are to successfully modernize. The Chinese Communist Party has taken the importance of supplying order to heart. Political order—what the Chinese regime calls stability—has become a central tenet of CCP rule, and to some, it is central to China's development model (Yang 2017).

However, the meaning and role of stability has changed over the past 40 years in China. The policy paradigm of stability has changed. Hall (1993, 279) describes a policy paradigm as a:

[F]ramework of ideas and standards that specifies not only the goals of policy and the kind of instruments that can be used to attain them, but also the very nature of the problems they are meant to be addressing. Like a *Gestalt*, this framework is embedded in the very terminology through which policymakers communicate about their work, and it is influential precisely because so much of it is taken for granted and unamenable to scrutiny as a whole.

The CCP has been talking about stability for decades, but the meaning of stability, the nature of the problem of stability, and solutions to pursue stability have changed. The change is difficult to see, but its effects are anything but subtle. We can observe the transformation of stability as a policy paradigm through the Dibao program.

When Dibao was first launched in the 1990s, the Chinese Communist Party saw political disorder as a consequence of economic liberalization and modernization. State-owned enterprise reform in the 1990s led to declining incomes for urbanites as firms, which faced greater competition and lower profits, had difficulty paying wages and pensions. Poverty in cities grew rapidly (Gustafsson, Shi, and Sicular 2008; Wong 1998), and by the late 1990s, China had up to 60 million unemployed urban workers (Solinger and Hu 2012; Solinger and Jiang 2016). Workers mobilized, and protest, unrest, and large-scale collective action intensified (Cai 2002; Chen 2000; Hurst and O'Brien 2002; Kernen and Rocca 2000; Lee 1998; Solinger 2000; Thireau and Linshan 2003).

During this period, the CCP saw the development of a new social welfare system as a way to solve the underlying reason—urban poverty—motivating social conflict and unrest. In 1992, Deng Xiaoping reaffirmed his support for economic reform during his "Southern Tour." A year later, during the third plenum of the 14th Central Committee of the Communist Party of China, the Central Committee adopted "Decision of the CPC Central Committee on Certain Issues in Establishing a Socialist Market Economy System." This CCP document called for the development of a "multi-layered social security system that provides urban and rural residents with a degree of security commensurate to China's reality so as to promote economic development and social stability." Dibao was one layer of this social security system. In 1999, when Dibao was launched nationally, then-premier Zhu Rongji said: "The Dibao's support of social stability and guarantee of the reform of the state firms has important significance; we should strengthen it, should fund it" (Tang 2003). Dibao was a policy concession made by the central government to address the problem of urban poverty. The thinking was that resolving the hardship of urban poverty would remove the impetus for social instability, which had resulted from economic liberalization. Thus, Dibao has always been linked to the preservation of political order—but in its early days, political order was a means of achieving the goal of modernizing, liberalizing, and growing the economy, and the Dibao program was one way to help resolve the factors generating poverty so that economic reform could continue.

However, at the turn of the 21st century, the relationship between Dibao and political order began to change. In April of 1999, over 10,000 Falun Gong practitioners surrounded Zhongnanhai, the central headquarters for the CCP and State Council, representing the largest collective action event in Beijing since Tiananmen in 1989. Falun Gong protesters mobilized not because of economic grievances but rather for social and political rights. It was not only workers and pensioners who protested, but diverse members of society from workers to intellectuals to party insiders. Falun Gong mobilization not only precipitated an immediate reaction from the regime, but also altered how the CCP conceptualized stability and their approach to pursuing it. Political order changed from a means of achieving economic modernization to the goal itself. The concepts of political stability (threats to CCP survival), social stability (social mobilization), and economic stability (economic growth) became fungible, with the CCP arguing that an increase or decrease in one aspect of stability would lead to parallel changes in the other aspects. In contrast to the 1990s when economic growth through economic liberalization was seen as a cause of social instability, by the end of the 2000s, economic growth was often described as a way of preserving and ensuring social stability. Dibao changed from being seen as a solution to the problems of poverty underlying protest and unrest, to a tool for addressing disorder by helping to control specific individuals deemed to be threats to social stability in the future. Because the terminology of stability has not changed, it can be difficult to see that the definition of the problem has changed.

The change in China's policy paradigm of stability has broad-ranging consequences for our understanding of Chinese politics. The CCP has not always been preoccupied with stability—the Cultural Revolution was anything but stable—and in the reform era, the CCP has not always been preoccupied with stability in the same way. Deng Xiaoping said to US President George H. W. Bush on February 26, 1989: "To China's problems, the overwhelming priority is stability. Without a stable environment, nothing can be achieved, and what has been achieved will be lost."[3] For Deng, stability was the priority, but it was not the ultimate aim of the regime; stability was a means of achieving and a means of

---

3. 中国的问题, 压倒一切的是需要稳定. 没有稳定的环境, 什么都搞不成, 已经取得的成果也会失掉. The unclassified memo of the conversation as recorded by the United States can be found at https://digitalarchive.wilsoncenter.org/document/116507 (accessed March 20, 2019).

preserving what had been achieved. When more recent Chinese leaders have spoken of stability, stability has been the priority *and* the aim of the regime. Over the past forty years, the concept of stability has been reiterated countless times in CCP documents, state media, and the speeches of China's top leaders, but stability in 2013 does not have the same meaning as it did in 1993, and if we, as scholars, reduce the concept to having a constant meaning over time, we risk misinterpreting the phenomenon we observe.

At the turn of the 21st century, the Chinese Communist Party doubled down on its strategy of maintaining stability through Comprehensive Management of Public Security. The idea of Comprehensive Management of Public Security emerged as an alternative to strike hard campaigns in the aftermath of the Tiananmen protests of 1989 (Wang and Minzner 2015). Strike hard campaigns were intensive but constrained time periods where the security apparatus was mobilized for mass arrests, imprisonments, and executions (Tanner 1999, 2000). In contrast, Comprehensive Management of Public Security in the 1990s strengthened incentives of officials to suppress social mobilization by embedding the priority of order into party institutions (Wang and Minzner 2015). The Chinese Communist Party controls access to key positions of power, allowing the ruling party to effectively mitigate intra-elite conflict by creating a mechanism for credible power sharing (Brownlee 2007; Haber 2007; Magaloni 2008; Magaloni and Kricheli 2010; Svolik 2012; Wintrobe 1998). What has received less attention from scholars of authoritarian politics and comparative politics is that China's party institutions do not simply offer a mechanism for power sharing. These institutions also aim to ameliorate principal-agent problems related to governance. Through a series of reforms implemented since the late 1970s, the CCP has linked career advancement for party committee members (and regime bureaucrats more generally) to their performance (Huang 1996). Lower-level officials must deliver certain outcomes in order to advance in political office. Performance outcomes initially emphasized conformity to regime ideology (Manion 1985; Whiting 2004), but with economic reform in the 1980s, they were increasingly tied to concrete achievements in economic and social areas (Edin 2003). After Tiananmen, avoiding large-scale social mobilization and growing the economy have consistently been identified as the most crucial targets for career advancement. Failure to meet these two targets can derail a political career even if performance is strong in all other areas (Edin 2003; O'Brien and Li 1999; Whiting 2004).

After the Falun Gong protests, responsibility for Comprehensive Management of Public Security expanded beyond the security apparatus to a broad array of government, party, mass organizations, and even public institutions (such as schools). This evolution of Comprehensive Management of Public Security forms the basis of what scholars refer to today as China's stability maintenance regime (Fewsmith 2012; Xu and Li 2011; Yang 2017). Many scholars have written about stability maintenance in China, but even the most expansive definitions of stability maintenance describe it as a delimited set of policies, practices, and actions. For example, Wang and Minzner (2015) focus on the institutional incentives to motivate lower-level officials' attention toward stability and order. Lee and Zhang (2013) focus on the discretionary nature of stability maintenance funds and activities. Yang (2017) describes stability maintenance as "a complex array of institutional arrangements and practices concerning social control, including cultivating grass-root state agencies and mass organizations, controlling media outlets and allowing various extralegal policing practices" (36). But even in this definition, stability maintenance is limited to institutional incentives and practices, the involvement of a broad range of organizations, media and information control, and policing.

This understanding of Comprehensive Management of Public Security and stability maintenance does not go far enough. Since the Falun Gong protests, the Chinese regime's pursuit of stability has seeped into unrelated policies and programs and has changed how resources are allocated in domains unrelated to public security. As a result, the goal of stability, and how the CCP pursues stability, shapes actions and outcomes across diverse domains. The empirical evidence of this book focuses on how exactly this occurs with the Dibao program and social assistance, but the seepage of political order is likely pervasive. For example, in September 2017, one month before the 19th National Congress of the Chinese Communist Party in Beijing, Chinese President Xi Jinping told security officials that stability was an absolute principle, and that stability must be maintained ahead of and during this important political meeting.[4] The regime utilized many tactics we might expect—increasing censorship, putting pressure on known activists and dissidents,[5] increasing police presence, and intensifying surveillance[6]—but the regime's pursuit of stability ahead of the 19th Party Congress was felt much more broadly. No event with more than 500 people could take place anywhere in China. This meant a film festival in the distant island province of Hainan had to be canceled.[7] Social science research, such as surveys, was deemed to be too sensitive, and projects were thus halted and delayed. In Beijing, where the meeting was to take place, malls, nightclubs, and restaurants

---

4. See https://reut.rs/2tHngaK (accessed January 26, 2018).

5. See https://bit.ly/2IuWurw (accessed January 26, 2018).

6. For examples, see https://bit.ly/2tC3uNS, https://bit.ly/2Ko8XCl, and https://bit.ly/2tC3uNS, https://bit.ly/2yKpcoT (accessed January 26, 2018).

7. See https://bit.ly/2ypmhRj (accessed January 26, 2018).

were temporarily closed.[8] Airbnb removed all Beijing listings, and some Alibaba produce deliveries were said to be delayed, presumably because of restrictions on transportation.[9] The seepage of political order into unrelated domains is not limited to high-profile political events. In their ethnography of stability maintenance at the street level in China, Lee and Zhang (2013) find that funds for education, environmental improvement, and general government administration are redirected to stanch local protests and social instability. While some policy areas are likely more affected by the seepage of political order than others, and some policies are likely more amenable to seepage than others, what I have found with regard to Dibao is very unlikely to be an isolated case.

1.2 Seepage

Seepage describes a process of institutional change where one government priority, goal, or orientation infiltrates, sometimes unintentionally, unrelated policies and programs without changing the formal rules of these other policies. Seepage generates change by altering the composition of resource allocation, and through this altered allocation, converts the goals of these other policies. The *Oxford English Dictionary* defines seepage as "the slow movement of water through the ground under the action of gravity." Similarly, policy seepage is often slow moving, difficult to observe, yet pervasive.

As the Chinese regime's understanding of and approach to stability changed after the Falun Gong protests, the priority of political order began to seep into Dibao. During the 2000s, the main formal change to the Dibao program related to the expansion of Dibao to rural residents. However, during this decade, public security and justice departments began issuing verbal instructions and policy documents that emphasized the provision of Dibao to populations they wanted to control, who, importantly, also met the formal eligibility requirements of Dibao. For example, in September 2003, during the National Conference on Comprehensive Management of Public Security, the minister of Civil Affairs and the vice minister of Justice said that targeted populations who meet eligibility requirements should be provided Dibao. In 2004, Cixi County in Ningbo Province began actively recruiting targeted populations for the Dibao program.[10] In 2008,

---

8. See https://bit.ly/2ypmhRj (accessed January 26, 2017).

9. See https://reut.rs/2Klo7Fh, https://on.wsj.com/2Kc7lL4 (accessed January 26, 2017).

10. See http://bit.ly/2tK1yEE (accessed May 16, 2015).

the departments of justice and civil affairs in Guangzhou issued a policy stipulating anyone undergoing re-education, which includes targeted populations, who is eligible for Dibao be helped to obtain it. In 2014, the city of Dongying in Shandong launched a campaign to mobilize government administrators and CCP cadres to visit the household of every family receiving re-education to help them obtain Dibao and reduced education expenses, and to facilitate other "charitable works."

By emphasizing the provision of Dibao for targets of repression, public security and justice departments shifted the allocation of funding for Dibao and changed the composition of Dibao recipients. Although Dibao in theory should have been made available to everyone whose income falls below the locally set Dibao line, the program is not fully funded; hence not every household eligible based on income receives the benefit. When Dibao was launched nationwide in 1999, local governments were given primary responsibility for financing, but local governments often did not have sufficient revenue to fund the program (Dabla-Norris 2005; Li 2007; Oi et al. 2012; Wong 1997). Even as the central government's share of funding increased, hard budget constraints remained because finance and civil affairs departments faced incentives and pressure not to make dramatic year-to-year changes to Dibao budgets. As a result, while Dibao was still provided to the poor, local administrators often denied Dibao to "ordinary" impoverished households but made sure that all impoverished households with individuals who were listed as targeted populations, who were ex-prisoners, and who were undergoing re-education received Dibao.

Over the past decades, political scientists' understanding of how institutions change has changed. Instead of viewing institutional change as the alternation between long periods of stasis and critical junctures (Krasner 1988; Mahoney 2000; Pierson 2000), the current view of institutional change is of incremental movement (Béland 2007; Hacker 2004; Hacker, Pierson, and Thelen 2015; Streeck and Thelen 2005; Thelen 2003, 2004). Thelen (2003) originated the ideas of layering and conversion, and Hacker (2004) the idea of drift. Layering involves "the grafting of new elements onto an otherwise stable institutional framework" (Thelen 2004:35). Drawing from the study of the US Congress by Schickler (2001), Thelen (2003) argues that layering occurs when new institutions are added because institution builders do not have the support or inclination to dismantle existing institutional arrangements. An often-cited example of layering is the addition of private savings accounts to pay-as-you-go pension systems (Pierson 1994). Conversion occurs when "existing institutions are redirected to new purposes, driving changes in the role they perform and/or the functions they serve" (Thelen 2003:226). Conversion can occur when new actors who are brought in alter the institutional role or core objectives of an institution. Drift was first described as "changes in the operation or effect of policies that occur without significant changes in those policies' structure" (Hacker 2004:246). In the United States, drift in social welfare occurred because existing programs could not accommodate the emergence of new and intensified social risks. In more recent years, drift has become defined more precisely as the process of holding back formal rule changes when contexts change so that the institutions' effects are altered (Hacker, Pierson, and Thelen 2015).

Thelen (2003) notes that there may be many modes of institutional change, and I see seepage as a different mode that is nevertheless related to existing concepts of incremental institutional change. Seepage describes one way in which conversion can occur. It describes a way for new goals to enter into existing institutions that do not entail the entrance of new actors. The public security agencies that emphasized the prioritization of Dibao for targeted populations are not beneficiaries, funders, nor administrators in the Dibao program. They do not have any particular vested interest in Dibao. Instead, new goals enter into Dibao because public security agencies emphasized the application of Dibao for a particular category of beneficiaries in order to serve their own priorities of implementing Comprehensive Management of Public Security.

Because there are no formal policy revisions or new institutions added, seepage also resembles drift. Hacker (2004) differentiates between "internal" policy changes and formal policy revisions, and conceptualizes drift as changes in internal policy that more likely occur when policies lack clearly specified and understood procedures and when front-line agents have discretion and vary policy implementation. Seepage also happens through internal policy changes, and it is also more likely to occur with policies that do not have clearly specified and understood procedures. However, the lack of clearly specified and understood procedures in seepage is not necessarily due to the fact that these procedures do not exist, but rather due to the fact that procedures become extremely difficult to understand because there are so many rules and contingencies. Seepage can thus occur when front-line agents do not have discretion to deviate from established procedure. In the case of Dibao, front-line agents have little discretion to deviate from the core tenets of the program, but the complexity of Dibao policies gives front-line workers the flexibility to apply slightly different procedures and rules to different people as dictated by upper-level priorities.

Perhaps the most important way in which seepage departs from drift, conversion, and other forms of incremental institutional change is that it does not result from the purposeful action (or purposeful inaction) of political actors engaged in contestation. Most of the current literature on institutional change comes from historical institutionalist studies of advanced democracies. This research is strongly informed by the dynamics of democratic politics, where replacement of existing institutions is difficult and where actors seeking change must do so through indirect pathways such as layering, conversion, and drift. Replacement of existing institutions, especially those that generate entitlements, can also be difficult in authoritarian regimes. Even powerful authoritarian regimes such as China are constrained by audience costs (Weeks 2008). Mass mobilization followed the breakdown of Maoist welfare institutions during economic reform. If Dibao were eliminated, it would likely become a focal point for contention and unrest. In autocracies, political actors may also rely on strategies such as drift and conversion to effect institutional and policy change. For example, the increasing emphasis on work in the Dibao program—making able-bodied workers essentially ineligible for Dibao—is likely influenced by political actors, such as local governments facing a multitude of fiscal pressures, who want the CCP to reduce welfare entitlements. By narrowing the scope of Dibao to those who cannot work, the regime is responding to financial and societal pressures to reduce Dibao without provoking those with vested interests in the material or symbolic value of the program.

This is not why seepage occurs. Seepage describes a process of change that occurs because of the influence of factors exogenous to the specific institution or policy being altered. By exogenous factors, I am not referring to the types of exogenous shocks—revolution, defeat in war—that lead to critical junctions as described in previous conceptualizations of institutional change. I am referring to forces outside of the specific policy or institution that are not oriented toward changing that policy or institution. This lack of intentionality contrasts with existing explanations of incremental institutional change. For example, even though drift refers to the lack of change in formal rules, this inertia is recognized by political actors who use it *deliberately* to serve their ends. In conversion, political actors *purposefully* redirect an institution or policy to new functions. By contrast, China's security apparatus did not set out with the goal of changing the function of Dibao. Under Comprehensive Management of Public Security, the regime mandated that all governmental, party, and societal resources be mobilized in pursuit of political order, and in this process, Dibao got redirected to new purposes. When public security departments and judicial departments emphasized the provision of Dibao to targeted populations, they intended to use Dibao as intended, as a social safety net for the impoverished. However, despite the lack of intention to change the function of Dibao, the goal of the policy and its effects were altered. Dibao, China's core social assistance program, became a tool of repression and surveillance. The fact that seepage does not result from the deliberate strategies of political actors engaged in contestation does not mean that seepage is apolitical. The seepage of political order into Dibao shapes political choices and outcomes.

Seepage highlights the importance of studying institutional change in non-democratic contexts. Institutions do not change gradually only in consolidated democracies with high levels of economic development. Policies and institutions can also evolve gradually in authoritarian regimes, especially longer-lasting ones such as monarchies and single-party regimes. The study of institutions occupies a central place in the study of authoritarian politics. Earlier decades of scholarship on authoritarian institutions examined change (Helmke and Levitsky 2004; Tsai 2006; Whiting 2006; Yang 1998), but the primary focus of scholarship in the past 10 years has been on how institutions such as parties, legislatures, and elections support authoritarian durability (Blaydes 2011; Boix and Svolik 2007; Bueno de Mesquita et al. 2004; Gandhi 2008, 2009; Gandhi and Przeworski 2006, 2007; He and Thogersen 2011; He and Warren 2011; Hou 2019; Lust-Okar 2006; Magaloni and Kricheli 2010; Malesky, Abrami, and Zheng 2011; Malesky and Schuler 2012; Svolik 2012; Nathan 2003; Wright 2008). As a result, we know relatively little about how authoritarian institutions evolve and transform over time. Seepage focuses on the gradual evolution of institutions in the absence of coups, wars, or other external shocks. In the case of Dibao, change happens as an indirect result of the strategy of Comprehensive Management of Public Security rather than through a process of learning or political competition between actors. Seepage is enabled by party institutions that make political advancement conditional on meeting goals of social stability. Do we observe seepage in other authoritarian contexts? What other forms of gradual institutional change occur in stable autocracies? How is gradual institutional change different or similar between democratic and authoritarian contexts? These and many other questions are unanswered but are important to our understanding of authoritarian politics and political institutions.

1.3 Repressive Assistance

When Dibao is prioritized to preempt disorder, it becomes a tool of repressive assistance. We usually associate political repression with physical sanctions and violence (imprisonment, mass killing), or at the very least, the threat of physical force (intimidation, surveillance). For example, Davenport (2007) describes repression as "actual or threatened use of physical sanctions against an individual or organization, within the territorial jurisdiction of the state, for the purpose of imposing a cost on the target as well as deterring specific activities" (2). However, physical sanctions, violence, and force are not the only means through which to impose costs on targets and deter specific activities. Older definitions of repression often did not specify any particular tactic to achieve these ends. Tilly defined repression as "any action by another group which raises the contender's cost of collective action" (Tilly 1978:100). Oberschall (1973) distinguishes between coercive forms of repression and what he calls channeling forms of repression. Channeling is intended to limit collective action and protest but does so without the application of force. More recent scholarship also has distinguished between these different forms of repression (Earl 2003; Frantz and Kendall-Taylor 2014; Way and Levitsky 2006).

The concept of repressive assistance builds on this recognition that repression need not be physically violent or threaten physical violence. In China, repressive assistance through Dibao provision occurs within the the context of re-education. Re-education does not refer to the acquisition of knowledge or skills, but instead to cognitive and behavioral reform. The goal of re-education is to transform the entire being, from innermost thoughts to outward behavior (Lifton 2012; Perry 2002b, 2017). Re-education goes beyond anti-recidivism, because it is not simply the prevention of actions of crime (change in behavior) but a change in the underlying thinking and psychology that lead to crime. Re-education takes place within China's penal system. It is also applied to released prisoners, and individuals suspected of having a higher propensity of committing crime in the future. Re-education has been applied to thousands of Falun Gong followers since 1999 (Tong 2009). Re-education is a core component of China's current mass internment of Uyghurs and other Muslims (Zenz 2019). For critics, re-education is synonymous with coercive repressive and human rights abuse; however, understanding re-education allows us to understand how Dibao represses. Re-education is carried out by teams—often composed of residents committee members, block captains, local police, neighborhood watch volunteers, and other community-level party activists and cadres—tasked with regularly visiting the target of re-education.

The distribution of Dibao to targeted populations deters activities such as social mobilization by increasing interactions between the regime and the target of repression. Each time a benefit is disbursed is an opportunity for contact between the regime and the person targeted by repressive assistance. For Dibao, cash transfers are disbursed monthly, and there are also additional disbursements of ad hoc cash and in-kind benefits. The disbursement of benefits serves as a natural starting point for conversations, which aids the gathering of private information by re-education team members. Surveillance is less noticeable when it is conducted as part of interactions related to the distribution of benefits. When re-education committee members bring news of a Dibao-related benefit, they will often follow up by asking whether the targeted person has any additional needs and desires and what s/he is thinking of doing about it. Private information is thus gathered through ordinary conversations about everyday matters. The distribution of benefits also makes targets of repression more likely to talk and to open up because these repeated social interactions can generate a sense of obligation. When grassroots representatives of the regime have come bearing "gifts" from the regime, the target of benefits may feel a stronger need to reciprocate by talking and sharing information or changing their stated beliefs and behaviors.

Even if targets of repressive assistance feel no sense of obligation, the distribution of benefits can constrain the behavior of beneficiaries as they become materially dependent on the assistance and socially isolated because of the stigma associated with welfare. Material dependence was a core strategy of control in pre-reform China (Walder 1988). Increasing incomes have broken material dependence for the bulk of the Chinese population, but for the very poor who are reliant on Dibao, material dependence continues to function as a means of control. Dibao benefits are not high enough to provide resources that enable recipients to mobilize against the regime, but they are just high enough to make the very poor dependent on the regime. Furthermore, there are features of the Dibao program, specifically the public display of the names of Dibao recipients in every neighborhood, that exacerbate feelings of isolation and shame among recipients (Han 2012; Solinger 2011, 2012), which deepens the dependence of Dibao recipients on the regime.

Although repressive assistance entails distribution of benefits, it differs from cooptation, clientelism, and contractual agreements. In cooptation, the provision of benefits serves to neutralize opponents, where benefits are distributed to "buy off" those who, in exchange, willingly forgo specific activities (Gandhi and Przeworski 2007; Svolik 2012).[11] In cooptation, targets decide that the value of the benefits is worth some change in their behavior. In repressive assistance, the distribution of benefits serves to make the recipients more legible to the state, more amenable to manipulation, and ultimately not only less willing but *less able* to engage in the activities the regime wants to suppress. Along these lines, repressive assistance is also not clientelistic or contractual. The individual receiving the benefits is not willingly entering into an agreement from which s/he can withdraw. The individual is not entering into a voluntary exchange of acquiescence for material benefit.

Repressive assistance bears many similarities to Albertus, Fenner, and Slater's (2018) concept of "coercive distribution," in which material benefits are

---

11. Some diverse examples of this form of cooptation include *panem et circenses* (bread and circuses), when Rome distributed grain to Roman citizens as a means of pacification to mitigate the threat of political activism (Ades and Glaeser 1994; Scullard 2010), the distribution of benefits to urban cities rather than rural areas in China (Hobsbawm 1973; Zipf 1941; Wallace 2014), and Emilio Medici's government expansion of social insurance to the Brazilian countryside to gain rural support in 1971 (Malloy 1979; Mares and Carnes 2009).

distributed to enmesh citizens in relationships of dependence on the regime. One difference between repressive assistance and coercive distribution is that repressive assistance does not only work through coercion, which is the existence of a conditional threat or the idea that nonconformity can lead to the loss of benefits. Repressive assistance can also work through obligation, where the actions of targets are constrained not because they fear the loss of benefits but because they feel obligated to satisfy social relations.

Another difference between repressive assistance and coercive distribution is that while coercive distribution refers to comprehensive, rather than particularistic or narrowly targeted, forms of distribution, repressive assistance can characterize welfare programs regardless of their scope. Albertus, Fenner, and Slater (2018) are interested in explaining why authoritarian regimes adopt comprehensive programs of distribution, and what role these programs serve. Coercive distribution assumes that the autocratic decision makers, at some point, make a conscious decision about launching or keeping the program. In contrast, repressive assistance can occur whether or not the welfare program is designed or intended to be repressive.

The fact that repressive assistance in the context of Dibao arises from seepage rather than from intentional design distinguishes this book from much of the research on authoritarian welfare institutions. The argument that welfare is used for controlling society is not at all new. Scholars have connected welfare to the suppression of social contention and opposition in countries and regions ranging from 17th-century England and Japan, to 19th-century Germany, to Africa and Latin America, to the United States in the 20th century, to the Middle East in the 21st century (Bates 1981; Brunschwig 1974; Cammett and Issar 2010; Cowgill 1974; Dawson and Robinson 1963; De La O 2013; Harris 2017; Isaac and Kelly 1981; Jennings 1979; Katznelson 1981; Koselleck 1969; Offe 1984; Piven and Cloward 1971; Skocpol and Amenta 1986; Steinmetz 1993; Wallace 2013; Yörük 2012; Zucco 2013). However, most of the research on authoritarian welfare sets out to explain why autocrats *adopt* welfare and distributive programs (Forrat 2012; Haber 2007; Mares and Carnes 2009; Tullock 1987; Wintrobe 1998). While researchers have provided a number of compelling explanations for the *adoption* of welfare programs by autocrats, repressive assistance describes a logic of distribution rather than a rationale for policy design. The implication for our understanding of authoritarian welfare is that social policies need not be designed at the onset to serve the political goals of autocratic elites. Authoritarian regimes can make narrow policy concessions that are converted to repressive purposes over time.[12]

---

12. Formal models of redistribution in authoritarian regimes typically theorize that narrow concessions are possible (Acemoglu and Robinson 2006; Chen and Xu 2017).

Although I have identified repressive assistance in China, repressive assistance is not necessarily limited to authoritarian regimes or even to state actors. That said, repressive assistance is more likely in some contexts and less likely in others. The provision of benefits is a way through the literal and metaphorical door of the target of repression. Repressive assistance requires there to be representatives of the government, party, or regime—who can be formal employees or volunteers—to make use of benefit distribution as an opportunity to surveil and repress. Because repressive assistance requires feet on the ground, it also requires some organization that can mobilize this activity and penetrate into the grassroots level. Countries with strong parties or administrative capacity are most likely to have the infrastructure required for repressive assistance. This would include communist single-party systems, but can also include parties in democratic contexts that have large networks of brokers who frequently interact with voters (Stokes 2005; Stokes et al. 2013).

Certain social policies are also more amenable to repressive assistance than others. Many of these characteristics are those identified by scholars of American and European welfare systems as those generating negative policy feedback—political demobilization—in democratic contexts (Campbell 2012). Pierson (1993) identified public policies as having "resource" and "interpretive" effects on the people who experience the policies. Social policies in particular can influence recipients by altering their level of resources, their feelings of political interest and efficacy, and ultimately, their probability of political participation and mobilization. Social policies with low-level but traceable and regular benefits that prevent proximity and concentration of beneficiaries are the most likely candidates for repressive assistance. Low levels of benefits foster dependence, yet prevent beneficiaries from obtaining sufficient resources to take independent political actions. Benefits that are traceable to the government and disbursed at regular intervals are more likely to generate an effect, including a repressive effect (Arnold 1990; Mettler 2011). Social policies that prevent the proximity and interaction of beneficiaries—for example, by generating stigma among recipients, by isolating recipients, by varying the duration of benefit provision—are also more amenable to repressive assistance because they make it harder for beneficiaries to coordinate and act collectively.

Does repressive assistance work in China? By subjecting individuals to repressive assistance, is the CCP successful in deterring specific behaviors and raising the cost of collective action? Repressive assistance is effective when recipients are closely managed and monitored. However, in China, heuristics—mainly tied to past behavior such as imprisonment—are used to identify individuals for repressive assistance, even when grassroots surveillance networks are strong. These heuristics, like all heuristics, are never entirely accurate (Tversky and Kahneman

1992). Many who are identified as targeted populations and subjected to re-education and repressive assistance are unlikely to threaten political order in the future. And often, individuals who end up causing disorder were not placed into targeted population lists. As a result, repressive assistance is unlikely, on average, to decrease contentious activity and mobilization among targeted populations, or if there is an effect, it is likely very small. In addition, not everyone who is identified for repressive assistance is closely managed all the time. There is a great deal of variation in the intensity of repressive assistance between neighborhoods and over time. Many neighborhoods do not have easy access to the manpower to carry out frequent interactions for long periods of time. Instead, surveillance and control ramp up during specific times of the year—before political meetings and around national holidays (Truex 2019). Overall, repressive assistance is effective when it is fully implemented on the right targets, but in reality, implementation varies between neighborhoods and over time, and many of those targeted are not individuals the regime may wish to target.

What is notable about repressive assistance is that it erases the delineation between repression and concessions. At the neighborhood level, the same individuals who facilitate the provision of welfare benefits also conduct surveillance. Residential committee members who process applications for Dibao and other social welfare benefits are the people who conduct re-education. Neighborhood block captains who visit households to check on receipt of benefits are the same people who gather information for local public security. Existing research on authoritarian regimes almost always conceptualizes repression as distinct from distribution, also called concessions or cooptation (Chestnut Greitens 2016; Earl 2003; Haber 2007; Magaloni and Kricheli 2010; Shadmehr 2014; Svolik 2012; Wintrobe 1998). There are debates about the relative importance of repression and concessions,[13] and some have suggested that repression and concessions are substitutes.[14] Even

13. For example, looking at the Chinese politics literature, Cai (2008) argues that it is difficult for local governments in China to make concessions, considering their financial and administrative costs, which prompts local governments to focus on attacking, harassing, and imprisoning protest leaders. Li and O'Brien (2008) arrive at a similar conclusion, that local governments focus on repression as a response to protesters. In contrast, Chen (2009) suggests that repression by the CCP is limited, and Lee and Zhang (2013) argue that material benefits are distributed in exchange for compliance, while repressive measures are sparingly used.

14. For example, the social contract thesis based on the Soviet regime suggests the state enters into a contract with the population whereby the population remains passive in exchange for desired social outcomes like secure employment, stable pricing, health, and education. This leads to the observable outcome of increased use of redistribution and decreased use of repression. See Bialer (1982); Breslauer (1978); Hauslohner (1987).

research recognizing that autocrats may use repression and concession in combination nonetheless treats them as distinct.[15] In contrast to these existing conceptualizations, this book shows that concessions and repression may not always be distinct strategies. The distribution of benefits can facilitate surveillance and control, and alter individuals' ability to act and to mobilize.

Repressive assistance sugarcoats repression so that it appears normal and benignly paternalistic. Because it appears so nonthreatening, repressive assistance may avoid backlash and other pitfalls associated with repression from the perspective of autocrats. Repression sometimes crushes mass mobilization (Brook 1998; Carey 1997; Walder 1989), and other times, it inflames dissent (Khawaja 1993; Kurzman 1996; Lichbach 1989; Moore 1998; Olivier 1991; Rasler 1996; Sullivan and Davenport 2017). Backlash results when repression generates anger rather than fear (Young 2017, 2019). As authoritarian regimes have entered into more international institutions, alliances, and agreements, they can face strong pressure to respect human rights and conform to Western democratic norms (Keohane 1988; Keohane and Nye 1974). At the same time, technological advances have made it increasingly costly for authoritarian regimes to suppress outflows of information. As a result, the international community is more likely to detect autocrats' use of coercive repression and sanction them for it. Repression that generates fear may create incentives for those who are repressed and those who witness repression to hide their true feelings (preference falsification), resulting in information problems for autocrats who can no longer accurately assess the extent of support or opposition (Kuran 1991; Wintrobe 1998). Repressive assistance avoids these outcomes because it is not easily discernible, and it does not match our common conceptions of what repression entails, so is unlikely to stir anger or outrage.

1.4 Backlash

The distribution of Dibao to repress does generate backlash. However, this backlash does not result from anger over repression but rather anger over distribution. The bulk of research on the effects of welfare and social policy focuses on effects for recipients (Campbell 2012; Pierson 1993; Schneider and Ingram 1993), but in the case of Dibao, it also makes sense to examine effects on non-recipients. Seepage shifted the resources and goals of the Dibao program without changing the way this program is described. This means the general expectations of the

---

15. Frantz and Kendall-Taylor (2014) argue that institutional cooptation allows autocrats to reduce indiscriminate repression; Shadmehr (2014) provides a formal model of mobilization of dissidents based on expectations of concession and repression by the state, and Cai (2008) states that while repression is favored by autocrats, repression and concessions can occur in combination.

program remained unchanged. As a result, Dibao leads to dissatisfaction and contention among those who do not receive the benefit but think they should be entitled to it.

As part of central government efforts to increase transparency in the Dibao program, the names of Dibao recipients are publicized in their neighborhoods.[16] Neighborhood residents can see exactly who is receiving Dibao and can compare the amount of Dibao subsidy to their own monthly earnings. This information prompts some neighborhood residents to approach the residents committee to try to apply for Dibao. However, because of the hard budget constraints on the Dibao program and the general policy of limiting Dibao to people who are not able-bodied, residents committees turn away many would-be applicants, especially those who appear physically and mentally capable of working. In neighborhoods where Dibao is prioritized for targeted populations, who often appear able-bodied, residents are more likely to engage in contention, both individual and collective, to demand benefits. This is especially true in neighborhoods where Dibao is distributed for repressive purposes and where residents engage in mutual surveillance. In these neighborhoods, residents know more about other residents, including Dibao recipients, so it is more difficult for residents committees to convince those agitating for Dibao that they are ineligible. Beyond the neighborhood level, cities with higher levels of Dibao provision for repressive purposes exhibit higher levels of welfare-related collective action than cities with lower levels of provision.

Contention over Dibao can be separated into two ideal types—rule-based resistance and bargaining—that differ in their goals, strategies, and perceptions of the Dibao program. Rule-based resistance draws from the concept of rightful resistance (O'Brien and Li 2006). Like rightful resistance, protesters engaged in rule-based resistance rely on established principles and deploy existing regulations and commitments in claim-making. However, rule-based resistance is solely about the adherence to preexisting rules, regulations, and policies governing Dibao and not does exhibit rights consciousness (Li 2010; O'Brien 2001; Perry 2007, 2009). Those engaged in rule-based resistance perceive Dibao as being unfairly implemented when they themselves do not receive it but other individuals who appear capable of work do. When rule-based resisters protest to the residents committee, they speak of the Dibao program as a commitment made by the Chinese government and Communist Party to help the poor. They describe their dire economic

---

16. If Dibao were seen by policymakers as a tool of stability maintenance, it would not make any sense for them to publicize who receives benefits. There is transparency because, as mentioned earlier, Dibao is not seen as a part of China's stability maintenance regime. The transparency associated with the Dibao program is a reaction to complaints of corruption that plagued the program in the 2000s.

circumstances, and they describe their lack of benefits as a failure of the regime to care for its people. Rule-based resisters point to Dibao regulations that describe eligibility based on means testing.

Protesters who engage in bargaining give no credence to the formal rules governing Dibao. They see Dibao as a resource to be negotiated and take the view that obtaining Dibao requires disturbing the current order. For bargainers, the CCP's preoccupation with stability creates a mechanism through which ordinary citizens can obtain concessions from the regime. Bargainers protest for Dibao because many other social welfare benefits are tied to Dibao status, but their goal is to obtain some concession from the regime, whether Dibao or something else. Unlike rule-based resisters, bargainers do not deploy rules or regulations to make their claims. Instead, they rely on highly visible tactics of dissent to gain the attention of neighborhood administrators (Fu 2017; Lee and Zhang 2013).

To deal with rule-based resistance, residents committees rely on the complexity of Dibao policies and their information advantage over protesters (i.e., they know more about the households receiving Dibao than the protesters know). Because grassroots administrators can truthfully say that they are simply following established government policies and procedures, rule-based resisters lose their anchor for resistance. If rule-based resisters learn that Dibao is prioritized for some able-bodied individuals because they are ex-prisoners or targeted persons, resisters' perceptions of the Dibao program may change. Instead of perceiving Dibao to be unfairly implemented (a problem with rule enforcement), they become opposed to the policy of prioritizing Dibao for ex-prisoners (a problem with rule making). However, most rule-based resisters do not exhibit a rights consciousness that leads them to press for policy or institutional changes. Instead, rule-based resisters may come to see appealing to rules and deploying commitments as futile and turn to bargaining instead, or they may be demobilized but resentful of Dibao and, by extension, the regime that produces it.

Grassroots administrators of Dibao have a strong interest in minimizing bargaining behavior. Visible disturbances greatly increase their workload without budgetary or career benefits. Bargaining can also escalate in ways that are damaging to their careers and the careers of their superiors, because when a protester successfully negotiates for a benefit, s/he has incentives to continue negotiating for more. To defuse bargainers, residents committees use policy justifications and threats. Just as they use the complexity of Dibao policy to discourage rule-based resisters, they do the same to deter bargainers. By referring to policy, residents committees show bargainers that their hands are tied and that they do not have room to maneuver or bargain. Grassroots administrators also threaten bargainers with coercion by pointing out, again truthfully, that bargaining can lead to monitoring, imprisonment, and an array of repressive outcomes.

Most protests over Dibao, regardless of whether they entail rule-based resistance or bargaining, are defused by residents committee and grassroots administrators, and protests remain small in scale and localized. However, even though people are demobilized, they remain resentful and unsatisfied. From the perspective of a person who experiences the Dibao program as a would-be applicant, the program appears arbitrary and restrictive. Some become disillusioned with the policy, others stop believing its rules have any real meaning, and still others are embittered by their failure in negotiating for benefits. All are left unsatisfied and resentful of the program, and this dissatisfaction and bitterness spills over into their perceptions of the government. In cities with higher levels of Dibao provision for targets of repression, the general public has a more negative assessment of the government's capabilities in managing stability, providing social welfare, responding to citizens, and reining in the behavior of the government. The legitimacy of the local government—specifically political trust and satisfaction—are also lower than in cities with higher levels of Dibao provision for targeted populations.

Although the distribution of Dibao to preempt disorder is associated with lower levels of legitimacy, overall, trust and satisfaction with the government is still high. The phenomenon of high levels of protests and high levels of legitimacy is often cited as characteristic of Chinese politics. China experiences frequent protests (O'Brien 2008; Perry 2002a), with estimates of up to 180,000 mass incidents each year (Wong 2012). The CCP regime is highly sensitive to the threat of collective action, but the prevailing view among scholars of China is that domestic protests do not pose an existential threat to the CCP because the regime is responsive and adaptive in the face of widespread protest (Florini, Lai, and Tan 2012; O'Brien and Stern 2007; Perry 2009; Wasserstrom 2009). Whether through cooptation (Lee and Shen 2014; Lee and Zhang 2013), repression (Deng and O'Brien 2013; Ong 2015), control of information (Dimitrov 2014a; King, Pan, and Roberts 2013; Lorentzen 2013), creation of quasi-democratic institutions (Chen, Pan, and Xu 2016; Distelhorst and Hou 2017), or some combination of these strategies, most empirical studies paint a picture of a highly capable regime, successful in mitigating the threat posed by public discontent and contention. What the results of this book suggest is that it may not be the existence or level of protest that threatens legitimacy but how protests and contention are resolved in the eyes of protesters. If protesters feel that they have been fairly treated, high levels of protests may accompany high levels of legitimacy. On the other hand, if the regime defuses protests (i.e., decreasing their number, size, and duration) but protestors are left dissatisfied, lower levels of protest may accompany decreased perceptions of government legitimacy.

Many works have recognized China's adaptability in the face of contention (Cai 2006; Florini, Lai, and Tan 2012; Heurlin 2016; O'Brien and Stern 2007;

Perry 2009; Wasserstrom 2009). The Chinese regime exhibits a great deal of resilience in its pursuit of stability—it can mobilize diverse resources quickly to serve the ends of political order. We see this in how Dibao is distributed to preempt disorder as well as how Dibao-related protests are defused. However, Dibao also reveals downsides of adaptability in service of stability. The regime's preoccupation with political order and the seepage of the primacy of political order into areas such as Dibao undermine the programmatic aspect of government commitments. Many have noted how the disconnect between government commitments and actual reality is problematic for stability (Gallagher 2017), but in the case of Dibao, it is the pursuit of stability itself that damages the government's programmatic commitments, leading to more protests and to a gently simmering dissatisfaction that has negative consequences for public assessments of government performance and legitimacy.

1.5 Surveillance and Preemptive Control

The distribution of Dibao to targeted populations is contingent on surveillance. Specifically, neighborhood-level networks of mutual surveillance are used to determine to whom to distribute Dibao, and the distribution of benefits in turn intensifies surveillance. However, mutual surveillance at the neighborhood level also fuels contention because it reveals the disparities of Dibao distribution. We are at the beginning of a new digital era characterized by explosive growth in individualized, digitized information, and fast-paced advances in computing power and machine learning. What are the consequences of digitization for surveillance, preemptive control, and China's preoccupation with political order?

Digital technologies help countries like China to collect much more information about their entire population than in the past, and to do so in a way that is less detectable to the public. Individuals generate huge amounts of detailed and continuous data about themselves that the government can use for surveillance without making the person aware that surveillance is happening. Digital technology also enables involuntary forms of mutual surveillance that governments can capitalize on, because governments can learn about a target of surveillance by obtaining the digital data of contacts in the target's social networks. These contacts have unknowingly and involuntarily enabled surveillance on their peers.

What does not change in China is the goal of surveillance. Some argue that surveillance in the digital age is *predictive* while traditional surveillance was *reactive* (Andrejevic and Gates 2014; Liang et al. 2018; Lyon 2016). Since the targeted population program began in the 1950s, the CCP has aimed to identify individuals from the entire population, so the regime can intervene in the behavior of these individuals to forestall future behavior. The task of surveillance for the CCP has, for a long time, gone beyond monitoring current behavior to include trying to predict the future.

What also remains unchanged is the fact that there will be errors in prediction, and, if anything, the scope of errors will expand with the adoption of digital technologies once we take into account China's preoccupation with political order. Traditional surveillance relied on heuristics of concrete past behaviors to implement preemptive control. From one perspective, these heuristics fail because they fail to capture many people who take actions objectionable to the regime but had not done so, or not done so in a detectable manner, in the past. From another perspective, these heuristics succeed because those who are monitored are, on average, more likely to disturb order than the general population, even if many who are monitored never intended to threaten political order. Furthermore, it may not matter to local police and administrators of the targeted population program that many who are listed as targeted persons are extremely unlikely to threaten the regime. Administrators can justify to their superiors the inclusion of these individuals because these individuals exhibited certain past characteristics, and they can fulfill quotas for the number of individuals they are tasked with monitoring and justify their budgets.

This does not change in the digital era. China is the world's biggest market for security and surveillance technology, and it is making significant investments in the use of large-scale data and machine learning—such as deep learning or artificial intelligence (AI)—for predictive policing. However, the probabilistic machine learning algorithms being used for predictive analytics are never right 100% of the time, and in particular, every system has to make a tradeoff between precision (minimizing false positives) and recall (minimizing false negatives). Local officials, who are tasked with implementing systems of preemptive control, want to avoid serious mistakes such as large-scale collective action events, while continuing to justify their budgets for maintaining stability. These incentives mean that recall would be prioritized over precision. Precision matters less because false positives—for example, people who do not pose a threats to political order but are deemed as threats to political order by a deep-learning surveillance system—are not problematic as long as false positives do not overwhelm true positives. People who pose no threat but who are identified as threatening can still be used to justify budgets, especially as local officials can defer responsibility to "scientific" machine algorithms that generate these predictions. In contrast, recall matters a great deal because false negatives—for example, people who do pose a threat to order but are missed by the system—could seriously damage the careers of local officials. The prioritization of recall over precision is what we see in the management of targeted populations described in this book. The growth in the amount of data that the Chinese government can gather about everyone, all the time, means that the government can minimize false negatives in ways that were not possible with traditional surveillance. However, because digital technologies will not eliminate error altogether and because there is always a tradeoff between precision and recall in machine classification systems, the dramatic expansion of information generated by digital technologies will likely expand the number of people trapped in programs of preemptive control. The resulting human costs will be high.

1.6 Data

Authoritarian governments do not publicize the phenomena—protest, surveillance, repression—I study in relation to social assistance in this book. To study these phenomena, I began with in-depth qualitative fieldwork and analysis of government documents. I conducted more than 100 semi-structured interviews with government officials, neighborhood administrators, and Dibao recipients from November 2012 to June 2013 in four Chinese provinces, and I spent time observing interactions between local administrators and residents at the neighborhood level.[17] Interviews are referenced by the type of interviewee (B for bureaucrats from the township and street level to the provincial level; N for administrators at the neighborhood level such as residents committee members, local police officers, and block captains; and D for Dibao recipients), the year of the interview, and an ID number.

When my fieldwork revealed seemingly contradictory patterns of Dibao distribution, I began to analyze government documents in depth. I gathered and read all news articles from the *People's Daily* pertaining to Dibao from 1993 to 2018; all major policies on Dibao issued by the State Council or Ministry of Civil Affairs; all publicly available documents from the Ministry of Public Security and Ministry of Justice mentioning Dibao; and documents returned by a systematic Baidu and Google search by city containing simultaneous mentions of Dibao and targeted population, as well as Dibao and re-education.[18] These analyses led

---

17. Most of my interviews were arranged based on introductions by Chinese academics, colleagues from my years working in China prior to my PhD, and subsequent introductions from those I interviewed. I conducted some of the interviews alone, but many of the neighborhood-level interviews and observations were conducted jointly with local college students I recruited and trained. These university students were trained on the research questions I wished to ask and would lead the interview in the local dialect preferred by the respondent; I would mostly observe and listen, and occasionally interject for clarification or follow-up questions.

18. I conducted analyses of government documents from 2013 to 2017. As I finalized the book in 2019, I realized that many of the URLs where I had obtained these documents were no

me to the concept of seepage, as well as ideas of how seepage influenced Dibao provision and its consequences for Dibao recipients and others denied benefits. I systematically test these ideas using five novel data sets I created.

The first novel data set is the result of an online field experiment across 2,103 Chinese counties to establish a causal linkage between disorder (the threat of collective action) and government action (responsiveness to Dibao applicants).[19] The second data set is an original survey of 100 neighborhoods from four Chinese cities that measures the micro-level dynamics and outcomes of Dibao provision, including the characteristics of Dibao recipients and the nature of grassroots surveillance and repression. To examine the consequence of distributing Dibao for political order, my third data set contains thousands of announcements related to Dibao that I gathered using automated algorithms and validated extensively with human coders. My fourth data set is a nationally representative survey asking 3,513 urban Chinese citizens whether they have received Dibao, about their experiences with collective action and future plans for it, and their assessment of government performance and legitimacy.[20] These data allow me to use fuzzy regression discontinuity design (RDD) to measure the causal effect of Dibao provision on future plans for collective action, and they allow me to examine the relationship between the provision of Dibao to targeted populations and perceptions of the regime. Finally, my last data set utilizes millions of social media posts to identify collective action events, capturing information on their prevalence, timing, and location. Studying collective action in China and in other authoritarian regimes in a quantitative manner is difficult because data on collective action are often kept from the public and from researchers.[21] China stopped publishing

---

longer available. This is true for almost all of the policy documents mentioning targeted populations available online just a few years prior. Whereas in 2017, county-level, city-level, and some provincial-level government policies pertaining to targeted populations were available online, most policies mentioning targeted populations have been removed as of 2019. I believe this reflects an initiative to remove the digital traces of this program rather than to eliminate it. This is because on the China National Knowledge Infrastructure—an archive of Chinese academic journals, dissertations, and other publications relevant for academic research—there are academic articles on targeted populations, mostly written by Chinese academics or practitioners in police academies and universities as recently as 2019. Most of the 2018 and 2019 articles pertaining to targeted populations focus on the application of AI and big data for identifying, monitoring, and managing targeted populations. If I could go back in time, I would not only have printed the web pages I found but also saved the pages on the Internet Archive.

19. Conducted as part of Chen, Pan, and Xu (2016).

20. From the 2015 China Urban Governance Survey conducted by the Tsinghua University Research Center on Data and Governance.

21. The qualitative study of collective action in authoritarian contexts is also challenging, but scholars have made greater inroads with qualitative methods.

data on collective action in 2005 and has imprisoned those who make information on protests and collective action public (Freeman 2010).[22] By using the two-stage text- and image-based deep learning classifier described in Zhang and Pan (2019), I identify real-world collective action events that I use to quantitatively assess the relationship between Dibao provision and protest.

The combination of qualitative and quantitative data allows me to make more robust conclusions in this book. Qualitative research helped generate the theories and hypotheses of the book, as well as valid ways of measuring the concepts of interest. Quantitative data and methods allowed me to test these theories and hypotheses, and in some cases to establish causal relationships.

1.7 Overview of the Book

This chapter has described the outlines of my main argument, introduced the key theoretical concepts and related literatures, and presented my methodological approach. The next chapter, Chapter 2, introduces the political context for how central authorities launched the Dibao program and shows how the relationship between Dibao and political order changed as the CCP's conception of stability shifted. This chapter discusses how the pursuit of political order shapes the incentives of local officials because party institutions embed the priority in the criteria for political advancement, and how the seepage of political order emerges. Chapter 2 also provides details on the Dibao program.

The first portion of the book, Chapters 3 and 4, provides empirical evidence of how political order shapes the Dibao program. Chapter 3 focuses on the results of my field experiment, which revealed that even very mild threats of collective action prompted government action. This chapter shows how Dibao provision is not only shaped by economic considerations. The findings of this chapter suggest that individuals who are impoverished but capable of work may also be prioritized for Dibao.

Chapter 4 focuses on the the dual logic of Dibao distribution using a combination of qualitative fieldwork and the survey of 100 neighborhoods, and illustrates the seepage of political order into benefit distribution. This chapter begins by showing how Dibao funds are constrained, limiting the number of Dibao recipients. The remainder of the chapter focuses on the urban neighborhood, which plays a crucial role in the Dibao application process as well as the surveillance and management of targeted populations. This chapter discusses the background of the targeted population program, how grassroots surveillance networks work,

---

22. It is rumored that there are over 180,000 mass incidents each year in China (Wong 2012), but detailed quantitative measures are lacking.

and how heuristics are used to identify targeted populations. Chapter 4 shows how Dibao is provided to the poor who cannot participate in the labor market, and it shows how targeted populations, when eligible based on income, are prioritized to receive Dibao while many other similarly impoverished households are turned away.

The second portion of the book, Chapters 5 and 6, turns to the consequences of prioritizing Dibao for targeted populations. Chapter 5 focuses on the consequences for targeted populations themselves. This chapter shows how Dibao works for repression and how the distribution of material benefits increases interactions between the regime and the target of repression, facilitating surveillance and control with dependence and obligation. Because heuristics are used to identify targeted populations, many who are targeted never intended to protest. There is also variation in the repression of targeted populations by neighborhood and over time. Using data from the nationally representative survey and news announcements related to Dibao provision, this chapter shows that repressive assistance may not decrease contentious activity on average among targeted populations. However, repressive assistance is effective in deterring specific activities for individuals when they are closely managed and monitored.

Chapter 6 captures the backlash triggered by prioritizing Dibao for targeted populations. Using data from the survey of 100 neighborhoods, this chapter shows that when targeted populations receive Dibao benefits, there is greater contention over Dibao distribution in the neighborhood. Those who are turned away from benefits are more likely to protest and bargain for Dibao. Examining overall trends in collective action, this chapter shows that welfare-related protests are higher among cities that have higher levels of Dibao provision for targeted populations than cities that have lower levels. Although local administrators are adept at defusing protests, and collective action remains small and localized, people are left resentful and embittered. Data from the nationally representative survey shows that cities with higher levels of Dibao provision for targeted populations have lower assessments of government capabilities, especially in welfare provision and public responsiveness, as well as lower levels of political trust and satisfaction.

I close the book in Chapter 7 by considering how China's pursuit of political order through preemptive control changes (or remains unchanged) in a digital context of rapidly growing data, computing power, and advances in machine learning. The goal of preemptive control, and the predictive surveillance that enables this goal, remain unchanged. What is more likely to change is an expansion in the number of individuals targeted for preemptive control.

2

Fixating on Political Order

Over the past four decades, China has transformed from a poor, underdeveloped nation to the world's second largest economy. In 1980, the Chinese economy contributed 2% of world GDP. In 2019, it represented nearly 20%.[1] More than 850 million people have been lifted from extreme poverty since China initiated reforms to liberalize the economy in 1978, contributing substantially to overall global declines in poverty (World Bank 1996; Zhang 1997).[2] Per capita national income increased more than eightfold, from $130 in 1978 to over $1,100 in 2015 (Piketty, Yang, and Zucman 2017).[3]

However, people in China have not experienced uniform gains. Income inequality has skyrocketed, increasing rapidly during the first half of the 1990s and during the early 2000s (Gustafsson, Shi, and Sicular 2008; Khan and Riskin 2001; Sicular et al. 2010). In 1978, the top 10% of income earners held 27% of national income, and the bottom 50% of income earners also held 27% of national income. By 2015, the share of national income held by the top 10% increased to 41%, while that held by the bottom 50% declined to 15% (Piketty, Yang, and Zucman 2017). Piketty, Yang, and Zucman (2017) note that "China's inequality levels used to be ... close to those observed in the most egalitarian Nordic countries—while they are now approaching U.S. levels."

Rising inequality resulted from economic liberalization, but China's welfare system exacerbated rather than reduced the gap between the rich and the poor. Gao and Riskin (2009) show that from the 1980s to the early 2000s, benefits in all major social welfare categories—pensions, health, housing, and food—were distributed regressively and enlarged inequality. Those who were better off benefited relatively more from China's welfare system while the poor benefited less.

---

1. Data from the IMF: World Economic Outlook Database via http://dataportal. opendataforafrica.org/wkmyjxf/imf-world-economic-outlook-weo-database-october-2018 (accessed June 21, 2019).

2. See https://www.worldbank.org/en/country/china/overview (accessed June 12, 2019).

3. Based on 2015 US dollars (USD).

The only category of social welfare in China that redistributed wealth to the poor and narrowed inequality was social assistance, centered around the Dibao program. Today, Dibao is the world's largest unconditional cash transfer program in terms of population (Gao 2017).

Why did China adopt Dibao? How does the Dibao program work? This chapter traces the evolution of Dibao, focusing in particular on its changing role in China's pursuit of political order. This chapter also provides background on the program and places it in the context of China's social policies.

2.1 Evolving Relationship between Dibao and Political Order

Almost all research about the Dibao program connects its adoption to the Chinese regime's concerns about social stability (Gao 2017; Heurlin 2016; Solinger 2005, 2008, 2010, 2014; Solinger and Hu 2012; Solinger and Jiang 2016; Tang 2003). However, what has not been said is that Dibao's relationship with stability has changed over time, reflecting changes in the regime's understanding of the concept of stability and the regime's strategies for pursuing it.

2.1.1 Origins of Dibao: Resolving Underlying Motives for Protest

State provision of welfare has a long history in China. Public welfare has been linked to state legitimacy as far back as the teachings of Confucius in the sixth century BC (Perry 2008). Historians have found the role of the state to be critical to famine relief in the 18th and 19th centuries (Edgerton-Tarpley 2008; Li 2007; Will 1990). The first programs that bear semblance to modern welfare policies were implemented in the Republican period (J. Chen 2012).

Starting in the 1950s, the Communist Party under Mao Zedong implemented welfare programs with vastly different goals and levels of benefits for urban versus rural areas. In urban China, the CCP aimed to create a productive society with full employment. China's labor insurance regulations adopted in 1951 stipulated that all benefits—including labor insurance, pensions, health care, housing, and distribution of consumer goods—be tied to employment. Entitlements differed depending on the status of a worker's unit and the seniority of the worker (Ahmad and Hussain 1991; Davis-Friedmann 1983; Frazier 2002; Whyte and Parish 1984). Welfare benefits far exceeded wage income and were typically pooled at the employer level, financed by a combination of employee and employer contributions (Ahmad and Hussain 1991). Urban social assistance—called the *Three Withouts* (三无)—was small in scale and provided meager benefits.

In rural China, benefit provision was centered around the rural collective, which pooled and distributed benefits. Rural benefits were much lower than those in urban areas (Ahmad and Hussain 1991; Parish and Whyte 1978).[4] The family was expected to remain the primary provider of welfare, as was the case prior to communist rule. Rural social assistance—called the *Five Guarantees* (五保)—covering food, clothing, medical care, housing, and burial expense were provided only to the elderly poor who did not have families to provide for their welfare (Parish and Whyte 1978).

China's economic liberalization dismantled this Maoist welfare system. Rural decollectivization in the 1980s eliminated rural social assistance and health care programs because the collective no longer existed to pool and distribute funds. By 1985, rural health insurance, which at its peak reached 85% of the rural population, survived in only 5% of rural brigades (Shao 1988). China transformed from a wholly state-controlled health care system to one of the most market-oriented health systems in the world (Wagstaff et al. 2009).

State-owned enterprise reform in the 1990s led to declining incomes for urbanites as firms, which faced greater competition and lower profits, had difficulty paying wages and pensions. China's 1951 labor insurance regulations mandated pension payment of up to 90% of worker salaries after retirement (at age 60 for men, age 55 for women) (Frazier 2010). However, firms did not set aside funds for pension obligations. Instead, pension payments were made through "pay-as-you-go" financing where benefits to retirees were paid directly out of contributions made by current workers. Between 1980 and 1990, the number of retirees increased from 8.2 million to 20 million, and many firms stopped or delayed pension payments because funds were insufficient (Frazier 2010; Hurst 2009). During this period, more than 30 million workers were laid off from state-owned enterprises (Hurst 2004). Poverty in cities grew rapidly (Gustafsson, Shi, and Sicular 2008; Wong 1998). By the late 1990s, China had up to 60 million unemployed urban workers (Solinger and Hu 2012; Solinger and Jiang 2016).

Protest, unrest, and collective action grew rapidly in urban areas, especially among former state enterprise workers (Cai 2002; Chen 2000; Hurst and O'Brien 2002; Kernen and Rocca 2000; Lee 1998; Solinger 2000; Thireau and Linshan 2003). The number of instances of collective action increased from 8,700 in 1993 to 25,000 in 1998 (Cai 2006). According to the Ministry of Public Security, the failure of state-owned enterprises to pay salaries and pensions to workers and laid-off workers accounted for one-third of all collective action events by 1998 (Cai 2006). Collective action events not only were numerous but also involved large numbers of people; for example, 9,600 people engaged in 575 collective action events in Shandong Province alone in 1998 (Cai 2006). There was also a great

---

4. The greatest expansions in rural benefits were in education and health care (Hsiao 1995).

deal of public sympathy for pensioners and workers. Hurst and O'Brien (2002) note that more so than other forms of social welfare in China, pensions "appear to be considered a truly sacred right in the eyes of both workers and the state" (360). In a 1996 survey of Guangzhou and Shanghai, Lee and Wong (2001) found that more than 90% of respondents felt that to "ensure social stability, the state has an obligation to provide retirement pensions for staff and workers" (85).

Faced with rising urban poverty and social mobilization, the Communist Party and its top leaders called for the development of a new social security system. After Deng Xiaoping's 1992 "Southern Tour" where he reaffirmed his support for economic reform, the third plenum of the 14th Central Committee adopted "Decision of the CPC Central Committee on Certain Issues in Establishing a Socialist Market Economy System" (中共中央关于建立社会主义市场经济体制若干问题的决定), hereafter Decision, in November 1993.[5] This document describes what is needed to establish a socialist market economy where "the market, under the macro-economic control of the state, plays a fundamental role in resource allocation" (市场在国家宏观调控下对资源配置起基础性作用). This central party document stated that one of the necessary conditions for establishing a socialist market economy is the creation of a

> [m]ulti-layered social security system that provides urban and rural residents with a degree of security commensurate to China's reality so as to promote economic development and social stability (多层次的社会保障制度，为城乡居民提供与我国国情相适应的社会保障).

The emphasis in the Decision on creating a *multi-layered* social security system reflected challenges with pension reform. Two years prior to when the Decision was adopted, a national pension reform policy had been promulgated. However, the pension reform effort had limited impact on increasing benefits for retirees because local-level governments fought for control of pension funds, resulting in high levels of fragmentation and under-funding. This fragmentation and under-funding persisted into the 2000s (Frazier 2004, 2010; Hurst 2004, 2009).

Local Experiments with Dibao

To create the multi-layered social security system described in the Decision, the government turned to social assistance. Shanghai was the first city to adopt Dibao in June 1993. Six other cities—Xiamen, Qingdao, Fujian, Dalian, Wuxi, and Guangzhou—soon followed suit. In those early days, Dibao was seen as a crucial part of creating a complete system of social security in order to resolve an

---

5. See http://www.gov.cn/gongbao/shuju/1993/gwyb199328.pdf for original text and http://www.bjreview.com.cn/special/2013-10/23/content_574000_2.htm for English translation (accessed June 21, 2019).

underlying cause of social instability and to bolster the legitimacy of the regime. On September 14, 1995, the *People's Daily* published an interview with Doje Cering, who was then head of the Ministry of Civil Affairs (MCA), the government administration tasked with running the program.[6] In this interview, the reporter asked why China needed Dibao when it already had pensions, health insurance, unemployment insurance, disaster relief, and traditional social assistance programs. Cering provided three reasons. The first reason was that the pre-existing benefit systems were limited and incomplete. He described how unemployment insurance could not be provided for more than two years, and how older assistance programs such as the Three Withouts did not have systematic coverage. The second reason for Dibao was to resolve the hardships faced by urban residents and to eliminate a cause of social instability. Cering was quoted as saying (emphasis added):

> With the Minimum Livelihood Guarantee System, the hardships encountered by urban residents can resolved in a timely and effective manner. It can help resolve social contradictions, improve the mood of the masses, and *eliminate all the sources and factors causing social instability*. It can more directly and more vigorously serve urban economic reform and promote social stability (有了最低生活保障线制度，市民生活困难能够得到及时有效地解决，有利于化解矛盾，理顺群众情绪，消除社会的不安定因素，更直接、更有力地为城市经济体制改革服务，促进社会的稳定).

The third rationale related to legitimacy of the government and of the Communist Party, with Cering describing how the implementation of Dibao showed the state's attentiveness to the plight of ordinary citizens and the superiority of China's socialist system.

In this early period of Dibao pilots, there are repeated references in official speeches and news outlets about how Dibao can solve the underlying motivations of social conflict and unrest. The *People's Daily* published an article in June 1996 encouraging local governments to expand implementation of Dibao by noting

---

6. From the *People's Daily* archive, titled "Major Reform of Urban Social Relief Work—Implementation of the Urban Minimum Livelihood Guarantee System, the Minister of Civil Affairs, Dorje Cering Responds to Reporter Questions" (城市社会救济工作的重大改革——就实行城市最低生活保障线制度民政部部长多吉才让答记者问), by Jia Zhaoquan (贾昭全), September 14, 1995.

how it ensures social stability.[7] This article described how economic reforms led to firm bankruptcies, full and partial production stoppages, and worker layoffs, and that as incomes decreased, a new class of urban poor emerged. This article stated that more than 100 cities had implemented or were preparing to implement Dibao, and that (emphasis added):

> Based on the experience of cities that have already implemented this system, Dibao's effects on society are very obvious. Not only has it reformed and improved the traditional social relief system, it has brought *resolution to social conflicts* and protected social stability (从已经实施这项制度的城市看，其社会效果十分明显，不仅改革和完善了传统的社会救济体制，而且缓解了社会矛盾，维护了社会稳定).

When Dibao was in its earliest stages, the Communist Party of the 1990s saw urban poverty as the direct result of economic restructuring, and it believed that a multi-layered urban social security system, of which Dibao was a part, would alleviate economic hardships for city dwellers and remove *the source* of social instability.

National Adoption of Dibao

On September 2, 1997, the State Council issued the "Announcement on the Establishment of the Urban Dibao Program Nationwide" (国务院关于在全国建立城市居民最低生活保障制度的通知), hereafter Announcement, mandating that all county and higher levels of government establish Dibao in all urban areas by the end of 1999.[8] The announcement declared that the State Council had decided to push forward the national implementation of urban Dibao because resolving the basic living challenges of urban residents was a key task facing China's economic and social development. In the days leading up to the Announcement, Cering, who was still the minister of Civil Affairs, penned an article for the *People's Daily* providing the rationale for nationwide adoption.[9] Cering makes a number of different appeals for why Dibao is necessary and feasible—for example, arguing that the people demand such a program, and

---

7. From the *People's Daily* archive, titled "More than 100 cities have implemented or are preparing to implement in the Urban Minimum Livelihood Guarantee System" (我国推进城市最低生活保障制度百多个城市已经实施或正在准备实施), by Chen Yan (陈雁) and Di Qiyun (翟启运), June 10, 1996.

8. For full text, see http://www.gov.cn/zhengce/content/2016-10/19/content_5121479.htm (accessed June 21, 2019).

9. From the *People's Daily* archive, titled "Actively Establish a Minimum Livelihood Guarantee System for City and Township Areas" (积极建立城乡最低生活保障制度), August 7, 1997.

equating government provision of Dibao to Mao's concept of serving the people (为人民服务). Most of these appeals, however, echo the regime's communications from the previous years that Dibao would alleviate urban poverty and remove the reason for the instability that accompanied economic reform.

From the fall of 1997 to the end of 1999, *People's Daily* articles on Dibao focused on showcasing Dibao's expansion and local implementation. For example, in January 1999, *People's Daily* reported on a visit by State Council member Ismail Amat (司马义·艾买提) to Yunnan Province to assess the implementation of Dibao prior to Chinese New Year. *People's Daily* quotes Amat as saying that Yunnan has implemented Dibao well, "helping the masses resolve their difficulties" (帮助群众解决困难).[10]

On September 28, 1999, the State Council promulgated the "Regulations on Guaranteeing Minimum Livelihood for Urban Residents" (城市居民最低生活保障条例), henceforth "Regulations," to govern the Dibao program.[11] In a *People's Daily* article that accompanied the Regulations, Vice Minister of Civil Affairs Fan Baojun said that Dibao reflected the CCP's and government's attentiveness toward caring for the urban poor,[12] and that it represented a new model for social welfare that is more extensive and systematic. As with other documents and speeches leading up to this national adoption, the *People's Daily* article emphasized how Dibao would solve the hardships of daily life accompanying economic reforms.

The Regulations made clear that Dibao was intended to act as a basic social safety net. The Regulations give local governments responsibility for implementation, with the Ministry of Civil Affairs and its subordinate offices taking the lead on administration. Civil affairs departments within the county governments as well as street-level and township government offices were given responsibility for program management and approvals, and neighborhood-level residents committees were tasked with day-to-day operations. Zhu Rongji, China's premier at the time of Dibao's adoption, said, "The Dibao's support of social stability and guarantee of the reform of the state firms has important significance; we

---

10. From the *People's Daily* archive, titled "Ismail Amat's Investigation in Yunnan Points Implementation of the Minimum Livelihood Guarantee System Should be Effective" (司马义·艾买提在云南考察指出　切实抓好最低生活保障制度实施), January 19, 1999.

11. For full text, see http://www.gov.cn/banshi/2005-08/04/content_20243.htm (accessed June 21, 2019).

12. From the *People's Daily* archive, titled "Guaranteeing the Basic Livelihood Rights of Urban Residents—Fan Baojun, Vice Minister of the ministry of Civil Affairs, Introduces the 'Regulations on Guaranteeing Minimum Subsistence for City Residents'" (保障城市居民基本生活权益—民政部副部长范宝俊谈《城市居民最低生活保障条例》出台), October 21, 1999.

should strengthen it, should fund it" (Tang 2003). Again, what is noteworthy about this quote is not only that Zhu Rongji, the second most powerful person in China at the time after Jiang Zemin, gave his support to the program, but that he linked Dibao to the task of economic reform and specified Dibao's role as one of providing social stability by solving daily hardships during economic transformation.

At the time Dibao was launched nationwide, four explicit goals were associated with the program: (1) establish and perfect China's socialist market economy, (2) establish and perfect China's social security system, (3) maintain social stability, and (4) meet the needs of comprehensive social development in China (Han 2014). These goals reflect the discussions and considerations leading up to the national adoption of Dibao. The first and foremost goal is economic reform, changing from a wholly state-led model of development to one where market forces allocate resources. Because economic reform was accompanied by layoffs and because people who had lost their source of income were mobilizing, the goal of perfecting China's social security system (goal 2) becomes essential to achieving a socialist market economy (goal 1) while maintaining social stability (goal 3) so that society can develop (goal 4) in the manner desired by the Communist Party.

2.1.2 Metamorphosis of Dibao: Serving the Comprehensive Management of Public Security

Gao (2017) notes that the period from 2000 to 2007 marked the expansion of the urban Dibao program and the adoption of the rural Dibao program. Indeed, in November 2001, the State Council issued a notice urging local levels to provide full benefits to all eligible households.[13] In 2003, the Ministry of Civil Affairs mandated that cash or in-kind benefits be provided to rural households not eligible for traditional social assistance funds.[14] And in July 2007, the State Council formally established the rural Dibao program.[15] During these years, state media coverage of Dibao focused primarily on successful implementation of urban Dibao and the need to expand Dibao to rural areas.

---

13. State Council November 12, 2011 "Notification about Further Strengthening the Urban Dibao Program" (国务院办公厅关于进一步加强城市居民最低生活保障工作的通知); for original text, see http://www.gov.cn/zhengce/content/2016-10/11/content_5117347.htm (accessed July 3, 2019).

14. Ministry of Civil Affairs April 2003 "Notification about Strengthening Social Assistance to Rural Families with Extreme Hardship" (Gao 2017).

15. State Council July 11, 2007 "Notification about Establishing the Rural Dibao Program Nationwide" (国务院关于在全国建立农村最低生活保障制度的通知); for original text, see http://www.gov.cn/zhuanti/2015-06/13/content_2878972.htm (accessed July 3, 2019).

However, an important change occurred in the Dibao program during this period that is not reflected in any change in Dibao policy. It is a change in the relationship between Dibao and stability, in Dibao's role in China's pursuit of stability. We can see this change in leaders' speeches and articles from party media outlets. For example, when the State Council issued the notice on strengthening the urban Dibao program in November 2001, an accompanying article in the *People's Daily* linked Dibao to the *security of the regime* in addition to social stability (emphasis added):[16]

> [Dibao] has great significance for improving the socialist market economic system, maintaining social stability, ensuring the smooth progress of state-owned enterprise reform, and *the long-term security of the country* (对于完善社会主义市场经济体制、维护社会稳定、保障国有企业改革的顺利进行和国家的长治久安具有十分重要的意义).

A few days later, on November 25, 2001, when state councilor Ismail Amat visited Chongqing to inspect the progress of Dibao implementation, he urged local governments to link Dibao work with stability maintenance (要把低保工作同社会稳定结合起来).[17] For those familiar with China today, the linkage of social policy to regime security and stability maintenance may sound like a familiar refrain, but prior to the 2000s, Dibao was not spoken of in this manner.

One year later, at the National Conference on Dibao in October 2002 (全国城市居民最低生活保障工作会议), Amat linked Dibao to ensuring stability during economic reform but placed less emphasis on Dibao achieving this by removing the sources of instability.[18] Amat was reported in the *People's Daily* as saying that Dibao "is a requirement for ensuring the general stability of reform and development" (是维护改革发展稳定大局的需要). The same article reported that in 2002, China's top leaders, Jiang Zemin and Zhu Rongji, heard numerous

---

16. See *People's Daily* article titled "The General Office of the State Council Issues Notice on Further Strengthening the Minimum Livelihood Guarantee for Urban Residents" (国务院办公厅发出通知进一步加强城市居民最低生活保障工作), November 11, 2001.

17. See *People's Daily* article titled "Ismamil Amat's Work in Chongqing Emphasizes the Importance of Grasping the Minimum Livelihood Guarantee for Urban Residents" (国务院办公厅发出通知进一步加强城市居民最低生活保障工作), November 25, 2001.

18. See *People's Daily* article titled "Ismail Amat Stressed at the National Conference on the Minimum Livelihood Guarantee for Urban Residents to Further Improve the Minimum Livelihood Guarantee for Urban Residents" (司马义·艾买提在全国城市居民最低生活保障工作会议上强调进一步做好城市居民最低生活保障工作) by Pan Yue (潘跃), October 25, 2002.

reports about the progress of urban Dibao, and wrote: "Ismail Amat emphasizes that all levels of government must treat 'Dibao' as an important political responsibility and include it as a major agenda item" (司马义 · 艾买提强调，各级政府必须把'低保'工作作为一项重要的政治任务，列入重要议事日程). These remarks from 2002 contrast with Amat's remarks about Dibao when he visited Yunnan in early 1999. In 1999, Amat emphasized how Dibao could solve the problems facing the poor to achieve social stability. By 2002, Amat no longer talked about Dibao as a solution to the problems underlying social security.

The metamorphosis of Dibao's relationship with stability is subtle. Dibao since its inception had been linked to preserving social stability during market reform. The key is that starting the the early 2000s, there is less and less emphasis in central party documents and speeches of leaders that Dibao ensures stability by *resolving* the reasons for contention and protest. This shift of Dibao from a way to resolve the motivations for protest and collective action to a more general tool for stability is gradual. The discussion of Dibao as a solution to the problems underlining protests does not disappear overnight but diminishes over time as the narrative of Dibao as a tool of stability maintenance increases.

This shift in how the Communist Party saw Dibao in relation to pursuing stability may be related to changes in China's pattern of large-scale mobilization, the state's response to these perceived social threats, and the regime's conceptualization of stability. In terms of the pattern of social mobilization, although protests over layoffs and declining wages continued into the 2000s, in April 1999 over 10,000 Falun Gong practitioners surrounded Zhongnanhai, the central headquarters for the CCP and State Council (Chang 2008). This was the largest collective action event in Beijing since Tiananmen in 1989, and The protesters were not over economic grievances but rather about social and political rights. This large-scale collective action event involved diverse members of society, from blue collar workers to white collar intellectuals, as well as party insiders such as police officers, government officials, and party members, who had come from all across China to participate (Amnesty International 2000; Chang 2008).

Falun Gong mobilization not only precipitated an immediate reaction from the regime (Noakes and Ford 2015), it also influenced the approach the CCP took to manage social and political threats. Specifically, it strengthened the Communist Party's long-term commitment to maintaining social stability through "Comprehensive Management of Public Security," which forms the basis of China's so-called stability maintenance regime (Yang 2017). The idea of Comprehensive Management of Public Security emerged as an alternative to strike hard campaigns to suppress crime and social unrest in the aftermath of the Tiananmen protests of 1989 (Wang and Minzner 2015). Strike hard campaigns were intensive but constrained time periods where the security apparatus was mobilized for mass arrests, imprisonment, and executions (Tanner 1999, 2000). Wang and Minzner (2015) show how, starting in 1991, Comprehensive Management of Public Security strengthened incentives of officials to suppress mobilization by tying public security outcomes to salaries and promotion of local officials, and facilitated the placement of more public security officials in positions of power over political and legal affairs within the Communist Party.

However, after the Falun Gong protests we observe a new dimension to comprehensive management of public security. In reaction to the Falun Gong protests of 1999, the Central Committee and the State Council issued a joint document, "Opinion on Further Strengthening the Comprehensive Management of Public Security" (中共中央国务院关于进一步加强社会治安综合治理的意见), in September 2001.[19] This document stated that party and government organs at all levels of government cannot only rely on the public security system to ensure political order but instead need to coordinate with other functional bureaucracies in managing public security. These other bureaucracies include the civil affairs system and the labor and social security system, as well as the education, health, and family planning systems. This contrasts with earlier documents from 1991 and 1993 describing Comprehensive Management of Public Security. In the early 1990s, Comprehensive Management of Public Security was functionally limited to the public security system and did not entail coordination with bureaucracies in other functional areas such as welfare and social policy.[20] By the early 2000s, the focus on coordination beyond the public security system is established. This is also when the emphasis on using Dibao to resolve the reasons for unrest and mobilization declines, while associations between social assistance and public security increase.

The shift in Dibao's role in preserving stability—from a way of resolving the reasons for protest to becoming a tool in the machinery of the public security

---

19. For full text, see http://www.gov.cn/gongbao/content/2001/content_61190.htm (accessed July 3, 2019).

20. See the 1991 "Standing Committee of the National People's Congress Decision on Strengthening Comprehensive Management of Public Security" (全 国 人 民 代 表 大 会 常 务 委 员 会 关 于 加 强 社 会 治 安 综 合 治 理 的 决 定), full text at http://www.npc.gov.cn/wxzl/wxzl/2000-12/05/content_4548.htm (accessed July 3, 2019) and the 1993 "Various Provisions Regarding Leadership Responsibility in Implementing Comprehensive Management of Public Security" (关于实行社会治安综合治理领导责任制的若干规定), full text at http://www.chinalawedu.com/falvfagui/fg22598/36444.shtml (accessed July 3, 2019).

apparatus—may also reflect a change that occurred in the 2000s in how leaders and cadres of the Communist Party conceptualized stability. Today, the CCP
conflates the concepts of political, social, and economic stability. Political stability refers to the continuation of CCP rule (政治稳定和长治久安), which
implies the absence of coups, revolutions, or other challenges to CCP survival.
Social stability (社会稳定) refers to control over the population, including controlling crimes such as murder and theft as well as suppressing mobilization over
social grievances that do not challenge CCP rule. Economic stability (经济发展)
refers to economic growth and prosperity. Scholars have carefully distinguished
these concepts from one another. For example, research has shown that protests
over economic and other social grievances (threats to social stability) do not dis-
pute CCP rule and pose no explicit threat to political stability (Lorentzen 2013;
O'Brien and Stern 2007; Perry 2008).

However, the CCP often argues that an increase or decrease in one aspect of
stability will lead to parallel changes in the other aspects (Benney 2016). For example, in response to peaceful protests in Hong Kong over electoral reform in March
2014, *China Daily*, a central government newspaper, published an article in its
Hong Kong edition titled "Economic Growth Depends on Social, Political Stability."[21] This article argues that Hong Kong's slower rate of economic growth can
be directly attributed to the presence of political opposition and to the presence
of social movements such as Occupy Central. In other words, the CCP regarded
a peaceful protest as a threat to social stability, to China's political power, and
to economic success and growth. The CCP has used similar tactics in its discussions of Tibet and Xinjiang, where the regime faces ethnic and religious conflicts
(Davis 2008; Goldstein 1997). At the second central working session on Xinjiang
in May 2014, President Xi Jinping emphasized that the overall objective of the
CCP's work in Xinjiang is the unified goal of social stability and long-term political stability, supported crucially by economic development and improvements in
prosperity.[22] Similarly, in August 2015, after the Sixth Central-level Work Conference on Tibet, a *People's Daily* editorial reiterated the need for social stability and
economic development to support political stability in Tibet.[23]

What is easy to forget is that the CCP did not always conceptualize political,
social, and economic stability in this way. In the early and mid-1990s, social unrest

---

21. See http://opinion.people.com.cn/n/2015/1022/c1003-27727236.html (accessed July 8,
2017).

22. See http://www.rmzxb.com.cn/c/2014-05-30/332517.shtml (accessed December 3, 2014).

23. See http://opinion.people.com.cn/n/2015/1022/c1003-27727236.html (accessed November 1, 2017).

(social instability) was seen as *a consequence* of economic growth. Economic liberalization greatly boosted growth but was seen as causing social discontent, rather than as a way to preserve social stability. Programs such as Dibao were seen as a solution to the problems of poverty underlying protest and unrest. By providing for the basic livelihood of the population, there would be fewer reasons for collective action and social mobilization, which would in turn allow economic reforms to continue without opposition. What we understand today as "political stability" enters into the equation only in the sense that the strength of the Communist Party would ensure that such policies were carried out. When reading documents such as the 1993 "Decision of Central Committee of the Chinese Communist Party on Setting Up the Socialist Market Economic System," we can clearly see that the goal is modernization. The Communist Party serves the task of pursuing socialist modernization, to ensure the creation of Deng Xiaoping's socialism with Chinese characteristics. Creating a social welfare system smooths the road to modernization by providing people across China (in both urban and rural areas) a degree of security so that social instability will not hinder the pursuit of economic reform and socialist modernization. In the time period when Dibao was first initiated, the CCP did not conceptualize social stability (absence of protest and unrest), economic stability (economic reform, growth, and modernization), and political stability (strength of the Communist Party and its continued rule) as fungible. Instead, they were treated as distinct concepts with specific relationships to one another.

2.2 *Suppressing Instability, Implementing Order*

Much of our current thinking on political order has its roots in Samuel Huntington's 1968 book *Political Order in Changing Societies*. Huntington makes a strong case for political order. He argues that liberty cannot exist without order, and contends that political order is essential for controlling social conflict during the course of modernization, which includes economic development and social mobilization. What is striking about this book for scholars of democratic politics, and one of the reasons it is popular among China's leaders, is that Huntington praises communist regimes for enforcing order during modernization. (Huntington 1968:8) writes:

> But one thing communist governments can do is to govern; they do provide effective authority. Their ideology furnishes a basis of legitimacy, and their party organization provides the institutional mechanism for mobilizing support and executing policy.... They may not provide liberty, but they do provide authority; they do create government that can govern.

In the absence of political order, Huntington describes a society characterized by relentless competition among social forces: "between man and man, family and family, clan and clan, region and region, class and class" (Huntington 1968:24). This competition generates conflict, violence, and corruption. North, Summerhill, and Weingast (2000) pick up this notion of political disorder and describe it more precisely as the condition when people fear for their lives, for their families, and for their sources of livelihood, arguing that political order is essential for long-term economic growth and the creation of successful societies.

2.2.1 Seeking Order through Party Institutions

The CCP pursues political order by firmly institutionalizing this goal so that it shapes the incentives of party and government officials. China is a single-party authoritarian regime with five levels of state administration: central, provincial, prefectural (also known as city), county (also known as district), and township (also known as street). At each level, crucial government and industry positions are held by members of a Communist Party committee, such as the local party secretary and vice party secretaries. For example, the governor of a province (government position) is often a vice party secretary of the province (party position), and the determination of who becomes governor is made by the Communist Party. I refer to these party committee members as the "top leaders" at each level of state administration.

Because the party controls access to key positions of power, it allows the ruling party to effectively mitigate intra-elite conflict by creating a mechanism for credible power sharing (Haber 2007; Svolik 2012; Wintrobe 1998). By offering opportunities for career advancement, the Communist Party can successfully coopt elites because political office allows for rent seeking, and higher political office allows for access to greater rents. This cooptation has been shown to lessen the risks of elite coup and conflict (Brownlee 2007; Magaloni 2008; Magaloni and Kricheli 2010). The CCP's control of key government positions and career advancement is often cited as an exemplar of this institutional design.

What has received less attention from scholars of authoritarian politics and comparative politics is that China's party institutions do not simply offer a mechanism for power sharing; rather, these institutions also aim to ameliorate principal–agent problems related to governance. Through a series of reforms implemented since the late 1970s, the CCP has linked career advancement for party committee members (and regime bureaucrats more generally) to performance criteria, the so-called cadre evaluation system (Huang 1996). Lower-levels officials must deliver certain outcomes in order to advance and benefit from greater opportunities for rent seeking. These outcomes are delineated by upper-level officials so that lower-level officials are working toward the same goals. This feature of China's party institutions has received a great deal of attention from scholars of China, especially as an explanation for China's spectacular growth (Burns 1989; Chen, Li, and Zhou 2005; Heilmann and Kirchberger 2000; Li and Zhou 2005; Maskin, Qian, and Xu 2000; Qian and Xu 1993; Xu 2011).

The cadre evaluation system initially emphasized the need for officials to conform to the regime's ideology (Manion 1985; Whiting 2004), but starting in the 1980s, evaluations were increasingly concerned with concrete achievements in economic and social areas (Edin 2003). By the mid-1990s, officials were evaluated against quantitative targets ranging from the population growth rate to the gross value of industrial output to education completion rates. As the cadre evaluation system evolved, China also implemented one-level-down management (下管一级), where the performance (and promotion) of top leaders at each level of government is evaluated by top leaders at the next level up (O'Brien and Li 1999).

Since the 2000s, avoiding large-scale collective action (social stability) and growing the economy have consistently been identified as the targets crucial for career advancement. Performance targets are ranked by importance—in ascending order soft targets, hard targets, and veto targets. The exact description of targets varies depending on the policy responsibility of that level of government and by region (e.g., between rural and industrial areas, between coastal and inland provinces). However, numerous researchers have independently identified social stability as a veto target, meaning that officials who fail to meet the veto target will not be promoted even if performance is strong in all other areas (Edin 2003; O'Brien and Li 1999; Whiting 2004). Whiting (2004) finds that in the mid-1990s, when unsanctioned levies on farmers generated unrest, central authorities prevented the promotion of any official disciplined for such levies. Edin (2003) shows that in a Zhejiang county, collective action events with 50 or more people would cancel out the achievement of targets in other areas. The importance of social stability for career advancement among officials has not declined (Broadhurst and Wang 2014; Gao 2016; Lampton 2014; Manion 2009; Wedeman 2004; Peter 2015). In March 2016, a few weeks after large-scale protests by coal mine workers in Heilongjiang Province in northeastern China, the General Office of the Central Committee of the Chinese Communist Party issued "Provisions for the Responsibility of Leadership to Implement Comprehensive Management of Public Security," which explicitly stated that the careers of party and government officials at all levels of the party, government, and industry would be vulnerable if they failed to defuse collective action and control unrest.[24]

---

24. For original text, see https://bit.ly/2J3JWIm (accessed July 1, 2017).

Based on internal documents that specify the criteria for political advancement from several central and eastern provinces that I gathered between 2015 and 2017, economic development and social stability remain heavily emphasized. For example, in one central province, prefecture and county governments can earn a maximum of 350 points in their annual performance evaluations. Of these 350 points, 98 are related to economic development, such as non-public sector GDP growth (six points) and total export volume (three points). The next largest category is social stability with 77 points, including 18 points for ensuring social stability and preventing collective action, and five points for managing petitions.

By making career opportunities conditional on performance, China's party institutions not only address the problem of intra-elite conflict but also aim to shape how lower-level officials carry out the goals and objectives of the regime. Through these party institutions, the central regime's goal of political order is perpetuated throughout the Chinese government, reaching county mayors, township party secretaries, and low-level officials across China.

2.2.2 Seepage of Political Order

How officials achieve political order is strongly influenced by the approach of comprehensive management of public security, which underpins China's stability maintenance regime. Stability maintenance in China is often described as involving a broad range of government agencies, grassroots party organizations, other communist mass organizations, and social institutions such as schools to maintain social order. Some have called it a form of "social management" (Xu and Li 2011). Yang (2017) describes stability maintenance as "a complex array of institutional arrangements and practices concerning social control, including cultivating grassroot state agencies and mass organizations, controlling media outlets and allowing various extralegal policing practices" (36). Fewsmith (2012) quotes former President Hu Jintao as saying in 2011 that stability maintenance involved "strengthening and making innovations in social management…to maintain social order" supported by eight key tasks: "supporting people's organizations'; forming 'scientific and effective mechanisms' for coordinating interests, expressing demands, and mediating contradictions; and improving the 'management of and services for' the transient population and special groups'" (1).

Scholars have focused on specific facets of how stability maintenance plays out. Wang and Minzner (2015) show how, under Comprehensive Management of Public Security, officials in the security apparatus have been promoted to key CCP positions. Lee and Zhang (2013) show how Comprehensive Management of Public Security results in bargaining between street- and township-level officials, who enforce stability, and the people they aim to control.

However, what has not been said is that China's intense preoccupation with political order generates what I call seepage. Seepage occurs when a goal of a regime impacts unrelated policies not by changing the core facets of those policies but by changing how the policy is implemented, and more specifically by changing how the resources associated with the policy are allocated. In this case, the goal is political order, the impacted policy is Dibao, and political order seeps into Dibao because Comprehensive Management of Public Security requires all resources of the regime to be available for stability maintenance. As the subsequent chapters will show in detail, even though Dibao is a welfare policy, it becomes prioritized for purposes of security and order. The Dibao policy is not changed, and core tenets of the policy (e.g., means testing, residency requirements) are not violated, but the priority of political order alters the logic of benefit distribution. Sometimes this altered logic is enshrined in official documents—for example, some cities in China will issue policy notices reminding low-level administrators to make sure poor people undergoing re-education obtain Dibao—but other times it occurs informally.

Seepage has organizational implications. In China and in the case of political order, it means that repression can permeate programs and policies that were not explicitly repressive. Bureaucracies such as civil affairs and family planning in China have played roles in state coercion since the Maoist era. The Ministry of Civil Affairs and its subordinate departments are crucial in exerting the regime's control over and suppression of civil society organizations (Ho 2001; Teets 2013; Yu 2011). The Family Planning system was long responsible for enforcing birth quotas (Greenhalgh and Winckler 2005). However, in the past, these ministries coordinated with China's public security apparatus in the implementation of specific policies that contained explicitly coercive goals. What changes in the early 2000s with Comprehensive Management of Public Security is that coordination was no longer limited to specific areas or targets such as birth rates or NGO registration, but instead seeped into many programs under the control of these bureaucracies that were not explicitly coercive.

Although this book is focused on Dibao, seepage of political order in China likely affects many other areas of policy making. In Lee and Zhang's (2013, 1486) ethnography of stability maintenance practices, they say:

> For instance, in order to prevent angry residents from demonstrating in the streets, a street government located in the embassy district in Beijing had to use its own funds to repair the water pipes during a protracted dispute between homeowners and the management company. In a housing-quality dispute involving low-income housing developed by the Shenzhen municipal government, officials sweetened the bargain with aggrieved

homeowners by building a new primary school for homeowners' children (counted as an education expenditure), improving the environment by planting shrubs (as an environmental improvement item), and providing "services," such as augmenting community security by adding a guarded gate, assisting unemployed residents to find jobs, and even providing some petty jobs in the community work station (run by the street government) to family members of the protest leaders.

Education is not regarded as part of China's stability maintenance regime, but when education funds are used to build a school to satisfy protesters, political order has seeped into education policy. The education policy itself has not changed—educational expenditures are spent on expanding access to education—but the logic guiding the distribution of educational expenditures has been altered. Environmental improvement is also not part of China's stability maintenance regime, but political order seeps into environmental policy when environmental improvement funds are used to plant shrubs to satisfy protesters. Again, the policy of environmental improvement has not changed, but how funds are allocated and distributed has changed. Job training is not part of China's stability maintenance regime, but when job training is prioritized for protesters, political order has seeped into job training policies—not by changing the written policy but by altering the logic of its distribution.

2.3 Basic Contours of the Dibao Policy

The rest of the book shows how political order seeps into Dibao provision and explores the consequences. But, before we get there, some basic background on the Dibao program and its financing is needed. The central feature of the Dibao program is cash transfers provided to households whose per capita incomes fall below a locally set Dibao line. This Dibao line is supposed to represent the amount of money needed to guarantee a basic subsistence with clothing, food, shelter, and, where appropriate, water, electricity/fuel, and education for minors. The Dibao line is set by city-level governments. Districts and urban counties subordinate to the city have a certain amount of latitude to adjust this line upward or downward.

The Dibao line and household registration (*Hukou*) status form the general eligibility criteria for Dibao. Participating households receive monthly cash subsidies up to the Dibao line. For example, let us suppose City A has a Dibao line of 400 Chinese Yuan (CNY) per month; this means each household with residency status in City A and per capita income below 400 CNY per month should, in theory, receive a cash subsidy so that the household's monthly per capita income reaches 400 CNY. In this case, a family with a household per capita income of 100 CNY per month would receive monthly per capita subsidies of 300 CNY per month; a family with a household per capita income of 350 CNY per month would receive monthly per capita subsidies of 50 CNY per month.

Individuals can obtain Dibao only in the locality where they hold *Hukou*, even if they are living or working in a different city. For example, if a married couple holding *Hukou* from Hebei is working in Beijing and their income falls below Beijing's Dibao line, they are not eligible for Beijing's Dibao program. If their income falls below the Dibao line of the city in Hebei where their residential permit is located, they can obtain the Dibao benefits of their *Hukou* residence. In practice, many considerations go into the determination of income, and residency status requirements are changing as the CCP works to narrow benefit gaps between rural and urban areas.

Participation in urban Dibao increased rapidly from 2.7 million when the program was launched nationwide in 1999 to 22.5 million in 2003 (solid line, left panel of Figure 2.1).[25] The number of urban participants stayed between 22 to 23 million between 2003 and 2011, and declined thereafter. As of 2017, there were 12.6 million urban Dibao recipients which is slightly less than 1% of China's population in 2017.

Various regions began piloting rural Dibao before its official national launch in 2007. There were already 3 million rural Dibao participants in 2001 when the Ministry of Civil Affairs first reported this number (dashed line, left panel of

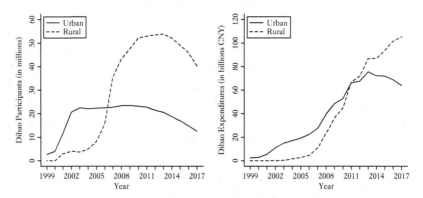

FIGURE 2.1 Dibao participants and Dibao expenditures

25. Data based on annual reports from the Ministry of Civil Affairs, found online at http://www.mca.gov.cn/article/sj/tjgb/ (accessed July 8, 2019).

Figure 2.1). When rural Dibao was officially launched in 2007, there were 35.7 million participants. Participation in rural Dibao peaked in 2013 with 53.9 million people. As of 2017, there were 40.5 million participants in rural Dibao (slightly less than 3% of China's population in 2017).

Government expenditures on urban Dibao increased steadily from 1999 to 2013, reaching a peak of 75.7 billion CNY (11 billion USD) in 2013.[26] Urban Dibao expenditures have since declined, reaching 64.1 billion CNY (9.3 billion USD) by 2017 (see solid line, right panel of Figure 2.1). Rural Dibao expenditures have continually increased, from 10.9 billion CNY (1.6 billion USD) at the program's nationwide launch in 2007 to 105.2 billion CNY (15.2 billion USD) as of 2017 (see dotted line, right panel of Figure 2.1).

The decline in urban Dibao participants and expenditures and the continued growth of rural Dibao reflect a priority of the Xi Jinping era to reduce the gap in welfare benefits between urban and rural areas (Solinger 2017). As Table 2.1 shows, in 2007, when rural Dibao was first launched, average annual expenditure per recipient was 1,220 CNY for urban Dibao participants and 306 CNY for rural participants. As of 2017, the gap has narrowed, but average expenditures for urban recipients (5,079 CNY) are still nearly twice that of rural recipients (2,600 CNY).

Table 2.1 also shows just how minimal the Minimum Livelihood Guarantee is. Average government expenditures of 5,079 CNY per year roughly translates to two dollars (14 CNY) a day for urban recipients, and average government expenditures of 2,600 CNY per year is roughly one dollar (7 CNY) a day for rural recipients. In comparison to average disposable incomes, average government expenditure per urban Dibao recipient was generally less than 10% of average urban disposable income in the 2000s, and since 2011 has remained steady at 14% of average urban disposal income. In rural areas, average government expenditure per recipient has increased since 2010 but remains less than 20% of average rural disposable income as of 2017.

Although the Dibao line is supposed to be at a level that covers clothing, food, housing, and other basic living expenses, Figure 2.2 shows that in most cities, the Dibao line falls below the city's average food expenditures.[27] In this figure, dotted lines represent the average monthly household food expenditures, and the solid line is the monthly Dibao line. For all 36 cities shown (representing all of China's provincial-level cities, provincial capitals, and sub-provincial level cities), which

---

26. All CNY to USD currency conversion based on 2019 conversion rate of 6.9 CNY to 1 USD from https://www.xe.com/currencytables/ (accessed July 8, 2019).

27. Food expenditure data from the 2011 *China City Economic Yearbook* (中国区域经济统计年鉴).

Table 2.1 Comparison of Dibao expenditures and disposable income

Year	Avg. govt expenditure per urban recipient	Avg. govt expenditure per rural recipient	Urban disposable income	Rural disposable income	Urban % of income	Rural % of income
2000	676		6,256	2,282	11%	
2001	461		6,824	2,407	7%	
2002	526		7,652	2,529	7%	
2003	670	71	8,406	2,690	8%	3%
2004	784	332	9,335	3,027	8%	11%
2005	859	307	10,382	3,370	8%	9%
2006	1,001	273	11,620	3,731	9%	7%
2007	1,221	306	13,603	4,327	9%	7%
2008	1,685	531	15,549	4,999	11%	11%
2009	2,055	763	16,901	5,435	12%	14%
2010	2,271	853	18,779	6,272	12%	14%
2011	2,898	1,258	21,427	7,394	14%	17%
2012	3,146	1,343	24,127	8,389	13%	16%
2013	3,666	1,609	26,467	9,430	14%	17%
2014	3,845	1,671	28,844	10,489	13%	16%
2015	4,228	1,900	31,195	11,422	14%	17%
2016	4,647	2,212	33,616	12,363	14%	18%
2017	5,079	2,600	36,396	13,432	14%	19%

Source: All values are in Chinese Yuan (CNY). Dibao data from annual statistical reports from the Ministry of Civil Affairs, 1999 to 2017; disposal income data from the 2018 *China Statistical Yearbook.*

serve as reference points for other localities, the Dibao line is at or below average household food expenditures, and in many cases the Dibao line has increased more slowly than food expenditures over time. Although average food expenditure does not reflect what a family would need to spend on food in order to avoid starvation, remember that Dibao funds are supposed to cover not only food, but also clothing, housing, and other basic living expenses. True to the program's name, Dibao benefits are extremely minimal, avoiding the provision of anything more than the absolute minimum needed to eke out an existence.

2.3.1 Related Social Assistance Programs

Dibao is one of two main social assistance programs in China. The other is the Assistance for the Especially Poor program, usually known as the *Tekun* program

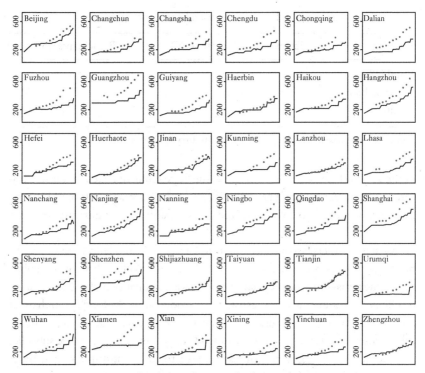

FIGURE 2.2 Dibao line and average food expenditures, 1997–2011

(特困人员救助). Dibao recipients cannot receive benefits from the Tekun program, and vice versa.[28] Most other social assistance benefits are dependent on being a participant in one of these two programs. Dibao is larger by far. In 2017, as shown in Table 2.2, urban and rural Dibao combined had six times as much funding as the Tekun program, and 11 times as many participants.

The Tekun program is the modern successor of two traditional social assistance programs—the Three Withouts for urban residents and the Five Guarantees for rural residents—that have been in place since the 1950s. While the rural Five Guarantees was always administered separately from rural Dibao, beneficiaries of the Three Withouts were largely absorbed into the urban Dibao program

---

28. See "State Council Opinions on Further Improving the Assistance System for the Especially Poor" (国务院关于进一步健全特困人员救助供养制度的意见), http://www.gov.cn/zhengce/content/2016-02/17/content_5042525.htm (accessed July 9, 2019).

Table 2.2 China's main social assistance programs

Program	Expenditure (billions, CNY)	Participants (millions)
Rural Dibao	105.2	40.5
Urban Dibao	64.1	12.6
Tekun	26.9	4.7

Source: 2017 annual statistical report from the Ministry of Civil Affairs.

in the 2000s (Gao 2017). In early 2014, the State Council issued "Interim Measures for Social Assistance" (社会救助暂行办法),[29] hereafter Interim Measures, that combined the Three Withouts and Five Guarantees programs into the Tekun program.

Most other social assistance benefits in China, such as medical insurance and housing subsidies, are available only to individuals who have been given Dibao or Tekun status—that is, they have been assessed as qualifying for participation in Dibao or Tekun.[30] Medical assistance provides subsidies for the purchase of government health care insurance as well as cash to cover out-of-pocket medical expenses.[31] In 2017, government expenditure on medical insurance subsidies was 7.4 billion CNY; government expenditure to cover out-of-pocket payments was 26.6 billion CNY. Education assistance provides fee waivers and subsidies for children in Dibao and Tekun households, as well as disabled children who otherwise cannot participate in compulsory education (six years of primary education, three years of secondary education). The housing subsidies program consists of access to low rent housing as well as subsidies for housing in urban areas for Dibao and Tekun households. Finally, the temporary assistance program is designed to provide Dibao and Tekun families facing extreme hardship, such as a disaster or illness, with additional, short-term cash and/or in-kind subsidies. In 2017, government expenditure on temporary assistance was 10.8 billion CNY.

The linkage of multiple social assistance programs to Dibao means that in addition to cash transfers, which is the central feature of the official Dibao program, Dibao households can receive a number of what I call "ad hoc benefits."

29. For full text see http://www.gov.cn/zwgk/2014-02/27/content_2622770.htm (accessed July 9, 2019).

30. The only exception from a national policy perspective is the Disaster Relief program for victims of earthquakes, flooding, and other natural disasters. In addition, the 2014 Interim Measures allows county and higher levels of government to designate other individuals to be beneficiaries of social assistance programs.

31. All descriptions of programs based on the 2014 Interim Measures.

These benefits are ad hoc not because they are informal—many are associated with the other social assistance programs described above—but because they can be issued at any time and often represent one-time distributions of benefits. The economic value of these benefits varies hugely. Access to low-rent housing can be thousands of yuan per month in value, while a cash subsidy for an education expense such as textbook purchase, can represent a one-time transfer of a few dozen yuan. This also means that while benefits are very minimal for most Dibao recipients, some recipients can receive benefits through Dibao and its associated programs that are much higher in value.

2.3.2 Dibao in the Context of Welfare in China

Welfare is the Chinese government's second largest category of spending, after education. Based on data from the 2018 *China Statistical Yearbook* (中国统计年鉴),[32] Table 2.3 shows that central and local governments together spent 2,451.2 billion CNY on welfare and unemployment programs in 2017, or slightly over 12% of all government expenditures. It is often noted that China's spending on domestic security, including armed police and stability maintenance funds, outstrips the country's spending on national defense, but what we can see from Table 2.3 is that spending on social welfare is nearly double that of either domestic security (1,246.1 billion CNY) or national defense spending (1,043.2 billion CNY).

However, only 3% of funding for welfare goes to social assistance programs. The majority goes to fund social insurance programs, and in particular to fund pension payments. Approximately 30% of the government expenditures on welfare (over 700 billion CNY) are government payments to pension programs, and another 30% are pension payments to public sector employees.[33]

The small share of government expenditures on social assistance relative to social insurance does not mean that social assistance is that much less important than social insurance. Instead, social assistance and social insurance play very different roles in public welfare; their sources of funding differ, and their level of flexibility differs. In social assistance programs, the government provides cash or in-kind assistance to individuals funded through tax or other government revenues. We can think of these programs as redistributing income. In governmental social insurance programs, various actors, including the government, employers, and individuals, contribute funds that are managed by the government and disbursed by the government at a later point in time. In other words, what we see

---

32. See http://www.stats.gov.cn/tjsj/ndsj/2018/indexch.htm, Table 7-3 (accessed July 8, 2019).

33. Based on social security data from 2017 from the China Fiscal Taxation Database (中国财政税收数据库), accessed from EPS China Data.

Table 2.3　Chinese government expenditures by category

Category	Total	% of Total	Central Gov't	Local Gov't
Education	3,015.3	14.8%	154.8	2,860.5
Welfare and employment	2,461.2	12.1%	100.1	2,361.1
Urban and rural community affairs	2,058.5	10.1%	2.3	2,056.2
Agriculture, forestry, and water conservancy	1,908.9	9.4%	70.9	1,838.0
General public services	1,651.0	8.1%	127.1	1,523.9
Medical and family planning	1,445.1	7.1%	10.8	1,434.3
Public security	1,246.1	6.1%	184.9	1,061.2
Transportation	1,067.4	5.3%	115.6	951.8
National defense	1,043.2	5.1%	1,022.6	20.6
Science and technology	726.7	3.6%	282.7	444.0
Housing security	655.2	3.2%	42.1	613.2
Interest payments for debt	627.3	3.1%	377.8	249.5
Environmental protection	561.7	2.8%	35.1	526.7
Exploration, power, information	503.4	2.5%	37.4	466.0
Culture, sports, media	339.2	1.7%	27.1	312.1
Affairs of land and water	230.4	1.1%	29.8	200.6
Management of grain and oil reserves	225.1	1.1%	159.7	65.3
Commerce and services	156.9	0.8%	5.0	152.0
Financial	114.8	0.6%	85.3	29.5
Foreign affairs	52.2	0.3%	52.0	0.2
Foreign aid	39.9	0.2%	0.0	39.9
Debt issuance expenses	6.0	0.0%	3.5	2.4
Other	172.9	0.9%	59.0	113.9
Total	20,308.5		2,985.7	17,322.8

Source: All values in billions of CNY. Data from the 2018 *China Statistical Yearbook.*

as government expenditure on social insurance are monies that come not only (or even primarily) from government coffers but represent what employers and individuals have contributed. We can think of these programs as redistributing risk. While both social insurance and social assistance programs can be used to change the structure of economic inequality, in China, social insurance programs are regressive—they privilege the wealthy over the poor—and exacerbate income inequality (Gao and Riskin 2009). Social assistance programs are the only welfare programs that redistribute wealth from the rich to the poor and reduce inequality.

The share of expenditures that comes from the central government is much greater for social assistance than for social insurance. Table 2.3 shows that only 4% of spending on social security and employment (100.1 billion CNY) came from the central government in 2017. However, in the same year, the Ministry of Civil Affairs reported that central transfers accounted for 42% of all government expenditures related to the provision of social services.[34] The 2017 report does not provide the share of central expenditures for the Dibao program; however, it is likely even higher. In 2014, when this number was reported by the Ministry of Civil Affairs, central government expenditure represented 71.9% of government expenditures on urban Dibao and 66.9% of expenditures on rural Dibao.[35]

Social assistance and social insurance programs differ in terms of their flexibility. Because individuals contribute to social insurance programs, it is difficult to provide benefits to an individual who has never contributed. And because individuals do not become eligible for benefits from social insurance programs until certain points in time (e.g., when they reach the legal retirement age for pensions), the timing of benefit provision is rigid. Finally, when conditions are such that individuals are eligible for social insurance disbursement, the benefits cannot be easily reversed and withdrawn.

In contrast, social assistance programs do not require prior contributions. They can be selectively targeted at particular individuals at any point in time, and they can be withdrawn at any point in time. These features make it easier for the communist regime to redirect social assistance to the goal of political order than to do so with social insurance. For social assistance programs, there is leeway in determining who receives the benefits, when, and for how long.

In sum, this chapter shows how the Chinese regime's understanding of and approach to stability changed over time, and how Dibao's role in the government's pursuit of stability changed in conjunction. In the Deng Xiaoping era, CCP documents suggest a view of stability that accords with Huntington and North's view of political order. Documents such as the 1993 Decision highlight modernization as the goal. In the 1980s and into the 1990s, political order served the goal of modernizing, liberalizing, and growing the economy. The Chinese

---

34. Based on the 2017 *Ministry of Civil Affairs Statistical Report* (2017 年社会服务发展统计公报), http://www.mca.gov.cn/article/sj/tjgb/2017/201708021607.pdf (accessed July 8, 2019).

35. See 2014 *Ministry of Civil Affairs Statistical Report* (2014 年社会服务发展统计公报), http://www.mca.gov.cn/article/sj/tjgb/201506/201506158324399.shtml (accessed July 9, 2019).

regime regarded social welfare and the Dibao program as the way to resolve the problems of poverty motivating collective action.

However, over time, political order became the goal. Order—the absence of social, political, and economic conflict—has been clearly, systematically, and institutionally linked by the CCP to its survival. Political order is no longer a means to achieve modernization. China is in an era where the primacy of political order reigns. Political order is an end, or perhaps the end in itself, for the CCP. When political order becomes the goal of a regime, it may be the case that most people, or many people, do not fear for their lives, for their families, and for their sources of livelihood. Many feel secure, and as a result are able to engage in activities that enrich society and boost the economy. However, such a system, as Huntington notes, does not provide liberty. Subsequent scholars of political order have expanded the notion of political order to encompass not only a strong and capable state but also the state's subordination to law and government accountability to all citizens (Fukuyama 2014). In the Chinese context, political order is focused on strength and control, where a large range of activities are viewed as problematic, deviant, and criminal. Peaceful protest and articulation of interests are seen as conflicts. Grievances against the government, against its policies, and against corrupt leaders are seen as conflicts. Conflicts are often criminalized. Activities that are protected in other countries as freedom of expression and assembly are, in China, grouped with common crimes such as murder, theft, and fraud, as well as with organized violence such as organized crime and terrorism. When order becomes the reason for the existence of a political regime, the imperative of order seeps into all aspects of governance, policy making, and policy implementation.

3

Reacting at the Threat of Disorder

That China is obsessed with political order is not a surprise to people who are familiar with China, but despite being aware of the phenomenon it is difficult to establish a quantitative, causal linkage between the pursuit of order and the specific actions of government or regime officials. In this chapter, I take advantage of local government online citizen complaint forums to conduct a field experiment to quantify the effect that fear of "instability"—in the form of an extremely vague threat of small-scale collective action—on the actions of local governments, specifically the responsiveness of county governments to Dibao applicants. This field experiment allows us to measure the causal effect on Dibao applications of concerns with ensuring social stability. The results shown in the chapter are part of a broader online field experiment described in Chen, Pan, and Xu (2016).

3.1 Experimental Design

Since the late 1990s, the Chinese government has promulgated three sets of regulations that require local levels of government to make information publicly available on the internet.[1] As a result of these regulations, the majority of local governments in China have set up government web portals, which contain online forums where individuals can submit questions or comments (Meng, Pan, and Yang 2017; Pan 2019). Figure 3.1 shows a 2016 screenshot of the "government–citizen interaction" (政民互动) page of the Changsha city government website, which is very typical of online government portals soliciting citizen complaints. The page contains several ways for individuals to interact with the local

---

1. These include the Government Online Project 政府上网工程, which encouraged government bureaus to make their documents, archives, and databases available online; Decree No. 17, "Guiding Suggestions on Constructing China's E-Government" (关于我国电子政务建设指导意见), which required every level of government to create its own web site and information databases; and the "Open Government Information Ordinance" (中华人民共和国政府信息公开条例), which delineated specific types of information that local governments must make public. For more details, see Pan (2019).

FIGURE 3.1 Changsha government web portal

government and shows visitors a curated set of questions and issues that other members of the public have raised. At the top of the main column is the *mayor's mailbox* (市长信箱), a government forum utilized by Changsha officials to collect inquiries and complaints.[2] The description of the mayor's mailbox reads:

---

2. Mayor's mailboxes are sometimes venues for private messages from individuals to the government. In the case of Changsha, content submitted to the mayor's mailbox is publicly viewable, so the mayor's mailbox acts as the government forum. For a list of comments and suggestions that are public, see http://www.changsha.gov.cn/zmhd/szxx/ (accessed March 7, 2016). In other localities, sometimes there is a forum for submitting questions that may be made public in addition to a mayor's mailbox that facilitates private messages.

The "mayor's mailbox" is an electronic email service set up by the Changsha Municipal People's Government on the city government portal to accept comments and suggestions from citizens, legal persons and other organizations related to the Changsha Municipal People's Government and associated departments. Your letter will be assigned and forwarded to the responsible departments after validation, and after a certain period of time, the response and result will be posted to the Changsha city government portal. Changsha's development cannot be separated from your wisdom and contribution, your comments and suggestions on the construction and development of Changsha are welcome.[3]

Below the description of the mayor's mailbox are recent questions that have been submitted. Further below in the main column are four other topics. From left to right and top to bottom, they are: (1) "consultation and complaints" (咨询投诉), which specifically focuses on complaints; (2) frequently asked questions (常见问题解答); (3) public opinion polls (民意征集); and (4) reports of responses to issues raised (结果反馈). The Changsha website specifies the types of comments that will be addressed, but typically there are no automatic rejections of posts based on content. However, across government portals, posts are almost always reviewed by website administrators before they are made public (Chen, Pan, and Xu 2016; King, Pan, and Roberts 2014).

Complaints on government portals range from clarifications on issues of policy to reports of government malfeasance. Lower-level governments carefully monitor online complaints: they direct complaints to the relevant bureaucracy to investigate and respond, and they bring issues, especially those related to protest and collective action, to the attention of top leaders at their level of administration (Pan and Chen 2018).

Because online complaints are monitored, by submitting requests related to obtaining Dibao that do and do not hint at threats to instability and measuring the resulting responsiveness, I can determine whether and how the goal of political order permeates into the Dibao program.

---

3. "市长信箱是长沙市人民政府在长沙市政府门户网站向社会公众设立的电子信箱，受理公民、法人和其他组织对长沙市各级人民政府以及政府工作部门的意见和建议的网上窗口。您的来信我们将通过审定、转发程序向有关责任职能部门交办，并在一定的时限在长沙市政府门户网站向您反馈处理意见或结果。长沙的发展离不开您的智慧与贡献，欢迎您对长沙的建设和发展提出宝贵意见和建议。"

This experiment was conducted in 2014, and online government forums were identified for 2,227 out of 2,869 Chinese counties (77%); 2,103 (73%) of these forums were functional.[4] For all counties with government websites, a detailed set of characteristics was recorded, including whether the website contains a public online forum or a place to contact local officials, as well as the requirements for posting to the forum or contacting officials.[5] A request for assistance in obtaining Dibao was submitted on public forums of the government website. The posting process as well as various dimensions of the government response were recorded.[6] Then, the forums were checked for responses 10 and 20 business days after the date of submission by at least two members of the research team for validation, and both the date checked and the date of the response were recorded.[7]

The outcome is the government response, which is measured in four ways: whether there was a response;[8] if there was a response, when the response was given; whether the response was viewable by the general public;[9] and, finally, the specific content of the response.

3.1.1 Treatment Conditions

The primary objective is to measure the causal effect of a threat of instability—in this case collective action—on Dibao. To do this, we create a control condition and a treatment condition that are identical except that the treatment condition contains a very vague threat of collective action. Two other treatment conditions, unrelated to stability, are tested in Chen, Pan, and Xu (2016). The control condition is as follows:

---

4. In the 124 counties with non-functional forums, attempts at submission led to errors in page loads after a lengthy wait. In each of these cases, at least three attempts were made at submission using different browsers. .

5. This experiment utilizes publicly viewable forums instead of private messaging options.

6. All posts were made from within China and submitted outside of the Lianghui period— the time of the "Two Meetings" when people's congresses and people's political consultative conferences meet—to avoid posting during a politically sensitive time period.

7. Most of the replies on government web portals—90.5%—include the date on which the reply was posted.

8. If a request for more information is the response, that is coded as a response. The protocol is to not provide further information to the government entity.

9. Based on pre-testing and previous research, responses can be made privately or viewable only by the individual submitting the request (King, Pan, and Roberts 2014).

Respected leader:

My wife and I have lost our jobs, and we have been unable to find work for a long time. Our economic situation is very difficult, and we cannot make ends meet. We have to support my elderly mother who is ill and for whom we have to buy medicine. We also have our son who is in school and has school fees and living fees that are difficult to bear. I have tried to apply for Dibao through my residents committee, but they say I am not eligible.

Can you help my family obtain Dibao? Much gratitude!

Yours,

[Common male name]

This message demonstrates existing knowledge of the Dibao program to try to increase the diversity and richness of government responses and to maximize the likelihood of a more personalized response. The inquiry states that the individual has already tried to apply for Dibao through the local residents committee but was turned away to decrease the chance of receiving replies that simply tell the applicant to go to the residents committee. The inclusion of an elderly, ill mother and school-aged child emphasizes the economic difficulties faced by this household, making the household a more likely candidate for Dibao status. This inquiry makes clear that the household faces severe economic hardships by stating that both the applicant and his wife have been unable to find work. At the same time, however, the inquiry also signals the presence of able-bodied workers in the household. Given the priority placed on work, we would expect this household to be turned away from Dibao under normal circumstances.

In the treatment conditions, the following two sentences are added:

People around me are in a similar situation, they face difficulties, and they also can't get *Dibao*. If you can't help, we'll try to figure out what we can do together about this situation.

This is inserted at the beginning of the paragraph prior to the phrase "Can you help my family obtain *Dibao*?"

This threat of collective action is oblique and weak. It is not threatening large-scale mobilization. It is not even saying for sure that there will be a protest. This is intentional due to ethical as well as theoretical considerations. If a strongly worded threat were used, this could lead the local government to investigate the post, resulting in greater use of government resources. As well, since I want to estimate the extent to which the goal of maintaining order, which is encompassing and vague, seeps into Dibao provision, this similarly vague treatment provides a more valid test.

If the provision of Dibao is motivated only by income and economic hardship, then there should not be any difference in how local governments respond to the treatment and control conditions. Similarly, if the provision of Dibao is motivated only by the desire to maximize work and labor, we also should not observe any difference in response rates to the treatment and control conditions. Both conditions signal the presence of two household members—the man writing the message and his wife—who are capable of working.

These two types of posts were randomly assigned to county government web forums stratified by prefecture so that counties within the same prefecture did not receive the same request. The posts were written to be similar in tone and length to existing content found on online government forums. Both conditions were pre-tested with Chinese citizens and officials to fine-tune their appropriateness for an online forum and their relevance to the concept tested. Because of the fragmentation of local government websites, and more generally of county governments in China, it is very unlikely that officials in one county would realize that a similar post had appeared in another county during the implementation of our experiment. Moreover, because the content of government forums is not always indexed by Chinese search engines, and because questions about social welfare and Dibao are common, the likelihood of identifying the posts as part of an experiment was low.

3.1.2 Ethical Considerations

This experiment entailed the use of deception. The decision to use deception was not made lightly (Desposato 2018; Pan 2020; Teele 2014; Whitfield 2019), but made in order to protect human subjects, to minimize disruption to the system being studied, and to protect the safety of the research team. The human-subjects aspects of our experimental protocol were pre-approved by Harvard's, MIT's, and Princeton's Institutional Review Boards.

One of the guiding principles in conducting this research was to minimize disruption to the system being studied. Since the experiment entailed submitting requests to government-managed websites, this meant minimizing the use of government resources. The submitted requests ask for government action in the form of a written response. Based on the subject of the inquiry, pre-testing, and analysis of online forums, it is unlikely that local governments would take any action beyond writing a response, and this prior expectation was borne out by the experiment. The subjects of the research, those responding to requests on government forums, were not debriefed in order to minimize the time government administrators would spend reading and potentially responding to a debrief notice. Minimizing disruption also involves making sure that future posts, whether from individuals or other researchers, are taken seriously. By not debriefing the subjects, disruption to government and risks to future applicants of the Dibao program are reduced.

To protect the safety of the research team and for logistical reasons, confederates were not used to submit informational requests. If confederates had been used, they would have needed to be individuals from households that qualify for Dibao in each of the localities where the experiment was conducted. Given the scope of the experiment, it would have been extremely difficult and costly to recruit the appropriate number of confederates, and confederates with similar enough characteristics to support our experimental design. In addition, by not using confederates, the potential for inconvenience that confederates submitting the information requests might face is eliminated.

3.1.3 Randomization and Balance

A quarter of China's 2,869 counties were assigned to the control condition (717) and a quarter to the collective action treatment condition (718). The remaining half of counties were assigned to two other treatment conditions discussed in Chen, Pan, and Xu (2016). Figure 3.2 visualizes the random assignment to the

FIGURE 3.2 Map of treatment and control assignment

treatment condition (dark gray) and the control condition (white) spatially. In this figure, the boundaries denote all 2,869 counties in mainland China.[10]

Table 3.1 shows the covariate balance across the control and collective action treatment groups on a number of different demographic, economic, and fiscal

Table 3.1 Covariate balance between treatment and control groups

	Control	Treatment	p-value
Log population	12.69	12.66	0.66
Log population (2000)	12.69	12.64	0.43
Population growth (2000–2010 %)	5.66	5.77	0.66
Gender ratio (female = 1.00)	105.97	105.64	0.4
Log population density (person/km²)	14.21	14.12	0.35
Migrant (%)	0.11	0.11	0.65
Non-agricultural household (%)	19.12	18.14	0.22
Permanent urban residents (%)	0.34	0.34	0.31
Average years of education	8.15	8.08	0.37
Illiteracy rate among age above 15 (%)	7.47	7.85	0.47
Unemployment rate (%)	0.02	0.02	0.48
Work force in agriculture (%)	64.12	64.96	0.49
Work force in industry (%)	16.22	15.34	0.27
Work force in services (%)	19.66	19.4	0.67
Ethnic minority (%)	20.76	22.26	0.48
Log GDP	4.06	4.03	0.62
Log agricultural output	2.41	2.37	0.52
Log industrial output	3.16	3.12	0.64
Log services output	2.9	2.87	0.66
Log total investment	3.68	3.65	0.66
Log total saving	2.02	1.91	0.23
Log total government revenue	0.92	0.91	0.93
Log total government expenditure	2.45	2.44	0.84
Enterprises above designated size	39.81	40.58	0.86
Average nominal GDP growth (2000–2010)	0.15	0.15	0.88

Note: Data are from 2000 and 2010 census and provincial statistical yearbooks. Variables were measured in 2010 unless otherwise noted.

---

10. Counties in light gray receive two other treatment conditions described in Chen, Pan, and Xu (2016).

factors. Demographic variables include population in 2000 and 2010, population density, gender ratio, the scope of the migrant population, the percentage of households with urban (or non-agricultural) *Hukou*, the percentage of permanent urban residents, average years of education, literacy rates, the unemployment rate, and the proportion of the work force concentrated in the agriculture, industry, and service sectors, as well as the proportion of ethnic minorities. Economic variables include GDP, per capita GDP, 2000–2010 nominal GDP growth, output by sector (agricultural, industrial, services), the number of industrial enterprises above designated size (above 5 million CNY), total investment from households, enterprises, and government, and total savings, which is the total outstanding bank deposits of rural and urban households at the end of 2010. Finally, fiscal variables include government revenue and expenditures. As can be seen from Table 3.1, randomization is successful and the treatment is balanced across all of the above dimensions.

In total, 519 posts in the control group were successfully submitted, and 525 posts in the treatment group were successfully submitted. Figure 3.3 shows that there is balance across the control and treatment groups for whether there is a government forum and whether posts are successful.

For each forum, information on the characteristics of the forum was collected, including whether existing posts and replies were publicly viewable—in other words, whether someone who does not have an account or is not logged in to the

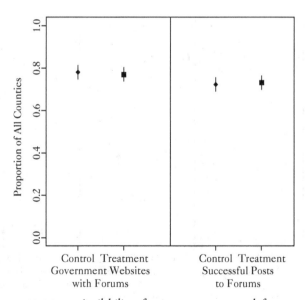

FIGURE 3.3 Availability of county government web forums

site can view posts and replies. Also recorded were the dates of the most recent posts and replies. Lastly, whether posts submitted were immediately viewable, or whether the posts were first reviewed by authorities before they were released to be publicly viewables was recorded. As shown in Figure 3.4, approximately 70% of forums have publicly viewable posts and replies. This means that for 70% of government forums, anyone who visits the forum URL can view posts and replies without creating an account or logging in. Approximately 40% of forums contain posts by the local government made within the past 30 days. However, less than 5% of forums immediately release submitted posts. This means that the vast majority of government forums first review the content of posts submitted before the posts are released to be seen by the general public. This finding is in line with the high prevalence of review found among government websites in prior research (King, Pan, and Roberts 2014). As seen in Figure 3.4, all of these forum characteristics related to openness are balanced across the control and treatment groups.

Finally, information was collected on the requirements for submitting posts to the government forum, including whether an email address is required, whether a name is required, whether a personal identification number (身份证号) is required, whether a phone number is required, and whether an address is required. Since the information of real confederates is not used, if an ID number, telephone number, or address is required, data is randomly generated to fill in these fields. The same, common name was used in all requests, and email accounts

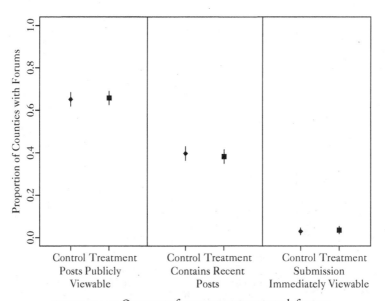

FIGURE 3.4 Openness of county government web forums

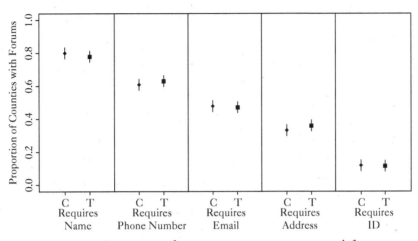

FIGURE 3.5 Requirements for posting to county government web forums

were created for the experiment. As shown in Figure 3.5, 80% of government forums require users to submit a name, 60% require a phone number, approximately 50% an email address, 30% to 40% an address, and only 10% a personal identification number. Posting requirements are also balanced across the control and treatment groups.

3.2 Threat of Collective Action on Government Responsiveness to Dibao Applicants

Under the control condition, 32% of county governments responded to the Dibao request,[11] and 21% of responses were publicly viewable.

The threat of instability increases government responses by 10 percentage points. Whereas only 32% of county governments responded to Dibao requests that describe the economic hardship faced by the household, 42% of county governments responded to Dibao requests that describe economic hardship and contain a vague threat of collective behavior. The black dot on the left side of Figure 3.6 shows the point estimate for the causal effect of providing information on future collective action on whether county governments responded to the Dibao applicant, and the black dot on the right side of the figure shows the point estimate for the causal effect of providing information on future collective action on whether governments responded publicly to the Dibao applicant. The

---

11. The denominator is the county websites where requests were successfully submitted.

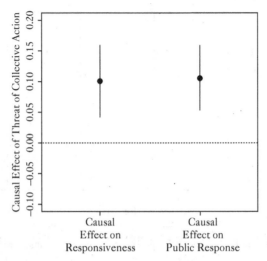

FIGURE 3.6 Effect of threat of collective action on government responsiveness to Dibao applicants

vertical lines are 95% confidence intervals.[12] When a Dibao applicant signals even slight potential to jeopardize social stability, county governments are one third more responsive to the applicant.

These results are stable to various model specifications and the inclusion of controls. Columns (1) to (3) of Table 3.2 show the results for all Chinese counties (unconditional models), where the coefficient estimates represent the causal effect of treatments on government response.[13] In column (1), government response is regressed on the treatment indicator. The model in column (2) performs the same analysis with the addition of control variables, showing that the coefficient estimates are very stable. Finally, the model in column (3) includes provincial dummy variables in addition to control variables, and again the coefficient estimates

---

12. Confidence intervals shown in the figures of the results section are based on a Welsh two-sided t-test. Although the data are binary, the large sample size and mean response rates give us confidence the central limit theorem applies. Confidence intervals based on alternative methods produce substantively identical results.

13. Results are based on regression adjustment. Treatment dummies and demeaned covariates, as well as their interactions with the treatment dummies, are included in the regressions (Lin 2013). Huber White robust standard errors are shown, though errors are virtually identical without using robust standard errors. Moreover, because treatment conditions are randomly assigned within each province (the variations of treatment are at the county level), standard errors clustered at the provincial level are qualitatively the same as those in Table 3.2. Control variables include log population, the proportion of non-agricultural households, the proportion of permanent urban residents, average years of education, the unemployment rate, and the proportion of ethnic minorities for the county in 2010.

Table 3.2 Causal effect of threatening collective action on government response

| | Government response (0 or 1) | | | | | |
| | Unconditional | | | Conditional | | |
	(1)	(2)	(3)	(4)	(5)	(6)
Threat of collective	0.077***	0.075***	0.074***	0.101***	0.101***	0.102***
action	(0.023)	(0.023)	(0.023)	(0.030)	(0.030)	(0.029)
Intercept	0.232***	0.233***	0.092***	0.320***	0.321***	0.176***
	(0.016)	(0.016)	(0.026)	(0.020)	(0.020)	(0.035)
Controls		YES	YES		YES	YES
Provincial dummies			YES			YES
Observations	1,435	1,435	1,435	1,044	1,044	1,044

Note: * p < 0.1; ** p < 0.05; *** p < 0.01.

remain stable. Columns (4) to (6) of Table 3.2 show the results for Chinese counties where requests were successfully submitted to the government web forum (conditional models). Column (4) shows the regression of government response on the treatment, similar to the unconditional model in column (1). Column (5) shows the regression of government response on treatment variables and control variables, and column (6) includes provincial dummy variables in addition to treatment and control variables. As expected, the causal effects of the treatment increase in the conditional models and remain very stable with the inclusion of control and provincial dummy variables. Together, the models in Table 3.2 show that these results are robust whether the analysis is based on all counties or on the subset of counties where posts were successfully made. The vague threat of small-scale social instability generates greater responsiveness from county governments to Dibao applicants.

The causal effect of threatening social instability on publicly viewable responses is also more than 10 percentage points. Whereas the overall rate of public responses is 21% for complaints that describe only economic hardship, the rate of public responses for complaints that also threaten collective action is 32%. This means adding a threat of disruption to the complaint increases the rate of public responses by nearly 50%. Table 3.3 shows that these results are also stable to various model specifications and the inclusion of controls. Table 3.3 shows the causal effect of threatening collective action on public responses, which are also robust to the inclusion of control variables and location dummies.

Table 3.3 Causal effect of threatening collective action on publicly viewable response

	Publicly viewable response (0 or 1)					
	Unconditional			Conditional		
	(1)	(2)	(3)	(4)	(5)	(6)
Threat of collective action	0.079***	0.079***	0.078***	0.106***	0.107***	0.108***
	(0.021)	(0.021)	(0.020)	(0.027)	(0.027)	(0.027)
Intercept	0.153***	0.154***	0.046***	0.212***	0.211***	0.097***
	(0.013)	(0.014)	(0.022)	(0.018)	(0.018)	(0.03)
Controls		YES	YES		YES	YES
Provincial dummies			YES			YES
Observations	1,435	1,435	1,435	1,044	1,044	1,044

Note: * $p < 0.1$; ** $p < 0.05$; *** $p < 0.01$.

I also examine the content of replies from county governments that responded to the Dibao applicant. Responses were hand coded into three categories: (1) Deferral, (2) Referral, and (3) Direct Information.[14] The content of these three categories roughly reflects increasing effort on the part of the government to respond constructively to the Dibao applicant.

Replies are coded as Deferral if the response does not provide an answer to the question of how to obtain Dibao. Sometimes a rationale for the lack of information is provided, but other times none is given. Oftentimes, the government response states that some piece of personal information is missing in the complaint. Replies in the Deferral category are on average the shortest replies, and likely require the least amount of effort on the part of the county government. The example below is a typical Deferral response:

Hello letter writer! Your question does not contain enough specificity, for example, your address.

Replies are coded as Referral when the government response suggests contacting another agency for further assistance, and provides the contact details of that agency. For example:

14. Intercoder reliability for agreement in classifying responses into these three categories was 99%.

Hello, you must meet certain requirements to apply for *Dibao*, based on the situation you describe, we cannot determine your eligibility. Please consult with the department of civil affairs for *Dibao* information. Telephone: ****373.

When replies state that the initial complaint does not provide sufficient information, but also provide details on how to obtain additional resources and assistance (e.g., a telephone number), the responses are coded as Referral instead of Deferral.

Finally, responses are coded as Direct Information when the reply directly provides the information required to answer the question posted by the Dibao applicant. These replies are generally the longest. Direct Information replies provide the most detailed information on what is required to obtain Dibao as well as specify the next steps for the prospective applicant, which may include contact information for relevant agencies. For example:

XX comrade, hello! First, thank you for your interest and support in our work on civil affairs. Eligibility for *Dibao* is based on household income. In your post, you did not specify your household income, nor did you specify whether you are a rural or urban household. For example, this year, in our city, the rural *Dibao* level is 2400 yuan. If your household's annual income is less than 2400 yuan, you have initial eligibility to apply for *Dibao*. But, whether you can receive *Dibao* is based on a rigorous set of criteria, which I cannot detail line by line here. Please go to the *Hukou* [household registration] office of the township civil affairs department to obtain detailed information. You can also obtain information by phone, our phone number is ****287. In addition, since the district-level civil affairs agency only has ability to review *Dibao* applications, and since the township government takes the lead in evaluation of *Dibao* eligibility, you can give your detailed information to the township office, who we believe will take your detailed information and provide preliminary advice on whether you are eligible to receive *Dibao*.

In this response, the county government not only provided information on the relevant agencies, but also provided details on what entity—the township government—makes the final decision on Dibao eligibility. Identifying the key decision maker improves the Dibao applicant's ability to obtain benefits.

Table 3.4 shows the number and percentage of responses for each of the content categories for the control and treatment conditions. Comparing the control and treatment groups, the proportion of responses in all three response categories,

Table 3.4 Content of government responses by treatment group

	No response		Deferral		Referral		Direct information	
Control	353	68.0%	33	6.4%	42	8.1%	91	17.5%
Threat of collective action	304	57.9%	36	6.9%	52	9.9%	133	25.3%

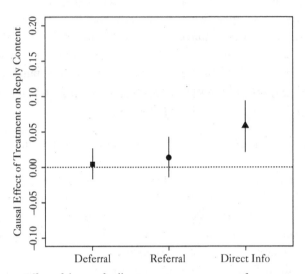

FIGURE 3.7 Effect of threat of collective action on content of government responses

but especially for the most helpful category of Direct Information, is higher when there is a threat of collective action.

Figure 3.7 shows the difference in means of each category of responses between the treatment group and the control group.[15] This difference in means represents the causal effect of the treatment on the content of the response. Providing information on the potential for future collective action has the causal effect of increasing Direct Information responses by six percentage points. In terms of speed of response, more than 20% of responses were provided within one business

15. The category of No Response exists for each group, but is not shown here. Because the differences in means are correlated with each other, a bootstrap procedure (of 1,000 iterations) is used to obtain the correct standard errors. In each round of bootstrap, prefectures are randomly drawn with replacement from the universe of prefectures to make sure the treatment conditions are balanced. Counties belonging to the newly drawn prefectures constitute a new sample.

day, and 70% of responses were provided within 10 business days. No significant differences in the speed of response were found between treatment and control groups.

This experiment provides a causal linkage between China's fixation on political order and government responsiveness to Dibao applicants. When a lower-level (county) government receives information that vaguely suggests a person has the potential for future actions that threaten social stability, the lower-level government is more likely to respond, more likely to respond publicly, and more likely to provide helpful/informative responses for obtaining Dibao.

The individuals responding to the complaints in this experiment are not top county-level leaders such as the county party secretary (县委书记) or county executive (县长), who face incentives through China's party institutions to quell collective action. However, the county government forums where this online field experiment was conducted are directly governed by top leaders at the county. The bureaucrats who head up the offices that manage these forums are directly controlled by the county's top leaders, and there may be social ties between bureaucrats running these forums and county leaders. The fact that we observe a causal effect throughout China suggests this is not driven by idiosyncratic behavior on the part of a few officials but rather is reflective of how the goal of political order seeps into China's government and bureaucratic apparatus, influencing how local governments respond to online grievances and how they treat Dibao applicants.

This experiment makes clear that Dibao provision is shaped not only by economic considerations. If income were the only factor deciding Dibao provision, we should not see any differences in the rate of response to the treatment and control inquiries, or any differences in the types of responses. The descriptions of economic hardship in the control and treatment conditions are identical. These results show that the prioritization of Dibao for individuals who are incapable of work is not the sole motivation of the program. Both conditions signal the presence of able-bodied workers in the household, so if turning away those who can work from Dibao is a key motivator of the program, then the response rates to both the treatment and control conditions should have been similarly low. The next chapter moves from Dibao application to Dibao distribution, where we see in detail how the goal of political order seeps into the logic of who receives Dibao benefits.

4

Distributing Social Assistance to Preempt Disorder

In the 1965 science fiction story by Philip K. Dick, "The Minority Report", three "precogs" foresee all crime before it occurs. These future crimes are reported to PreCrime, a specialized police department that arrests suspects before the crime is committed. Although there are no precogs in China, the Chinese regime would also like to round up, or at least monitor, would-be protesters and would-be dissidents before they can complain and protest, and in fact, the Chinese regime has designated a special class of individuals—targeted population or *zhongdian renkou* (重点人口)—to do this very thing. Public security departments across China manage lists of individuals who are suspected of being likely to damage political, social, and economic stability in the future. These individuals are placed under intense surveillance, and all resources available to the regime are brought to bear to control their behavior. One of these resources is Dibao.

It is perhaps not surprising that an actual policy in China so closely resembles the fictional depiction in "The Minority Report", which was written because of Dick's concerns about authoritarian suppression of personal autonomy. What is more surprising is that most people are unaware of the targeted population program—few academics have studied it,[1] few journalists have reported on it, and few people living in China, including individuals on targeted population lists, are aware of its existence. This is by design. Information about who is targeted is treated as classified state secrets, and "Even the concept of *zhongdian renkou* is now treated as an internal term, any use or discussion of which outside the police system is strictly prohibited" (Wang 2005:106–107).

This chapter begins by discussing the financing of Dibao before focusing on the urban neighborhood, where the identification, surveillance, and repression of

---

1. One exception is Wang (2005), whose book on China's *Hukou* system deals extensively with the management of targeted populations. Other exceptions are researchers working in Chinese police academies and research institutes associated with the public security apparatus (M. Wang 2016; Wang 2018).

targeted populations often take place. Through in-depth interviews I conducted from 2012 to 2013 with nearly two dozen residents committee party secretaries and directors, residents committee members, block captains, and public security personnel, as well as more than 50 residents in Jinan, Qingdao, Zhengzhou, Wuhan, and Zibo, I stumbled upon the targeted populations policy. I did not set out to study the policy, and it was only because I wanted to understand some puzzling patterns of Dibao distribution in the context of limited funding that it became apparent how Dibao provision was linked to a repressive program managed by the public security apparatus. I test this linkage between Dibao provision and repression, to the extent possible given its secrecy, through an original survey of 100 neighborhoods in four cities in East, Central, and West China.

4.1 *Financing and Fiscal Constraints*

Each level of government plays a specific role in the implementation of Dibao. The central government establishes general guidelines and principals. Provincial-level governments establish more precise policies based on central directives and provide supervision to lower levels of government. City-level governments set the Dibao line, determining which households are eligible for Dibao and the level of benefits Dibao and ad hoc benefits households receive. County-level governments can amend the Dibao line; if a county government increases the city's Dibao line, it usually has to shoulder the additional fiscal responsibility this entails. Both city and county levels of government can exercise discretion in refining the rules of eligibility for the program. The county-level civil affairs bureau is tasked with conducting checks of randomly selected subsets of Dibao households to ensure they meet official eligibility criteria. Civil affairs administrators with street-level governments typically screen and approve Dibao application materials.[2] The neighborhood residents committee manages the day-to-day activities related to Dibao applicants and recipients.

In terms of financing, in its initial pilot stages, localities explored two financing mechanisms for Dibao. The first—*Finance Covers All* (财政统包)—split financial responsibility between the prefecture and county levels of government. For example, in Dalian during the pilot phase, the prefecture government paid for 70% of local Dibao expenditures, and the county government paid for 30% (Min and Chong 2018). The second financing mechanism—*Split Burden, Finance Guarantee* (分别负担, 财政兜底)—made Dibao financing dependent on the

2. In some localities, approval rests with the county-level civil affairs department.

background of the Dibao recipient. Dibao payments were supposed to be made by the former employer, and if the employer could not make the payments, government finance took over the responsibility. Dibao came into being during a time of mass layoffs and enterprise reform, where employers of potential Dibao recipients often had severely constrained fiscal capacity. As a result, the first mode of financing dominated.

When Dibao was launched nationwide in 1999, local governments were given primary responsibility for financing. In 1999, the central government contributed less than 17% of financing for Dibao.[3] However, financing became a major bottleneck in Dibao implementation. The late 1990s and early 2000s were characterized by unfunded mandates (Dabla-Norris 2005; Li 2007). Local governments were given fiscal responsibility for funding a vast array of programs, but after tax recentralization in 1994, many local governments did not have sufficient revenue to fund these programs (Oi et al. 2012; Wong 1997). This was a problem for the Dibao program, so in 2001, the central government began to increase fiscal transfers to local governments in the form of earmarked subsidies (专项补助) for Dibao. Earmarked subsidies are designated for specific bureaus—in the case of Dibao, for civil affairs bureaus—and usually require local matching funds (Park et al. 1996). To minimize diversion of earmarked subsidies, local finance bureaus are often required to establish designated accounts for these funds (专户管理, 封闭管理) so spending and balances can be more easily audited by upper levels (Liu et al. 2009). This is the case for Dibao. By 2002, central transfers represented over 40% of expenditures on urban Dibao, and by 2011, central transfers accounted for over 70% of expenditures.[4]

Under the current financing model, the central government estimates an annual budget for Dibao based on total revenues and local Dibao thresholds. How much is allocated to each province is based on a formula that takes into account the number of participants, past spending, and local financial capacity (Gao 2017). Then, the province allocates this central funding downward based on local formulas to its subordinate prefecture, and prefectures do the same for counties.

Since local governments also have to supply their own funding for Dibao, the department of civil affairs proposes an annual budget based on previous and

---

3. Based on the 1999 *Ministry of Civil Affairs Statistical Report*; (1999年民政事业发展统计报告), http://www.mca.gov.cn/article/sj/tjgb/200801/200801150093969.shtml (accessed July 8, 2019).

4. Based on annual Ministry of Civil Affairs statistical reports; see http://www.mca.gov.cn/article/sj/tjgb/ (accessed July 8, 2019).

anticipated numbers of beneficiaries and the Dibao line. This budget is presented to the local departments of finance, pricing, and statistics for comments and feedback. The revised budget is submitted to the local people's congress for consideration and approval. In practice, the budget approved by the local people's congress has been pre-approved by the local party secretary and head of government, who shape overall budgetary decisions. Approved budgets are final. Localities do not exceed the budget even if it means withholding benefits from eligible households, because exceeding the budget suggests the budget proposal was poorly done and may negatively influence future allocations.

Local governments face a hard budget constraint when it comes to funding for Dibao. This budget constraint means that Dibao funds are often insufficient to cover all individuals who are impoverished and who, based on income, qualify for the program. When Dibao was first implemented nationally, local government revenue shortfalls prevented all eligible households from receiving benefits, and benefits that were received were often too low to even provide for subsistence-level survival. Throughout the 2000s, the Ministry of Civil Affairs recognized the inadequacy of Dibao coverage and promulgated policy documents to try to improve standards. For example, in 2004, policy documents were issued by MCA calling for increasing standardization of Dibao policies.[5] In 2011 MCA, in conjunction with the National Development and Reform Commission, the Ministry of Finance, and the National Bureau of Statistics, released detailed guidelines on how localities should calculate Dibao standards using basic living expenditures, Engel's coefficients, or consumption expenditure ratios.[6]

While these regulations were intended to increase Dibao's coverage of households in poverty, they did not do so because there are strong incentives for path dependence in budget calculations. At central and local levels, future budget allocations are based on past performance, where good performance means that spending of allocated funds matches approved budgetary proposals. Large jumps in budget requests signal problems with previous budgets and calculations, and finance personnel and government officials want to avoid negative evaluations. We can observe the path dependence of Dibao budgets. At the central level, after larger increases in central transfers in the 2000s, central government expenditures on Dibao grew at steady rates. For example, government documents regarding the 2019 central budget set the growth in central transfers for urban Dibao at 5%.[7]

---

5. See http://bit.ly/1LSxisX (accessed August 12, 2013).

6. See http://bit.ly/1ze5iG3 (accessed August 12, 2013).

7. See "Report on The Implementation of the Central and Local Budgets for 2018 and the Draft Central and Local Budgets for 2019" (关于2018年中央和地方预算执行情

This is a top-down calculation slightly above consumer food inflation, rather than a bottom-up calculation based on the number of impoverished households. [8]

At the local level, adjusting the Dibao line is difficult because it has broad budgetary implications. For almost all Chinese localities, the level of unemployment insurance is set below minimum wage, and the Dibao line is set below unemployment insurance. A finance department official in Henan told me that when the Dibao line is increased, unemployment insurance and minimum wage also have to be increased (Interview, B2012_521). He, along with other finance officials in Beijing and Hubei, said that adjusting the Dibao line requires extensive negotiations between a number of different bureaucracies.

Opposition to social welfare also limits financing for Dibao.[9] A number of county-level officials told me that while Dibao is essential for helping the truly destitute, Dibao can make people "lazy," and some applicants are better off working (Interview, B2012_631). A provincial-level Dibao administrator in northern China said that the Civil Affairs bureau had received pressure from local business representatives in the Provincial People's Congress (PPC) to limit the number of Dibao recipients (Interview, B2013_113). These PPC delegates were concerned that Dibao benefits were going to able-bodied workers, decreasing the availability of low-wage workers and thereby increasing costs and decreasing profits for local employers. The Beijing People's Political Consultative Conference also recommended that the municipality limit Dibao benefits for "able-bodied" workers and instead encourage them to seek employment (Han and Yu 2012). The Chongqing People's Congress criticized the provision of Dibao to those who were "idle" and "lazy." They recommended providing Dibao for only a short period of time unless the Dibao recipient is elderly or infirm. A finance department vice-director from a city in central China told me that top leaders in the city government had made clear that expenditures on Dibao should not increase in the coming years, and since central authorities were mandating that the Dibao line be set in a certain way, capping Dibao expenditures meant limiting the number of individuals who participated in the program (Interview, B2013_627).

It is hard to say to what extent local government concerns with the deleterious effect of Dibao provision are based on real labor market concerns of a need

---

况与2019年中央和地方预算草案的报告) at http://www.gov.cn/guowuyuan/2019-03/17/content_5374492.htm (accessed July 11, 2019).

8. Consumer food inflation was 4.1% in March 2019 compared to a year prior.

9. Opposition to social welfare is by no means unique to China; however, it is important to note that in China, as is the case elsewhere, business interests are not uniformly opposed to social welfare programs (Estevez-Abe, Iversen, and Soskice 1999; Gordon 1994; Hacker and Pierson 2002; Mares 2003; Martin and Swank 2012; Swenson 1991).

to preserve the pool of low-wage labor, on local adherence to central government guidance to get able-bodied individuals off Dibao, or on the persistence of traditional values placed on work in China. These factors likely all play some role, and the consequence is that financing for Dibao is insufficient to meet the needs of all households with local residency whose income falls below the local Dibao line. Studies have consistently shown that Dibao suffers from abnormally high levels of exclusion error, which refers to the exclusion of people who should be eligible from means-tested programs. One study conducted by the World Bank in conjunction with China's National Bureau of Statistics in the early 2000s and another done by the Chinese Academy of Social Sciences in the late 2000s both found that only 20% to 30% of households eligible for Dibao end up receiving the much needed support (Chen, Ravallion, and Wang 2006; Yang 2012). In other words, 70% to 80% of eligible households are excluded from the program (high exclusion error). While means-tested programs frequently suffer from exclusion error, 70% to 80% is abnormally high. In other developing contexts, including countries in South Asia and Africa that we would usually think of as having lower state capacity than China, it is more common to see exclusion rates of 40% to 50% (AusAID 2011).

4.2 *Limiting Dibao to Maximize Work*

When local governments are faced with a situation where they have to selectively distribute Dibao to a subset of impoverished households, how do they decide who should get Dibao? And how are these decisions carried out when Dibao is a programmatic policy governed by a large number of rules and regulations? To answer these questions, we have to examine not only government policies but also the neighborhood residents committee, which plays a key role in the provision of Dibao to maximize work, as well as the identification, surveillance, and control of targeted populations and the prioritization of Dibao for targeted individuals who are impoverished. Although neighborhood administrators do not have the power to approve Dibao applications, they facilitate the selective distribution of Dibao benefits by changing the likelihood that a Dibao application will be approved.

4.2.1 Residents Committees

The neighborhood is the smallest urban level of governance, equivalent to the village in rural China. Neighborhoods fall outside of China's formal governmental administrative structure.[10] In large cities, urban neighborhoods typically include

---

10. China's formal administrative structure ends at the township (street) level.

2,000 to 3,000 households. Residents committees, which administer these neighborhoods, are usually staffed with a half dozen to a dozen individuals, including a
director, a vice-director, and administrators focused on different policy areas such
as family planning, Dibao, petitions, and public security. Figure 4.1 shows bulletin
boards located outside of residents committee offices containing information on
residents committee staff, including their names and areas of responsibility.

Residents committees are described in official documents as grassroots organizations that allow residents to self-govern.[11] In reality, however, residents committees are firmly under the control of the Communist Party (Tomba 2014). Key
administrators are Communist Party members who run the neighborhood Communist Party branch. Generally, the physical location of the residents committee
office is also where the party branch meets and conducts business.[12] This means
residents committees are organs of China's single-party regime that interact most
directly and most frequently with urban residents on a wide range of issues.

Residents committees were used during the early communist period to reach
city dwellers, such as unemployed housewives, who had no other connection
to the regime (Zheng 2005). In the 1980s and 1990s, faced with economic
reform and urban transformations that generated layoffs as well as an influx of
migrant workers, residents committees were reformed and reemphasized as a way
to increase the "infrastructural power of the Party-state" (Heberer and Göbel
2011:5). Reform was led by the Ministry of Civil Affairs, the same bureaucracy
that administers Dibao, with the goal of increasing the relevance of the residents
committee for urban residents (Benewick, Tong, and Howell 2004; Bray 2006;
Derleth and Koldyk 2004; Dutton, Lo, and Wu 2008; Kojima and Kokubun
2005; White and Shang 2003; Wong and Poon 2005).

The key responsibilities of the residents committee, according to the Residents Committee Law, include publicizing and educating residents about
national laws, regulations, and policies; managing the affairs and welfare of residents; mediating disputes; helping to maintain social order; administering public
programs for residents; and communicating the opinions and suggestions of residents to the government. As of 2017, there were 106,000 residents committees
across China.[13]

---

11. See http://bit.ly/1Ib41Kx for text of *People's Republic of China Organization Law of Urban
Residents Committees* (accessed January 5, 2015).

12. If there are 50 to 100 party members, the party branch is called a *dangzongzhi* (党总支); if
there are three to 50 party members, the branch is called a *Dangzhibu* (党支部).

13. See *2017 Ministry of Civil Affairs Statistical Report*, http://www.mca.gov.cn/article/
sj/tjgb/2017/201708021607.pdf (accessed July 8, 2019).

FIGURE 4.1 Residents committee bulletin boards

4.2.2 Gatekeepers of Dibao

For anyone who wants to obtain Dibao, the process starts at the neighborhood residents committee. The residents committee collects and ensures the veracity of all materials submitted to street-level officials for approval. Assessing income, which can include all forms of income as well as assets, is a primary concern of the residents committee. Read writes that "neighborhood leaders are not at liberty to make an up or down decision about welfare benefits on their own authority, they are preliminary fact finders, and advise higher level agencies" (Read 2012, 121–122). While this statement is correct, the difficulty of ascertaining income turns residents committees from fact finders into gatekeepers.

Many Dibao applicants work informally, so there is no employer to provide verified income information. The residents committee can go to great lengths to gather income information. Residents committees are required to conduct household visits and interviews with applicants. Residents committee members, often accompanied by other neighborhood administrators and block captains, go into the prospective Dibao applicant's home to speak with family members. One local residents committee member told me that during visits, she is looking to see whether the household has assets like a color television, a vehicle, or pets (Interview, N2012_622). She is looking closely at what type of phones family members use, as well as the quality of clothing family members wear. Residents committee members also conduct visits and interviews with neighbors, employers, and other acquaintances to verify information in the application. A residents committee member in Wuhan informed me that for Dibao applicants who are vegetable sellers, she will go to the market where they set up shop and catalog their goods and observe their sales transactions to estimate daily revenues and profits (Interview, N2013_629). Residents committees also organize "participatory" appraisals of Dibao applicants, where at least seven members of the community, which includes residents committee members and block captains, are brought together to review the applicant. Finally, the residents committee is required to publicly display the names of Dibao applicants in the neighborhood. In this process of income verification, there are many opportunities at the margins for residents committees to increases or decrease an applicant's chance of success.

The complexity of the administrative process also makes the support of the residents committee crucial for applicants. In a neighborhood in Wuhan's Jianghan district, applicants are required to submit an application form, a copy of their personal identification card, a copy of their urban *Hukou*, a marriage certificate, validation of their income or validation of unemployed status if they have no source of income, documentation of illness and/or disability, a copy of lease or housing ownership, and monthly utilities statements (Interview, N2013_621). A

Dibao applicant must obtain these forms from a variety of government bureaus and offices, and often those agencies require additional paperwork and verification in order to provide the documents. Given the complexity of gathering the required documentation, the support and assistance of the residents committee can mean the difference between a successful or failed application.

The power of the residents committee can result in corruption, but corrupt practices are relatively rare in China's urban Dibao program. Conferring Dibao to friends and relatives who do not fulfill the eligibility criteria is called *favor Dibao* or *relationship Dibao* (人情低保, 关系低保). National-level studies of Dibao show this phenomenon is limited, but *favor Dibao* has garnered a large share of media attention in recent years, resulting in government efforts to crack down on the phenomenon. Echoing a 2006 nationwide study, a 2012 study by the Chinese Academy of Social Sciences based on a nationally representative survey found that only 1.75% of households not eligible for Dibao receive the benefit (Chen, Ravallion, and Wang 2006; Yang 2012).

4.2.3 Limiting Dibao to the Infirm

Because Dibao was adopted in the 1990s in response to mass layoffs and rising urban poverty, many recipients in the 1990s and early 2000s were unemployed workers who could not find jobs. Table 4.1 shows the breakdown of participants in urban Dibao in 2002, where 44% of recipients were laid-off or unemployed.[14]

Dibao marked a departure from the norm of China's traditional welfare programs, such as the Three Withouts and Five Guarantees, which excluded those who were able-bodied and able to carve out a subsistence through their own labor. However, Gao (2017) notes that the value and emphasis placed on work continues to shape the development of social assistance. Solinger (2017) finds that even in the 2000s, local governments exhibited a tendency of being unwilling to provide Dibao to those capable of work, and, starting in 2009, the central government began formally prioritizing those who were unable to participate in the labor market for Dibao. My fieldwork, conducted from 2012 to 2013, confirms that encouraging those who can work to seek employment rather than obtain Dibao is a dominant logic in the provision of Dibao benefits.

This prioritization of work is clearly spelled out in the "Interim Measures for Social Assistance issued by the State Council in 2014". The Interim Measures

---

14. Data from the 2002 *Ministry of Civil Affairs Statistical Report* (2002年民政事业发展统计公报), from http://www.mca.gov.cn/article/sj/tjgb/200801/200801150093829.shtml (accessed July 8, 2019).

Table 4.1 Urban Dibao participants by category

Category	Population (millions)	Percentage of Total
Employed	1.9	9%
Laid-off	5.5	27%
Retired	0.9	4%
Unemployed	3.6	17%
Family members	7.8	38%
Three Withouts	0.9	4%
Total	20.6	

Source: 2002 Ministry of Civil Affairs Statistical Report

make clear that if members of a Dibao household are able-bodied, the county government needs to ensure that at least one family member is employed. The Interim Measures require that all Dibao households where someone is able to work are provided with job training subsidies, job placement subsidies, and public service job placements. If someone who is able-bodied refuses an offer of work three consecutive times, the civil affairs department at the country level can suspend the household's Dibao status or reduce the household's Dibao allowance. Some cities have implemented even more extreme measures to move individuals capable of work out of Dibao. For example, in 2017, Zhejiang passed "Zhejiang Province Measures Regarding the Minimum Livelihood Guarantee" to make "able-bodied workers who refused to work" ineligible for Dibao even if they meet income requirements.[15]

The difficulty of determining income for impoverished households means that residents committees at the neighborhood level have a great deal of leeway to turn away potential applicants. Many poor households whose members can work are turned away so that Dibao is focused on those who cannot participate in the labor market, such as the elderly, disabled, or ill.

Between 2009 and 2016, the Ministry of Civil Affairs reported the number of Dibao recipients by their characteristics in their quarterly statistical reports.[16] Based on this data, Figure 4.2 shows the proportion of Dibao recipients who were classified as disabled, *sanwu* (without ability to work, without income, without

15. See https://bit.ly/2IiUwLO (accessed June 14, 2017).

16. See http://www.mca.gov.cn/article/sj/tjjb/dbsj/?2 (accessed April 3, 2017).

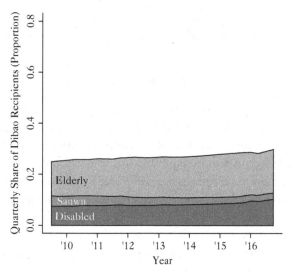

FIGURE 4.2 Proportion of Dibao recipients officially classified as disabled, *sanwu*, and elderly

family support), and elderly from 2009 to 2016.[17] The share of these recipients who have no ability to engage in labor increased from 25% in the third quarter of 2009 to 30% in the last quarter of 2016.

However, these official statistics do not fully capture the logic of limiting Dibao for those who cannot participate in the labor market. Dibao recipients who are classified as disabled include only those who are formally certified as such by the China Disabled Persons' Federation (CDPF, 中国残疾人联合会). According to CDPF, there were 85 million disabled Chinese people as of 2010. However, CDPF's definition of disability is stringent, and if the World Health Organization's definition for disability were used, there would be upwards of 200 million disabled people in China (Y. Wang 2016).

Furthermore, individuals who are unable to work because they have been injured or ill would not be classified by either CDPF or the World Health Organization as disabled, yet they are also more likely to receive Dibao because of their inability to participate in the labor market. In my survey of 100 neighborhoods, among the neighborhoods reporting data on Dibao recipient characteristics, 74% of the neighborhoods said that most Dibao recipients were people unable to work

---

17. The categories of elderly, *sanwu*, and disabled are not mutually exclusive. The same person can be classified into two or three of these categories, resulting in double- and sometimes triple-counting.

because of physical or mental impediments, including disability but also including illnesses. An additional 10% said most Dibao recipients were the elderly or infirm.

4.3 Prioritizing Dibao to Preempt Disorder

The logic of limiting Dibao distribution to maximize work is governed by documents issued by the Ministry of Civil Affairs, which runs the Dibao program, and it is carried out at the grassroots level by residents committee members. In contrast, while the logic of distributing Dibao to preempt disorder is also carried out by residents committee members, they are guided by programs and policies initiated by China's judicial and public security ministries. It is in this sense that while the logic of limiting Dibao to maximize work is the main focus of the program when we examine Dibao policy documents, the logic of prioritizing Dibao for targeted populations reflects the seepage of political order into the Dibao program.

4.3.1 Background on Targeted Populations

Targeted populations encompass individuals designated as potential threats to political, social, and economic stability. These are individuals for whom the state does not have evidence to prosecute or convict now, but whom the state wants to control, through surveillance and repression, to prevent them from taking certain actions in the future. The category of targeted population is a crucial part of China's tiered population management system (Wang 2005).

The term *targeted populations* was first used in 1956 when the Ministry of Public Security issued "Interim Provision on Management of the Targeted Population" (重点人口管理工作的暂行规定). Prior to 1956, these populations were referred to as *special populations* (特种人口), which included landlords (地主), rich peasants (富农), and counterrevolutionaries (反革命分子). In 1956, targeted populations shifted away from a focus on class to focus exclusively on *suspected* counterrevolutionaries (行反革命可疑的分子 and 可能有反革命罪恶尚未查清的分子), criminals, class enemies (敌对阶级分子), and other bad elements (其他坏分子). Monitoring of targeted populations often led to their arrests and incarceration. For example, in the late 1950s, 291 targeted people were under surveillance in Urumqi in Western China. Subsequently, sufficient information was gathered to send 75 of these individuals to re-education through labor camps.[18] As with many other government activities, the management of targeted populations was mostly halted during the Cultural Revolution from 1966 to 1976.

---

18. See http://bit.ly/2v5y2Hg (accessed May 22, 2015).

Focus on targeted populations resumed in the early 1980s, and by 1985, the Ministry of Public Security issued "Regulations for Management of the Targeted Population" (重点人口管理工作规定). In these 1985 regulations, the scope of targeted populations expanded to six types of individuals deemed as threats to social stability: (1) suspected counterrevolutionaries (有反革命活动可疑的); (2) suspected criminals other than counterrevolutionaries (有其他刑事犯罪活动可疑的); (3) suspected threats to social order (有危害社会治安可疑的); (4) people suspected of possibly committing violent crimes due to civil disputes (因民事纠纷激化,有行凶闹事苗头的); (5) individuals who have been sentenced to prison, parole, house arrest, and other forms of detention (被依法判处管制、剥夺政治权利、缓刑、假释、监外执行和被监视居住、取保候审的) and 6) those who have been released from prison or re-education through labor for three or less years (刑满释放、解除劳动教养、解除收审不满三年的).

Since the mid-1980s, regulations governing targeted populations have been updated several times, with the most recent update in 1998. The current stated goal of managing targeted populations is to "prevent, discover, and fight unlawful criminal activity; educate, manage, and save those engaged in unlawful activity, in order to maintain social safety."[19] Identifying and mitigating *potential* threats to social stability is central to the management of targeted populations. In a document titled "How to Manage Targeted Populations," public security officials emphasize the need to control individuals with the *potential* to harm social security, stability, and national safety.[20]

The 1998 regulations identified 19 types of targeted populations falling into four main categories. In more recent years, additional categories have been added by various lower-level governments. Table 4.2 lists the 19 types from the 1998 regulations, as well as newer additions in parentheses.[21]

---

19. In Chinese: 为预防、发现、打击违法犯罪活动,教育、管理、挽救有违法犯罪行为的人员,维护社会治安.

20. "对有可能危害社会政治稳定和国家安全的重点人口无漏管、失控现象;" see http://bit.ly/1TvGhUw (accessed May 22, 2015).

21. For information on more recent types of targeted populations, see the 2012 "Guizhou Province Provisional Measures for Management of the Targeted Population by Public Security Organs" (贵州省公安机关重点人口管理工作暂行办法); see http://bit.ly/1J52fuw (accessed May 24, 2015). These categories and types in Chinese are: Category 1 有危害国家安全活动嫌疑的: 1、有从事颠覆国家政权、分裂国家、敌投叛变叛逃等活动嫌疑的; 2、有参与动乱、骚乱、暴乱或者其他破坏活动,危害国家安全和社会稳定嫌疑的; 3、有组织、参加敌对组织嫌疑,或者有组织,参加其他危害国家安全和稳定的组织活动嫌疑,或者与这些组织有联系嫌疑的; 4、有参加邪教、会道门活动或者利用宗教进行非活动嫌疑的; 5、有故意破坏民族团结,抗拒国家法律实施等宣传煽动活动嫌疑的; 6、有从事间谍或者窃取、现时探、收买、非法提供国家秘

Table 4.2 Categories of targeted populations

1. Those suspected of endangering state security	Those suspected of participating in public disturbances, riots, revolts, and other actions that threaten national security and social stability (including terrorism)
	Those suspected of organizing or participating in organizations that threaten national security, or having links to these organizations
	Those suspected of participating in cults, sects, secret societies, or illegal religious activities
	Those suspected of seeking to damage national unity or inciting unrest
	Those suspected of engaging in espionage, or providing state secrets or intelligence
	Others suspected of endangering national security
2. Those suspected of serious criminal activity	Those suspected of murder, rape, and human trafficking
	Those suspected of robbery, theft, fraud, or other violations of private property
	Those suspected of arson, bombing, poisoning, illegal arms and ammunition manufacturing, trafficking, stockpiling, seizure, or theft
	Those suspected of drug trafficking, transportation, and manufacturing
	Those suspected of participating in organized crime, both domestic and international
	Those suspected of forgery, the sale and purchase of counterfeit currency, other activities sabotaging financial order
	Those suspected of monetary fraud and other financial fraud
	Those suspected of organizing gambling
	Those suspected of organizing prostitution
	Others suspected of serious criminal activity

Table 4.2 *Continued*

3. Those who because of conflicts and disputes have a potential to create a disturbance, engage in violent retaliation, or act recklessly	(Those suspected of causing instability) (Key petitioners) (Mentally ill persons capable of creating trouble)
4. Those who have been released from prison or labor reform within the past five years	
5. (Drug users)	

The first category of targeted populations comprises of individuals suspected of threatening CCP rule or jeopardizing state security. This category includes individuals suspected of participating in disturbances, riots, and revolts, as well as suspected spies, suspected participants in certain religious groups, and those suspected of having linkages to organizations dangerous to the regime. This category reflects what the regime perceives as major threats to its survival, which is in turn a reaction to social unrest in China. After the 1999 Falun Gong protests, religious groups were added to this first category. Terrorism and ethnic conflict were not mentioned in previous definitions of targeted populations and reflect global geopolitics as well as more recent outbreaks of ethnic unrest in Western China.

The second category focuses on activities unrelated to political and social dissent, which would in most countries be considered criminal behavior—murder, rape, human trafficking, theft, fraud, arson, drug trafficking and so on. However, unlike in most countries where such behavior is considered criminal, targeted

---

密或者情报嫌疑的；7、有其他危害国家安全活动嫌疑的. Category 2 有严重刑事犯罪活动嫌疑的：1、有杀人、强奸、伤害、拐卖妇女儿童等侵犯公民人身权利嫌疑的；2、有抢劫、盗窃、诈骗等侵犯公私财物嫌疑的；3、有放火、爆炸、投毒、非法制造、买卖、运输、储存或者盗窃、抢夺枪支、弹药、爆炸物品等危害公共安全活动嫌疑的；4、有走私、贩卖、运输、制造毒品嫌疑的；5、有参与境外黑社会组织的渗透活动或者参加境内黑社会性质的组织及犯罪团伙嫌疑的；6、有伪造、变造货币、国库券及有价证券或者出售、购买、伪造、变造的货币等破坏金融管理秩序活动嫌疑的；7、有使用诈骗方法非法集资、贷款或者进行金融票据、信用证、信用卡、保险诈骗等金融诈骗活动嫌疑的；8、有经常聚众赌博或者聚赌抽头嫌疑的；9、有组织、强迫、引诱、容留、介绍卖淫活动嫌疑的；10、有其他严重刑事犯罪活动嫌疑的. Category 3 因矛盾纠纷激化、有闹事行凶报复苗头,可能铤而走险的. Category 4 因故意违法犯罪被刑满释放、解除劳动教养不满五年的. Category 5 吸食、注射毒品人员，以及司法强戒所和公安强戒所的出所人员.

populations track individuals who have not been convicted or even accused of such crimes but simply suspected of having the potential to commit them in the future.

The third category of targeted populations consists of individuals who may resort to troublemaking and revenge because of interpersonal or inter-group disputes. Over the past decade, this category has been expanded to explicitly include those suspected of causing social instability, such as individuals who have petitioned repeatedly, those who have organized collective petitions, and those suspected of being likely to engage in protest and collective action in the future.[22]

The fourth and fifth categories of targeted populations are ones in which individuals are not identified based on suspicion alone but identified based on concrete prior activities—imprisonment and drug use. The fourth category of targeted populations includes individuals who have been released from prison or other forms of detention such as re-education through labor camps. While we do not know the total number of people imprisoned in China because extrajudicial detention is not reported in official statistics, we can look at official reports of criminal prosecutions to get an estimate of the minimum number of people imprisoned for social and political dissent.

Table 4.3 shows the number of people prosecuted by the People's Procuratorate for different categories of crimes in 2017. Since conviction rates in China are often over 99.9%, this gives us a sense of the proportion of activities leading to judicial incarceration, and the characteristics of ex-prisoners.[23] The largest single category of China's criminal prosecutions is obstruction of social order, which primarily focuses on penalizing participation in collective action, participation in certain religious activities, and protests against the government.[24] In 2017, over half a million people were prosecuted for obstructing social order, representing over 30% of all individuals who were prosecuted through the criminal system. The second largest category is infringement of property, such as robbery, theft, and

---

22. For examples or more recent government documents that explain this category in greater detail see "Guizhou Province Provisional Measures for Management of the Targeted Population by Public Security Organs," http://bit.ly/1J52fuw; "Protecting Livelihood, Striving for Innovation, Improving Dibao Management in Yakeshi," http://bit.ly/1Ceqsqy; "Haiyuan strengthens management of targeted populations by category," http://bit.ly/1MMRfQf (accessed May 24, 2015).

23. In 2017, the China Drug, Crime and Detention Database shows that for crimes of harming public security (危害公共安全罪), only 0.015% of cases resulted in a verdict of not guilty, see http://www.lse.ac.uk/united-states/international-drug-policy/IDPU-China-drug-database (accessed July 14, 2019).

24. This category of crimes also includes defacing the national flag and national emblems, drug trafficking, prostitution, and pornography.

Table 4.3 Criminal prosecutions by category

Category	Chinese	Number of People	Percentage
Obstruct social order	妨害社会管理秩序	521,064	30.55%
Infringement of property	侵犯财产	448,375	26.29%
Harm public safety	危害公共安全	367,500	21.54%
Violate personal rights	侵犯公民人身、民主权利	223,845	13.12%
Destroy socialist market order	破坏社会主义市场经济秩序	103,511	6.07%
Corruption and bribery	贪污贿赂	33,580	1.97%
Dereliction of duty	渎职侵权	7,379	0.43%
Harm national interest	危害国防利益	322	0.02%
Other	其他	196	0.01%

Source: Number of Criminal Prosecutions by the People's Procuratorate in 2017 from the 2018 *China Statistical Yearbook*, Table 24-8, http://www.stats.gov.cn/tjsj/ndsj/2018/indexch.htm.

fraud, comprising 26% of prosecutions. The third largest category, representing slightly less than 22% of people prosecuted, is harming public safety, which includes arson, destruction of property, and terrorism, as well as the illegal sale of arms and ammunition. The fourth category is the violation of personal rights—including murder, manslaughter, injury, rape, and human trafficking—at 13% of prosecutions. The fifth category of damaging the socialist market order includes smuggling, forgery, financial fraud, and violation of intellectual property. The next two categories—corruption and bribery, as well as dereliction of duty—represent crimes of official cadres and total 2.5% of prosecutions. The last category of harming state security includes impediments to military activities.

Although prosecutions for disrupting social order comprise the largest share of individuals prosecuted in the Chinese criminal system, these numbers underestimate those imprisoned for political and social dissent because they do not include the many more who are imprisoned through extrajudicial means (Human Rights Watch 2009). Between 1957 and 2013, extrajudicial detentions were mainly carried out through re-education through labor camps, which were run by the justice or public security systems.[25] These camps were used to imprison individuals—ranging from petitioners to drug users—considered threats to social

---

25. In both China's prisons and re-education through labor camps, physical labor is used. As a result, China's prison system is sometimes known as the reform through labor (劳动改造 or 劳改) system.

Table 4.4 Scope of judicial and extrajudicial detention

Type	Chinese	Number of Centers	Number of People	Year of Data	Ministry
Prison	监狱	674	1,649,804	2015	Justice
Drug detention & isolation	强制隔离戒毒所	775	357,000	2016	Public Security
Peace and health hospital	安康医院	23	?	2016	Public Security
Custody & education	收容教育所	90	15,000	2014	Public Security
Re-education through labor	劳动教养所	320	190,000	2009	Justice, Public Security
"Black jails"	黑监狱	?	?		Public Security

Source: The China Drug, Crime and Detention Database http://www.lse.ac.uk/united-states/international-drug-policy/IDPU-China-drug-database).

stability who could not be prosecuted through China's criminal justice system. As Table 4.4 shows, in 2009 the Chinese government's official statistics reported 190,000 individuals imprisoned in 320 re-education through labor sites. Some human rights organizations put this number much higher, at up to 2 million people imprisoned.[26] Although China abolished the re-education through labor system in 2013, extrajudicial detention continues through so-called "black jails" run by the public security apparatus and private security companies.[27] The Chinese government officially denies the existence of black jails, so we do not have a sense of their scale. The government does acknowledge and publish statistics on three other types of extrajudicial detention centers: 1) drug detention and isolation centers (强制隔离戒毒所) designed to imprison drug users, 2) peace and health hospitals (安康医院) designed to detain people with mental health issues, and 3) custody and education centers (收容教育所) designed to incarcerate sex workers and their clients. Although these centers are intended for drug users, the mentally ill, and sex workers, there are reports that protesters, petitioners, and

26. See *Laogai Handbook* from the Laogai Research Foundation, archived at https://bit.ly/2Jzn5Io (accessed July 14, 2019).

27. See http://bit.ly/1BwUkx1, http://bit.ly/1ySAizL, and http://bit.ly/1uHAYTk (accessed December 6, 2014).

Falun Gong practitioners have also been detained at these sites.[28] The upshot of this is that a sizable share of ex-prisoners were imprisoned because of their political, social, and religious beliefs and activities and not for activities considered to be criminal in many democratic countries.

The CCP sees management of ex-prisoners as important to the continued social stability of the country, and has emphasized the need for their continued reform as they integrate back into mainstream society.[29] Officials speak of the need to "rectify deviant influences and go back to the straight and narrow to return to society" (改邪归正回归社会), where the term *deviant* alludes to participation in religious organizations such as Falun Gong. Prior to the 2010 World Expo in Shanghai, the Shanghai Bureau of Justice issued a "Four things to avoid" (四个不发生) order targeted at former prisoners. Of the four things to prevent, two echo policing tactics that could be found elsewhere in the world—to prevent former prisoners from committing another crime and to prevent any major criminal cases involving former prisoners—but the other two relate to social unrest: "to prevent former prisoners from participating in petition and mass incidents, and to prevent former prisoners from disturbing social stability and participating in any large-scale collective events."[30]

The final category of targeted populations focuses on drug users and those who have been released from mandatory drug detoxification. This category was added in August 1999.[31] The addition of this category may reflect increased concern over drug use; however, because individuals who engage in political and social dissent have also been imprisoned in drug detention centers, the inclusion of this category into targeted populations may also reflect social and political concerns.

As Table 4.2 shows, the Chinese government's conceptualization of targeted populations conflates political dissent, religious practices, and social mobilization with common crimes such as murder, theft, and human trafficking, as well as individuals afflicted by mental illness and drug addiction. In the eyes of the Chinese regime, all are forms of social conflict that threaten political order. All are criminal

---

28. See the China Drug, Crime and Detention Database (中国毒品、犯罪和拘留数据库), http://www.lse.ac.uk/united-states/international-drug-policy/IDPU-China-drug-database (accessed July 14, 2019).

29. See http://bit.ly/1zVbzoo.

30. In Chinese: "不发生刑释解教人员重新违法犯罪, 不发生刑释解教人员参与上访、闹访和群体性事件, 不发生刑释解教人员重大恶性刑事案件, 不发生刑释解教人员参与影响社会稳定的重大群体性事件."

31. Ministry of Public Security "Notice on the Classification of Drug Users as Targeted Population" (关于将吸毒人员列为重点人口管理的通知).

behaviors. China's criminalization of dissent is not unique. Other authoritarian regimes, both past and current, such as East Germany, Cuba, and Saudi Arabia, also criminalize political dissent.

4.3.2 Neighborhood-Level Surveillance

Responsibility for targeted populations, along with management of the *Hukou* system, falls to the Ministry of Public Security. Police officers within local police stations (派出所), including household registration police, are responsible for the day-to-day tasks of identifying, monitoring, and controlling targeted populations (Dutton 1992; Wang 2005).[32] Police officers face tremendous challenges in identifying and monitoring targeted populations because of internal migration. In 2018, there were 288.36 million rural *Hukou* holders who worked in areas outside of their *Hukou* registration.[33] China's residence permit system was designed to control internal migration and by extension, enable surveillance (Cheng and Selden 1994). However, as people's place of work has become increasingly disconnected from the official location of the *Hukou*, *Hukou* has become less valuable as a tool for local surveillance (Chen and Hu 2013).

Neighborhood residents committees have been charged with aiding local police in enforcing social control since the earliest days of the communist era (Dutton 1992). However, prior to the initiation of economic reforms, their role was auxiliary to that of employer work units. Since the early 2000s, there have been efforts by the public security system to strengthen coordination with the neighborhood on surveillance.[34] A 2015 public security report on targeted populations from Wenzhou in Zhejiang Province emphasizes reliance on information from neighborhoods where targeted populations reside.[35] A report from a neighborhood in Xinjiang details how the neighborhood residents committee members, grid captains, block captains, volunteer police, and local party members are involved in closely monitoring households with targeted populations.[36]

---

32. Sometimes, targeted populations are jointly managed between the local police station and the criminal investigations unit.

33. See http://www.stats.gov.cn/tjsj/zxfb/201904/t20190429_1662268.html (accessed July 15, 2019).

34. See "Opinions on Strengthening the Construction of Community Policing" at http://bit.ly/1GQmnhO (accessed May 20, 2015).

35. "Pingyang County Public Security Bureau Three Words Tactic to Control Targeted Populations," http://bitly.com/1MMR33B (accessed May 25, 2015).

36. See "Investigation and Reflections on Management of Targeted Populations," http://bit.ly/1GgMiKE (accessed May 24, 2015).

Management guidelines for targeted populations from Sichuan Province detail how neighborhoods are given responsibility for gathering information on targeted populations to ensure that every individual remains under "surveillance and control."[37] This reliance on neighborhood resources is echoed in provinces all over China, from rich coastal provinces such as Zhejiang, to heartland provinces such as Henan, to poor regions with ethnic minorities such as Yunnan.[38]

Block Captains

Wang (2005) reports that for every 500 hundred to 700 hundred households, there is one police officer who is supposed to be familiar with the details of each household, but sometimes one police officer is responsible for up to 2,000 households. It is impossible for one individual to closely monitor the activities of thousands without additional assistance. For the same reason, it is not residential committee members, a dozen of whom may be responsible for 2,000 households, who engage in day-to-day surveillance. Through my fieldwork, I found that it is block captains (门楼张) who most often engage in day-to-day surveillance and act as the so-called eyes and ears (耳目) of the public security system. Because they are embedded in the neighborhood, the neighborhood becomes a central point for surveillance.

Block captains are responsible for residential blocks, typically apartment buildings with one or more entryways like those that proliferate across China. Figure 4.3 shows maps posted to community bulletin boards of two neighborhoods I visited. The first map shows a neighborhood in Xi'an where each rectangle corresponds to a residential block. Block captains are responsible for one to three of these rectangles. The second map contains a poster of a neighborhood in Wuhan. The poster says there are 3,034 households with 7,960 residents, and each rectangle corresponds to a residential block. In this neighborhood, there were approximately 50 block captains, and most were responsible for one of the rectangles shown in the second map of Figure 4.3. According to my neighborhood survey, described in detail below, the number of block captains per neighborhood ranged from 10 to 130, and the number of households each block captain was responsible for ranged from 13 to 280. On average, neighborhoods had 40 block captains, so that each block captain was responsible for approximately 80 households.

---

37. See "Management Guidelines for Targeted Populations in Jinjiang," http://bit.ly/1JVCoH2 (accessed May 25, 2015).

38. For additional examples, see http://bit.ly/1MMR33B, http://bit.ly/1J51VMu (accessed May 2015).

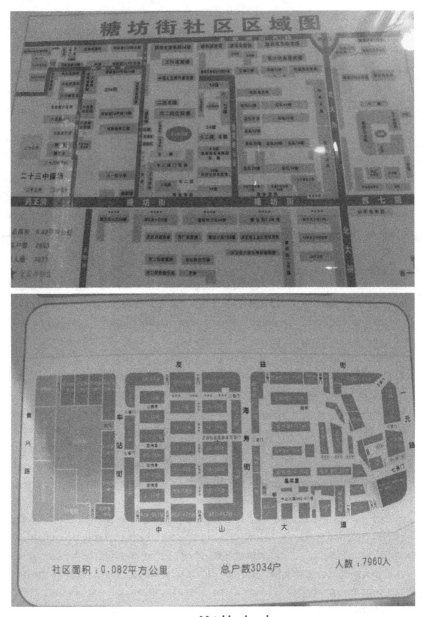

FIGURE 4.3 Neighborhood maps

Block captains are typically selected and then recruited by other block captains and residents committee members. They are almost all women. They live in the neighborhood. They are often retired, unemployed, or laid-off workers. There is no formal mechanism to compensate block captains for their work, but they receive gifts and in-kind benefits. In some neighborhoods, block captains travel for gatherings and retreats, and they may have a small budget for food at meetings.

These networks of block captains have supported residents committees and local police in surveillance since before economic reforms.[39] During the Cultural Revolution, they reported which youths sent down to the countryside secretly returned to cities. During the crackdown on Falun Gong in the late 1990s, block captains helped identify practitioners. During the 2003 SARS epidemic, anecdotes circulated of block captains taking temperatures and imposing quarantines.[40]

Variation in Surveillance Capabilities

Based on my fieldwork, I found that while almost all neighborhoods have block captains, the surveillance capabilities of block captains differed greatly. In some neighborhoods, block captains are well-recognized and trusted members of the community who interact frequently with residents. They energetically communicate state policies to residents, organize residents for officially sanctioned activities, resolve conflicts among neighbors, and gather information about residents, including identifying and monitoring those belonging to targeted populations. In these neighborhoods, when walking with the block captain around the neighborhood, I observed them greeting residents by name and asking after their families. Residents I spoke with knew their block captains and could point to the apartments where they lived.

In other neighborhoods, "block captain" was simply a title, and those with this title had little or no interaction with residents or the residents committee. Block captains did not interact frequently or regularly with residents. Residents either had no idea whether there was a block captain or had some vague notion that someone who went by that title existed. When asked about the role of the block captain, residents would say they were not sure. In his study of urban neighborhoods, Read (2012) notes that block captains have a reputation for getting into

---

39. As Read (2012) notes, residents committees have their roots in the communist period rather than earlier traditions of community governance such as the *baojia* (保甲) system of community law enforcement originating in the Song Dynasty.

40. For example see http://www.salon.com/2003/06/19/sars_2/.

other people's business (爱管闲事). While this reputation absolutely reflects the situation in some neighborhoods, in others it did not apply. In some neighborhoods, block captains were deeply penetrated into their communities. As a result, they were trusted and able to effectively gather private information for surveillance. In other neighborhoods they were indistinguishable from other resident and had little capacity to gather information. Because surveillance depends on integration and penetration into the community, I use whether or not residents in the neighborhood said they knew their block captain as a measure of grassroots surveillance capacity. When residents know their block captain, I consider this neighborhood to have strong surveillance capacity. When residents do not know their block captain, I consider this as lacking strong surveillance capacity. Table 4.5 shows the number of neighborhoods with block captains and the number of neighborhoods with strong surveillance capacity from my survey of 100 neighborhoods. Table 4.5 shows that although almost all neighborhoods (96%) have block captains, just over 30% of neighborhoods have high surveillance capacity. This means that the majority of neighborhoods with block captains do not have strong surveillance capabilities because their block captains are not penetrated into the neighborhoods.

These differences in the integration and penetration of block captains lead to differences in the level of information about neighborhood residents they could provide to residents committees and local police. In neighborhoods where block captains had deeply penetrated into their communities, government administrators were well informed of the goings-on of the neighborhood. In these neighborhoods, there are often regular (weekly or biweekly) meetings between block captains and residents committees, as well as local public security officers. In the meetings I observed, information about residents was shared and discussed. In these neighborhoods, local administrators not only had information related to official programs (e.g., the number of pregnant women for family planning, the number of veterans for veterans' services, the number of residents enrolled in public health insurance programs), they also had access to much more personal information—which neighbors were fighting, which husbands and wives were

Table 4.5 Surveillance capability of neighborhoods

	Number of neighborhoods	Percentage of neighborhoods
Block captains	92	96%
High surveillance capacity	28	32%

experiencing familial discord, which families had children who were not doing well in school, which households were not disposing of trash properly, which residents had been posting handbills in inappropriate places, and the list goes on.

In contrast, in neighborhoods where block captains had not penetrated into their communities, local administrators seemed to know very little about the neighborhood's residents. In these neighborhoods, often there were no meetings between the residents committee and block captains, or a meeting only once a year. While these residents committees could report numbers of residents participating in various public programs, they knew very little about the lives of local residents. In these neighborhoods, it seemed that what neighborhood administrators knew about residents came mostly from residents who proactively approached the committee with questions about programs or access to services.[41]

There is an inherent challenge in an effective block captain's ability to conduct surveillance and collect information. On the one hand, a block captain must enjoy a certain level of trust among residents in order to be integrated in the community and to obtain private information. On the other hand, a block captain might be seen as betraying that trust if others knew she was transmitting private information to local administrators and local police. Block captains try to balance this tension by engaging heavily in persuasion. They do not merely transmit private information to the residents committee, but work to address the underlying sources of discontent. For example, if a block captain finds out that a resident is thinking of petitioning, she will inform the residents committee and local public security officials, but she will also participate in conversations with the resident to try to persuade that person against petitioning. However, this balance can easily be lost, which in part explains why block captains have reputations for being intrusive.

Grid Captains

The CCP seems aware of this variation in the quality of its urban grassroots surveillance organization. In the early 2010s, a new grassroots structure—called *grid captains* or *grid personnel* (网格长, 网格员)—was launched in neighborhoods with support from the public security apparatus. Grid captains were predominantly young women in their 20s or 30s, who were relatively well educated with community college or even college degrees and who generally did not

---

41. My work does not delve into the question of why some neighborhoods have networks of block captains that are deeply penetrated into their communities while other neighborhoods do not. The work of other scholars suggests that this variation could be due to differences in the level of CCP penetration in urban areas and the historical legacies of conflict (Koss 2015), or to the type of housing and stability of residency (Read 2012).

live in the neighborhood. Their appointed tasks were very similar to the traditional responsibilities of block captains. They were supposed to engage in social work to identify, communicate, and solve problems residents faced (了解民情, 转达民情，解决民情). The grid structure was closely tied to efforts by the public security apparatus to upgrade their grassroots surveillance capabilities more evenly across neighborhoods. Grid captains often received training from local public security personnel and interacted regularly with them.

However, during my time in the field between 2012 and 2013, most residents committees said their grid management systems were still in the process of being implemented.[42] Figure 4.4 shows a map of the grid network in a neighborhood in Zhengzhou and a map of one in Wuhan, both of which were publicly posted on community bulletin boards. Figure 4.4 shows that neighborhoods were divided into fewer grids than blocks. The Zhengzhou neighborhood was divided into four grid sections (each of the three sections on the left side of the Zhengzhou map are distinct grids while all three sections on the right side of the same map belong to the same grid). The Wuhan neighborhood was divided into nine grid sections, which are numbered in Figure 4.4. With fewer grids, there were also fewer grid captains than block captains, and not all grid captain positions had been filled. Importantly, when I spoke with local residents, few were aware of the existence of grid captains. Grid captains did not appear to play a key role in surveillance at the time of my fieldwork.

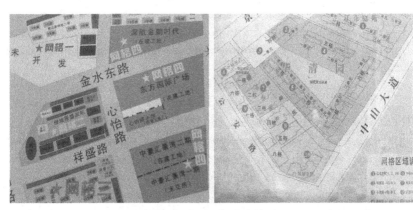

FIGURE 4.4   Grid network maps

42. The creation of the grid management system is usually attributed to Zhou Yongkang during his tenure as minister of Public Security. It is rumored that as his fortunes fell under Xi Jinping, this grid management system also fell by the wayside.

Heuristic of Ex-Prisoners

Although individuals who have been released from prison or detention are only one category of targeted populations, they represent a large share of individuals who appear on lists of targeted populations because they are relatively easier to identify. If someone has never participated in or organized a protest, has never petitioned, has never done anything the regime associates with social unrest, it would be extremely difficult, if not impossible, to know that they are planning to protest before the fact. Even with the help of grassroots surveillance networks, police cannot closely monitor everyone who has ever complained or expressed an interest in social causes, because doing so would inundate them with false leads. During my qualitative field work, of the 23 targeted persons I learned about, all but two were ex-prisoners.

Focusing on released prisoners becomes a heuristic whose effectiveness is debatable. On one hand, by focusing on ex-prisoners, the regime may miss many would-be dissidents and protesters. Most individuals who have been incarcerated do not wish to run afoul of China's laws after their release, especially those who were released decades ago.[43] The inability of local police to identify everyone who should be placed on targeted population lists is frequently identified as the major problem of targeted population management in Chinese language studies of the topic (Y. Wang 2016; Wang 2018). On the other hand, even if targeted populations were composed entirely of ex-prisoners (which is not the case), the rate at which released prisoners commit crimes is still likely higher than the rate among the general population. If the system of identifying targeted populations based on these heuristics were a machine learning system, we would say that the system has higher precision (reduces Type I error) compared to random chance because it likely uncovers more activities objectionable to the government than monitoring the entire population would, but low recall (increases Type II error) because many who engage in objectionable activities are not identified.

The identification of ex-prisoners by local police and residents committees is not always seamless. This is because prisoners are managed by the judicial system while targeted populations are managed by public security, and there is fragmentation and lack of data sharing between these two bureaucracies, especially at lower levels of government. When an individual is incarcerated, their prior *Hukou* is canceled and registered in the location of their incarceration. Roughly a month

---

43. While it is possible that surveillance effectively prevents these individuals from engaging in activities deemed by the regime to be undesirable, there are many whom the regime would like to place under surveillance who are not included in targeted populations because they are extremely difficult to identify.

before an individual is to be released from prison, the penal institution is supposed to notify the individual's family, former place of work, and local public
security office, and transfer all relevant materials about the individual—including
the individual's personnel files, or *dang'an*—to the local police station wheres/he
will live upon release. The public security office is then supposed to notify the
local government and administration, including the local civil affairs bureau to
facilitate social assistance and the local administration of industry and commerce
to facilitate job training and re-employment (Standing Committee of Guangdong Provincial People's Congress 1994). However, upon release, some prisoners
originally from urban areas are assigned *Hukou* in remote towns or rural areas
to prevent them from moving back to cities upon release (Wang 2005). While
this may have been effective in the 1980s and 1990s, given the amount of internal migration, the local police station where the released prisoner ends up is
often not informed of his/her arrival. The local police station may only find out
about a released prisoner because the individual self-reports upon arrival, or if
neighborhood surveillance networks manage to identify the person.

In theory, an individual's personnel file, which includes information such as
school performance, employment record, and political history, as well as criminal and administrative records, should alert local police about released prisoners;
however, the personnel files of targeted populations are often incomplete, with
low-quality and out-of-date information.[44] Government documents describe
how, after many years of incarceration, the *dang'an* cannot be updated because
local police personnel may have changed many times, the released prisoner no
longer resembles his/her former self, and in many cases there is no communication between the detention facility and the local police where the released
prisoner is living.[45] Furthermore, extrajudicial forms of detention, such as internment in psychiatric hospitals and drug detention centers, do not always appear in
the *dang'an*, so even though these centers are all managed by the public security
system, information gets lost over time.

Block captains who are penetrated into their neighborhoods discover ex-
prisoners because they are actively monitoring activities in the neighborhood. In
one neighborhood in Wuhan, a block captain described how she saw that a man
in her block was often at home during the weekdays (Interview, N2013_632). This
was atypical, so she approached him and found out that he was at home because
he could not find work. After several conversations, the block captain realized he
was recently released from prison. She then told the residents committee, which

44. See http://bit.ly/1G5c3i3 (accessed May 25, 2015).

45. See "Problems in Managing Targeted Populations," http://bit.ly/1G5c31s (accessed May
24, 2015).

in turn informed the local police station. Neither the residents committee nor the local police station had been informed of his arrival. If the block captain had not been familiar with the dynamics of the neighborhood and reported this information, the individual would have gone unidentified. Among the dozens of neighborhoods I visited, in only two (one in Qingdao and one in Zhengzhou) had block captains identified targeted populations belonging to categories based on suspicion of future activities alone. In the neighborhood in Zhengzhou, the block captain had a neighbor, Mr. Huang, who had been encouraged into early retirement (Interview, N2013_534). He had been promised a pension by his former employer, but after a year still had not received any payments. Mr. Huang made repeated visits to his former employer and local social security bureau, but that did not yield any results. The block captain knew Mr. Huang was getting increasingly agitated and believed he was at risk of "creating public disturbances." The block captain communicated this information to the residents committee, which liaised with the local police station. Mr. Huang became classified as a targeted population and was placed under surveillance. In the neighborhood in Qingdao, a Mr. Wu was placed on the targeted population list after he and several other parents complained to various district-level government offices (the education bureau, the district court, the office of letters and visits) that teachers and administrators at their children's elementary school were charging illegal fees and shirking their teaching duties (Interview, N2012_431). Because neighborhood administrators feared Mr. Wu would escalate and organize a parent protest, they placed him under surveillance. While I do not know the outcome of Mr. Huang's case, in Mr. Wu's case the residents committee helped him obtain a number of social welfare benefits, including Dibao and education assistance.

Local public security personnel are not only required to identify targeted populations but also to obtain detailed information about them on a regular basis. Local police are generally required to be familiar with an individual's name and aliases, gender, age, ethnicity, address, suspected "crime," physical characteristics, associates, places frequented, sources of income, and behavior. In some localities, local security personnel are tasked with assessing the psychological state of targeted populations.[46] Dossiers on targeted individuals include information on the person's name, gender, date of birth, personal identification number, ethnicity, highest level of education, province of birth, other names/aliases, accent (e.g., Shanghainese), address based on residence permit, current place of residence, blood type, height, body type (e.g., "fat and strong" 胖、结实), face shape (e.g., round), shoe size, foot length, identifying features (e.g., a scar on his left forearm),

---

46. See "Pingyang County Public Security Bureau Three Words Tactic to Control Targeted Populations," http://bit.ly/1MMR33B (accessed May 25, 2015).

family members and their characteristics (e.g., a father who is a worker in a chemical factory, a mother, and an aunt), friends and romantic relations (e.g., one female friend), and previous crimes (e.g., disturbing order in the work unit in 2005). The dossier also includes information on the public security personnel assigned to the individual, as well as the name and contact information for informants tasked with day-to-day monitoring.

Surveillance is supposed to occur at regular intervals, determined by the level of threat assigned to that individual. For example, some localities in Shandong require quarterly updating of targeted populations dossiers. Police in Shenzhen separate targeted populations into three groups based on their level of threat—1 is the lowest threat and requires occasional monitoring; 2 is medium risk, requiring regular monitoring; and 3 is high risk, requiring constant monitoring and active management.[47] Police in Guizhou Province color code targeted populations into blue (low risk), yellow (medium risk), and orange (high risk). For targeted populations in the orange category, local police are required to respond within one hour if alerted of a potential problem and to report back on the situation within 48 hours.

Monitoring is supposed to intensify during sensitive political periods such as major holidays and political meetings (see Chapter 5 for additional details). Police in Qujing Prefecture of Yunnan Province in southwest China are told to do the following around these sensitive time periods:

> During major festivals such as National Day, Chinese New Year, New Year's Eve, May Day, the Two Meetings,[48] the emphasis must be on prevention through high quality preventative public security measures, to ensure stability and security of the neighborhood. The first point of the approach is to focus on targeted populations, to have conversations with them, to gather materials about them, and for those that cannot be seen in person, to know their whereabouts and current status; not a single person can be missed to ensure that targeted populations do not result in problems.[49]

Police in Qiqihar City of Heilongjiang Province in northeast China are instructed to be especially vigilant during major holidays and to immediately report

---

47. See "Longgang Police Station, 'Three In Place' To Strengthen The Control of Targeted Populations," http://bit.ly/1CeqM8D (accessed May 24, 2015).

48. Two Meetings refers to People's Congress and Political Consultative Committee meetings that occur annually in every locality within a few days of each other.

49. See "10 How To's for Public Security," http://bit.ly/1J51VMu (accessed May 24, 2015).

potential issues in order to prevent snowballing and expansion of protests.[50] Police in Beijing's Haidian District are encouraged to intensify monitoring during key holidays.[51]

The amount of surveillance conducted generally does not live up to these formidable standards. A study of targeted populations management in Henan found that local police often do not have the time or resources to conduct regular monitoring (Chen and Hu 2013). The resources available to local police are constrained, as is their time. Greater priority is given to dealing with existing problems rather than latent threats.

4.3.3 Distributing Dibao to Targeted Populations

Targeted populations are not only under surveillance, they are managed through *re-education assistance* (帮教), where a team of people are organized at the neighborhood level to supervise and re-educate targeted persons.[52] Re-education assistance, which is an aspect of the strategy of Comprehensive Management of Public Security, often involves facilitating access to social assistance benefits such as Dibao.

Political order seeps into Dibao provision because public security and judicial departments require a broad array of governmental resources to be available for the populations and people they want to control. In the case of Dibao, the Dibao policy itself remains unchanged, but public security and justice departments make announcements and issue policy documents that prioritize Dibao for targeted populations, for ex-prisoners, and for those undergoing re-education. When these directives are followed, a different logic guiding Dibao distribution is generated.

In September 2003, during the National Conference on Comprehensive Management of Public Security, the minister of Civil Affairs, Li Xueju, and the vice minister of China's Ministry of Justice emphasized the importance of education assistance and living support for targeted populations.[53] Minister Li said that targeted populations who meet Dibao eligibility requirements should be provided

---

50. See "Training to Improve the Quality of Grid Captains in East Lake Neighborhood," http://bit.ly/1IPSxcD (accessed May 25, 2015).

51. See "College Road Sub-District Explores New Model of 'Grid Management, Group-based Mentoring,'" http://bit.ly/1FnBMRc (accessed May 24, 2015).

52. According to "Ministry of Public Security Regulations of Targeted Populations," re-education assistance is provided to all targeted populations; see copy at http://bit.ly/2tAA9F3 (accessed June 1, 2017).

53. See news report at http://bit.ly/2sIkkJt (accessed June 1, 2017).

Dibao status and funds. In 2004, Cixi County in Ningbo Province in Western China began to actively recruit targeted populations for the Dibao program.[54] Starting in 2005, there have been news reports of neighborhoods across Zhejiang Province proactively helping former prisoners obtain Dibao.[55] The Nanjing Bureau of Justice wrote that for targeted populations who meet the eligibility criteria of social welfare programs, education assistance committees must introduce the details and procedures of these programs and help these individuals obtain benefits such as social assistance, job training, and jobs.[56] A program designed to control targeted populations in Hubei suggests that major holidays are an opportunity to visit the home of targeted populations and ensure their material needs are met:

> Major holidays are an opportunity to regularly visit their homes to "bring warmth and offer love," to help those facing economic hardship who are eligible for Dibao obtain the Minimum Livelihood Guarantee, to help those who can be employed find a job, to coordinate resources so loans and other resources are available.

Some cities—for example those in Shandong, Jilin, and Anhui Provinces—have explicit policies in place that guarantee Dibao to prisoners immediately upon release.[57] For example, in 2008, Chaoyang District in Beijing issued "Implementation Rules for Social Relief Work for Individuals Undergoing Community Correction and Released Prisoners who Face Financial Hardships" (朝阳区生活困难社区服刑人员和生活困难刑释解教人员救助工作实施细则), which required the provision of social assistance benefits such as Dibao to these populations. Other localities do not have explicit policies, but provide resources to help released prisoners obtain Dibao as part of broader programs for targeted populations.[58]

There are also explicit policies linking Dibao to re-education assistance. For example, in July 2008 the Guangzhou city departments of justice and civil affairs

---

54. See http://bit.ly/2tK1yEE (accessed May 16, 2015).

55. For examples see http://bit.ly/1JROAHl, http://bit.ly/1MI3IVB, and http://bit.ly/1MZjA6M.

56. For details see http://bit.ly/2sX0TDZ (accessed June 1, 2017).

57. For examples see http://bit.ly/1zVbz00 (accessed November 15, 2013).

58. For just a few examples, see http://bit.ly/1C4dQE2, http://bit.ly/1DkSggr, http://bit.ly/18T85iO, http://bit.ly/1D3MMWX, and http://bit.ly/1xw7N5R (accessed December 7, 2014).

jointly issued "Notice on Further Improving Provision of Minimum Living Guarantee for Released Prisoners and Targets of Community Corrections" (关于进一步做好符合低保条件的刑释解教人员及社区矫正对象最低生活保障工作的通知) to emphasize how neighborhoods need to proactively help anyone undergoing re-education who is eligible for Dibao to obtain it.[59] In 2012, the city of Xi'an launched a policy where released prisoners who lacked family support, a home, and work would be eligible for Dibao.

These policies often are not initiated by the Civil Affairs Ministry or lower-level civil affairs departments, and when we examine key Dibao policy documents, we do not see the prioritization of Dibao for these populations. However, when the public security or justice departments issue these policies, they do involve the civil affairs department at the corresponding level. The core policy, Dibao, does not change. Administration and funding still go through the civil affairs system.

To more systematically assess the distribution of Dibao to targeted populations, I conducted a survey of 100 neighborhoods in four cities in Eastern (Hangzhou), Central (Wuhan, Zhengzhou), and Western (Xian) China from March to June 2013 with the help of students from local universities whom I trained. These cities exhibit different levels of economic development, income, and inequality, as well as coverage of the Dibao program, and were selected to help generalize my findings to different regions of China. Responses were obtained in 97 of the 100 neighborhoods. A total of 103 residents committee members were surveyed, and while in the neighborhood, enumerators also interviewed 382 residents of these neighborhoods in order to create the measure of surveillance.[60] Details about the survey implementation and geographic coverage can be found in Appendix A.5.

I am primarily interested in gathering data on the distribution of Dibao to targeted populations; however, because the program is secret, it is not possible to ask direct questions about it without endangering the research team. To overcome this difficulty, the neighborhood survey asks residents committees whether

---

59. See http://www.gdzf.org.cn/gdsgzdt/gz/201209/t20120911_317464.htm (accessed July 24, 2019).

60. Because of the timing of the visits, during weekdays between 9a.m. and 4p.m., residents interviewed were primarily individuals who were not working, such as retirees and mothers on maternity leave. These are the people who spend the most time in the neighborhood and are most likely to know about neighborhood programs and to interact with the residents committee and block captains. Interviewed residents are not meant to be representative of any broader population. The goal of the survey of residents was simply to measure the surveillance capabilities of the neighborhood block captains. Because of the small number of questions, which did not deal with sensitive topics, the majority of residents were willing to be interviewed, and those who did not want to be interviewed typically declined because they did not have time for a conversation.

ex-prisoners reside in the neighborhood and whether they are among the Dibao recipients. Using released prisoners as proxies for targeted populations has some limitations. When not all targeted populations are captured, it is possibile that Dibao is going only to released prisoners and not all targeted populations. By focusing on released prisoners, I do not have a falsifiable test of whether the identification of targeted populations relies on heuristics. While the results of the neighborhood survey should be interpreted with both considerations in mind, neither limitation calls into question the main focus of my analysis—whether Dibao is selectively distributed to those thought to be more likely to engage in activity the regime views as threatening to political order. Ex-prisoners are included in targeted populations precisely because of the regime's perception of their potential for future actions. As a result, while we cannot conclude from this neighborhood survey that all targeted populations are prioritized for Dibao, we can see whether this is the case with one subset of targeted populations.

Out of 97 neighborhoods surveyed, 13 neighborhood residents committees said released prisoners resided in the neighborhood, 75 said there were no released prisoners among residents, and nine refused to answer the question. Table 4.6 shows the number of neighborhoods with released prisoners for each city.

To gather information on who receives Dibao, residents committee members are asked whether Dibao recipients, whose names and addresses are often listed on community bulletin boards, include released prisoners as well as other official population categories such as the disabled and elderly.[61] Seventy-eight neighborhoods provided information on Dibao provision.

Because the distribution of Dibao to ex-prisoners may be influenced by the quality of the neighborhood surveillance network, I measure surveillance

Table 4.6 Released prisoners by neighborhood by city

	Has released prisoners	No released prisoners	Refused to answer
Hangzhou	5	10	3
Wuhan	0	21	3
Zhengzhou	3	21	1
Xian	5	23	2
Total	13	75	9

61. Figure 6.1 in Chapter 6 shows photographs of these bulletin boards.

Table 4.7 Released prisoners and neighborhood surveillance capacity

prisoners	Number of neighborhoods with:		% of neighborhoods with known released prisoners
	Known prisoners	No known released released prisoners	
Low surveillance capacity	7	48	13%
High surveillance capacity	6	19	24%

capacity by measuring the extent to which block captains are known among residents.[62] To ensure that my measure of neighborhood surveillance is not instead measuring social capital, I ask residents whether they stop by and visit with their neighbors (串门) to measure of the level of social connectedness in the neighborhood.[63]

As expected, there is a strong correlation between neighborhood surveillance capacity and the identification of released prisoners. Table 4.7 shows that among the 80 neighborhoods for which I have data on both the presence of released prisoners and surveillance capacity, released prisoners are found in only 13% (seven) of neighborhoods with low surveillance capacity, while they are found in 24% (six) of neighborhoods with high surveillance capacity. Neighborhoods with stronger surveillance capacity are nearly twice as likely to identify released prisoners. This relationship holds even after controlling for social connections and other neighborhood-level characteristics (see Appendix Table A.3).

Most importantly, the neighborhood survey shows that ex-prisoners are prioritized for Dibao. In all but one of the 13 neighborhoods that identified

62. We ask residents whether they can recall the surname of their block captain. If any resident surveyed can provide the surname of their block captain, which is then verified with the residents committee, then this neighborhood is considered as having high surveillance capacity. Despite the small number of residents surveyed, block captains are supposed to be familiar with every resident under their care, so by extension these residents should all be familiar with the block captain. Note that this measurement strategy dichotomizes surveillance capacity into high and low. While surveillance capabilities may fall along a broader continuum, my qualitative fieldwork showed that most neighborhoods have either high or low surveillance capacity.

63. In half of neighborhoods (48), all residents said they regularly visit with their neighbors. In 43 neighborhoods (45%), some proportion of residents regularly visit their neighbors, and in five neighborhoods (5%), none of the residents interviewed said they visit their neighbors.

Table 4.8 Released prisoners and Dibao status

	Neighborhoods with released prisoners	Released prisoners receiving Dibao
Hangzhou	5	4
Wuhan	0	0
Zhengzhou	3	3
Xian	5	5
Total	13	12

ex-prisoners among residents, ex-prisoners received Dibao.[64] Table 4.8 shows the number of neighborhoods with released prisoners receiving Dibao for each city. Five neighborhoods in Xi'an had released prisoners among Dibao recipients; four neighborhoods in Hangzhou had released prisoners among Dibao recipients; three neighborhoods in Zhengzhou had released prisoners among Dibao recipients, and no neighborhoods in Wuhan reported having released prisoners among Dibao recipients.[65] These results show that released prisoners are extremely likely to receive Dibao in cities across different regions of China that have very different levels of economic development.

Among those 12 neighborhoods where released prisoners were among Dibao recipients, in eight neighborhoods, all of the released prisoners received Dibao. In the remaining four neighborhoods, some subset of released prisoners received Dibao, while other released prisoners participated in different social welfare programs (e.g., job training or job placement programs). In the one neighborhood in Hangzhou where no released prisoners received Dibao, there was only one ex-prisoner in that neighborhood, and this person had been incarcerated for drug abuse. Because the residents committee still believed this person to be a drug user, he was deemed not eligible for Dibao.[66] Given the relationship between neighborhood surveillance capacity and the identification of released prisoners, the survey also shows that in neighborhoods with stronger surveillance capabilities, Dibao benefits are more likely to be given to released prisoners and less likely to be

---

64. Information on who receives Dibao and the presence of released prisoners was available in 78 neighborhoods. Among these 78 neighborhoods, 13 neighborhoods had released prisoners among their residents.

65. In several neighborhoods in Wuhan, residents committees refused to provide information on released prisoners.

66. In some localities, people who use use drugs or gamble are ineligible for Dibao. See http://bit.ly/2tJG6xR (accessed May 15, 2017).

given to the disabled than in neighborhoods with weaker surveillance capabilities (see Appendix Section A.1.2).

The neighborhood survey clearly shows how Dibao is prioritized for released prisoners. Providing Dibao to targeted populations who are low-income does not violate Dibao regulations. However, public security and justice ministry documents that emphasize the prioritization of Dibao for individuals they have deemed threatening to political order contrast with Ministry of Civil Affairs policies that emphasize the need to limit Dibao provision to the poor who are infirm. The eagerness with which residents committees help targeted populations obtain Dibao also stands in stark contrast to the barriers and burdens that residents committees impose on most other Dibao applications. The seepage of political order into Dibao ultimately results in a second logic guiding the distribution of Dibao benefits in a context of hard budget constraints. While the logic of maximizing work is clearly spelled out in government documents on Dibao, the logic of distributing benefits to preempt disorder is an indirect result of how wide-ranging resources and policies are contorted to serve the needs of political order and stability in China.

5

Repressing with Social Assistance

The last week of December 2012 was particularly cold in the city of Xi'an. But this did not deter Mrs. Yang, a 49-year-old block captain, from making her weekly visit to the Zhao household (Interview, N2014_939). Mrs. Yang had been going to the Zhaos' apartment for months. Mr. Zhao was an engineer working for a private company. Mrs. Zhao made money doing housework. Their son was five. The summer before, Mrs. Zhao's mother, who lived with them, had been diagnosed with lung cancer. The family was on solid financial footing prior to this illness, but surgeries, hospitalization, drugs, and other medical expenses bankrupted them.

Around this time, Mrs. Zhao became a member of the Association of Disciples, or Mentuhui (门徒会), a religious movement with Christian origins founded in 1989 in Shaanxi, the province where Xi'an is the capital. The Chinese government officially classifies Mentuhui as a cult (邪教). Following the Falun Gong protests in 1999, the CCP's concern with religious movements, which had the potential to facilitate cross-class and cross-regional mobilization, intensified. As of 2017, the Chinese government considered 20 groups—often religions with stronger organizational capacity and larger followings—to be cults (Irons 2018). If a person is discovered to be a member, the state will aim to re-educate the individual using whatever means necessary until they recant their belief.[1]

Against expectations, Mrs. Zhao's mother's cancer went into remission. Soon after, Mr. Zhao and Mrs. Zhao's mother both became adherents of Mentuhui. In the spring of 2012, Mr. Zhao was detained by police for "illegally collecting money" for Mentuhui, and imprisoned for re-education and transformation (教育转化). The family was flagged for surveillance and monitoring. Mrs. Yang soon began making her visits. Sometimes she would visit the family alone. More often, she would visit with residents committee members, public security officers,

---

1. Participating in organizations officially designated as cults is punishable by imprisonment; see Article 300 of China's criminal code, https://www.fmprc.gov.cn/ce/cgvienna/eng/dbtyw/jdwt/crimelaw/t209043.htm (accessed July 17, 2019). Re-education takes place within criminal detention and outside of it.

and other community members. Mrs. Yang believes she is assisting in the "ideological transformation" (思想转化) of the Zhao family and "rescuing" (挽救) them from dangerous beliefs. Mrs. Yang's goal is that each member of the Zhao family renounce their faith in Mentuhui, eliminate all practices associated with Mentuhui (such as prayer) from their lives, and desist from participating in any activities associated with the organization.

Mrs. Yang describes her most effective tools as "delivering warmth" (送温暖) and "solving practical difficulties" (解决实际困难) for the family. The family has been given Dibao, as well as health and educational assistance benefits. When Mrs. Yang visits, she asks Mrs. Zhao about her mother's health and about how her son is doing in preschool. She asks Mrs. Zhao if there is anything the community can do to help. She tells Mrs. Zhao about the free medical check-ups available for Dibao families. She tells Mrs. Zhao that the residents committee will be delivering rice and oil to some Dibao households in a few weeks for Chinese New Year. Talking about these practical matters and benefits makes it easier for her to engage Mrs. Zhao and for Mrs. Zhao to open up to her. Mrs. Yang feels that she has gotten close to the family and has a good sense of what is going on with them. Mrs. Yang thinks that the Zhao family knows they can rely on the government and the Communist Party.

The previous chapter showed how Dibao is prioritized for targeted populations and ex-prisoners. This chapter focuses on the results of such benefit distribution—what I call *repressive assistance*. The Zhao family's experience illustrates some facets of how benefit distribution represses by facilitating repeated interactions and the development of social bonds that enable surveillance, dependence, and obligation. This chapter first situates the concept of repressive assistance in the broader literature on repression and authoritarian welfare provision, contrasting it with related concepts such as channeling, relational repression, and coercive distribution. The chapter then shows how repressive assistance works, then examines its effectiveness.

5.1 *Repression without Coercion*

We usually associate political repression with physical sanctions and violence— imprisonment, mass killing—or at the very least, the threat of physical force— intimidation, surveillance—by security forces managed or contracted by the government. The threat or application of force is often a part of how repression is defined. For example, Stockdill (2003) defines repression as "any actions taken by government authorities (or other elites) to impede mobilization of social movement participants; harass and intimidate activists; divide organizations; and physically assault, arrest, imprison, and kill movement members" (121). Davenport (2007) describes repression as "actual or threatened use of physical sanctions against an individual or organization, within the territorial jurisdiction of the state, for the purpose of imposing a cost on the target as well as deterring specific activities" (2). Wrong (1988) defines repression as "a mechanism of force wielded by the government—an overtly manifest device, always available to political authorities—that restricts the freedom and/or inflicts bodily pain/injury on citizens up to and including the destruction of human life itself" (24).

However, physical sanctions, violence, and force are not the only means through which to restrict freedom, impose costs on targets, deter specific activities, or impede the mobilization of social movements. Older definitions of repression often did not specify any particular tactic to achieve these ends. Tilly defines repression as "any action by another group which raises the contender's cost of collective action" (Tilly 1978:100). Oberschall (1973) distinguishes between coercive forms of repression and what he calls channeling forms of repression. Like coercion, channeling is intended to limit collective action and protest, but does so without the application of force. Earl (2003) incorporates channeling into her typology of repression and provides examples of channeling such as the Pinochet government's obstruction of funding to opposition organizations, tax laws that limit revenues for social movement organizations, and laws that restrict when and how protests can occur. Other scholars have also differentiated between repression that uses physical sanctions and repression that mostly avoids it. Way and Levitsky (2006) distinguish between "high intensity coercion," which includes killing of demonstrators and assassinations of opposition leaders, and "low intensity coercion," such as surveillance, targeting by tax police, and the use of legal actions against opposition. More recently, Frantz and Kendall-Taylor (2014) separate repressive strategies that lead to physical harm, "physical integrity rights repression," from "empowerment rights repression," such as censorship and restrictions on assembly.

The concept of repressive assistance builds on this recognition that repression need not be physically violent or threaten physical violence. Repressive assistance differs from channeling, low intensity coercion, and empowerment rights repression because it does not restrict, limit, or take away. Repressive assistance may result in the suppression of activities, mobilization, or contention, but the strategy is not inhibitive. Previous typologies of repression generally remained focused on repressive strategies that involve placing *restrictions* on material and physical resources that in turn limit protest and mobilization—for example, preventing an organization from accessing funding or other resources, or preventing a person from taking action. In contrast, repressive assistance involves the provision of material resources—cash and in-kind benefits—to increase the cost of collective action and limit contention. Rather than take away resources to achieve its goals, repressive assistance provides resources.

However, even though repressive assistance entails distribution of benefits, it differs from cooptation, clientelism, and contractual agreements. Cooptation was traditionally conceptualized as the inclusion of rival elites and other strategic actors into positions of power to neutralize the threat they pose (Gerschewski 2013; Selznick 1949). In more recent years, political scientists often treat cooptation as the provision of benefits to achieve the same goal (Gandhi and Przeworski 2007; Svolik 2012). Repressive assistance is functionally similar to this latter definition of cooptation because in both cases benefits are distributed in order to prevent some action or activity from taking place, but their mechanisms differ.

In repressive assistance, the value of the material benefits provided is not the only thing doing the work of neutralizing opposition. In cooptation, the value of the material benefit is central. The provision of benefits buys off the target, who is then willing to forgo specific activities. The target decides that the value of the benefits is worth some change in their behavior. In repressive assistance, the distribution of benefits serves to make the recipients more legible to the state, more amenable to manipulation, and ultimately not only less willing but less able to engage in the activities the regime wants to suppress. For this same reason, repressive assistance is not clientelistic or contractual. The individual receiving the benefits is not willingly entering into an agreement from which s/he can withdraw. The individual is not entering into a voluntary exchange of acquiescence for material benefit. In the case of the Zhao family, they were not told, "If you give up your religion, we will give you Dibao"; Dibao was provided to them because community cadres knew they were impoverished and eligible for Dibao, and Dibao opened the Zhaos' home to the regime.

Repressive assistance bears many similarities to Albertus, Fenner, and Slater's (2018) concept of "coercive distribution." Coercive distribution describes comprehensive distribution programs that enmesh citizens in relationships of dependence to the regime. Repressive assistance is similar to coercive distribution in that it also regards the provision of material benefits as a form of repression. In describing coercive distribution, Albertus, Fenner, and Slater (2018) write that "distribution—so often considered as an alternative to repression—can, in fact, be one of its most effective expressions" (3). Like coercive distribution, repressive assistance also changes people's ability to challenge the regime because of "legibility, dependence, narrowed political horizons, and the marginalization of alternatives" (Albertus, Fenner, and Slater 2018:15).

A key difference between repressive assistance and coercive distribution is coercion. Albertus, Fenner, and Slater (2018) define coercion as a "form of forceful compulsion in which a more powerful party credibly threatens severe sanctions against a weaker one should the latter fail to comply with terms imposed by the former" (12). The key aspect of what makes something coercive is a conditional threat. In most discussion of repression, this is a threat of physical sanction. In coercive distribution, this is a threat of revoking or reducing material benefits. While repressive assistance can involve coercion—for example, Mrs. Yang could tell the Zhao family that if they return to Mentuhui they will no longer be able to get Dibao—coercion is not necessary for repressive assistance.

Contemporary philosophical accounts of coercion have been influenced by Nozick's framework of coercion where P is said to coerce Q if P intends to keep Q from some action A; P communicates to Q that if Q performs A, P will bring about consequences that would make it less desirable for Q to do A than not do A; P's claim is credible to Q; Q does not do A, and part of the reason is that avoiding A lessens the likelihood P will bring about the consequences P claimed (Nozick 1969). While this framework has been heavily debated, most philosophers treat conditional threat—the consequences P would have applied to Q had Q done A—as essential to coercion. In order for there to be a conditional threat, P has to communicate the conditions and make the consequences known to Q. Repressive assistance need not be coercive, because P may not set out any conditions to Q. P may purposefully avoid making the consequences clear and explicit. P may not make explicit threats. P may instead focus on building social relations so that Q would be obliged to avoid A. In other words, Q may avoid A not because of fear of consequences but because of a sense of obligation. Mrs. Yang does not threaten the Zhao family. She has invested a great deal of time to become close to them, and because she has brought them "warmth" they will in return owe her (and the party that she represents) their gratitude.

Instead of coercion, repressive assistance can work through mechanisms described in relational repression, where social ties are used to demobilize protesters (Deng and O'Brien 2013). In applying relational repression, Deng and O'Brien (2013) describe how officials seek to "'engineer emotions' by mixing 'practical incentives and psychological pressures' and tapping a 'Confucian stress upon social bonds and obligation'" (548). This description can be applied to the social and psychological pressures repressive assistance is intended to generate, and captures how repressive assistance can shape the actions of those targeted without conditional threats. In repressive assistance, the provision of benefits opens the door so that community cadres can, ideally, build social bonds with the targeted individual or, at the very least, gather some information.

Another difference between repressive assistance and coercive distribution is that while coercive distribution refers to comprehensive, rather than particularistic or narrowly targeted, forms of distribution, repressive assistance can characterize welfare programs regardless of their scope. Albertus, Fenner, and Slater (2018) are interested in explaining why authoritarian regimes adopt comprehensive programs of distribution, and what role these programs serve. Coercive distribution assumes that the autocratic decision makers, at some point, make a conscious decision about launching or keeping the program. In contrast, repressive assistance can occur whether or not the welfare program is designed or intended to be repressive. The previous chapters showed how Dibao evolved into a tool for social control as it was redirected to new purposes. The implication is that repressive assistance need not be the entire or even main goal of a distributive program. Many Dibao recipients are given the benefit solely because they are desperately poor and have no means of earning a living, not because they are targets of political repression. In contrast, coercive distribution captures the raison d'être of comprehensive distribution programs in authoritarian regimes.

5.2 *Conversion of Social Assistance for Repression*

The argument that welfare is used for controlling society is not at all new. Scholars have connected welfare to the suppression of social contention and of political opposition in countries and regions ranging from 17th-century England and Japan, to 19th-century Germany, to post-colonial Africa and Latin America, to the United States in the 20th century, to the Middle East in the 21st century (Bates 1981; Brunschwig 1974; Cammett and Issar 2010; Cowgill 1974; Dawson and Robinson 1963; De La O 2013; Harris 2017; Isaac and Kelly 1981; Jennings 1979; Katznelson 1981; Koselleck 1969; Offe 1984; Piven and Cloward 1971; Skocpol and Amenta 1986; Steinmetz 1993; Wallace 2013; Yörük 2012; Zucco 2013). The concept of repressive assistance and the provision of Dibao to targeted populations in China very much build from this literature.

However, repressive assistance departs from much of the research on authoritarian welfare institutions because it does not assume that authoritarian regimes implement social policies for repressive purposes by design. Instead, repressive assistance recognizes that authoritarian regimes could make narrow policy concessions that are converted to repressive purposes over time.[2]

Most of the research on authoritarian welfare sets out to explain why autocrats *adopt* welfare and distributive programs (Albertus, Fenner, and Slater 2018; Forrat 2012; Haber 2007; Mares and Carnes 2009; Tullock 1987; Wintrobe 1998). This line of questioning is based on the recognition that the first major welfare state initiatives in Western Europe and the majority of social policies all over the world first came into being under autocratic rule. In the past 10 years, researchers

---

2. Formal models of redistribution in authoritarian regimes typically theorize that narrow concessions are possible (Acemoglu and Robinson 2006; Chen and Xu 2017).

have provided a number of compelling explanations for the *adoption* of welfare programs by autocrats. Repressive assistance refers to the deterrence of protest, contention, and mobilization through welfare provision. A country could purposefully design social policies so that they enable repressive assistance, but a country's programs could also evolve to take on characteristics of repressive assistance. Repressive assistance describes a form of repression that entails distribution rather a rationale for policy design.

In the Chinese case, as seepage of political order occurred, the Dibao program underwent policy conversion, resulting in repressive assistance. Thelen (2003) puts forth the concept of institutional "conversion" to explain institutional change. Conversion occurs when "existing institutions are redirected to new purposes, driving changes in the role they perform and/or the functions they serve" (226). Focusing on developed, Western, democratic countries, most scholars attribute conversion to changes in the nature of political opposition (Hacker 2004; Thelen 2004; Hacker, Pierson, and Thelen 2015). For example, in the 1960s, American social assistance programs became tools of racial equality through a process of conversion (Thelen 2003). In China, as Dibao resources were directed to targeted populations following changes in the CCP's strategy for maintaining political order, seepage resulted in conversion of the Dibao program. Instead of Dibao serving as a basic social safety net of last resort for the destitute, Dibao now also serves the goal of repression.

Scope Conditions

Repressive assistance could characterize social policies and distributive programs in authoritarian regimes and in democracies. It can even characterize welfare provision by non-state actors (Cammett 2014; Cammett and MacLean 2014). That said, where are we more or less likely to see repressive assistance? Repressive assistance requires strong organizational or state capacity. The provision of benefits is only a way into the (literal and metaphorical) door of the target of repression. Repressive assistance requires there to be representatives of the government, party, or regime—who can be formal employees or volunteers—to make use of benefit distribution as an opportunity to surveil and repress. Because repressive assistance requires feet on the ground, it also requires some organization that can mobilize this activity and penetrate into the grassroots level. Countries with strong parties or administrative capacity are most likely to have the infrastructure required for repressive assistance. This can include communist single-party systems. This can also include parties in democratic contexts that have large networks of brokers who frequently interact with voters (Stokes 2005; Stokes et al. 2013).

There are certain characteristics of social policies that make them more amenable to repressive assistance. Many of these characteristics are those identified by scholars of the American and European welfare systems as those generating negative policy feedback—political demobilization—in democracies (Campbell 2012). Pierson (1993) identified public policies as having "resource" and "interpretive" effects on the people who experience the policies. Social policies in particular can influence recipients by altering their level of resources, their feelings of political interest and efficacy, and, ultimately, their probability of political participation and mobilization. American social assistance programs such as Temporary Assistance for Needy Families generate negative policy feedback and undermine political participation because extremely meager benefits that are short in duration do not increase the resources of political engagement, and administration of the program by case workers increases mistrust among recipients and alienates them from formal channels of political participation (Soss 1999, 2002).

Repressive assistance is demobilizing, which means social policies with low level but traceable and regular benefits that prevent proximity and concentration of beneficiaries are more likely candidates for repressive assistance. Low levels of benefits foster dependence yet prevent beneficiaries from obtaining sufficient resources to take independent political actions. Benefits that are traceable to the government and disbursed at regular intervals are more likely to generate an effect (Arnold 1990; Mettler 2011). Mental accounting may make a visible and traceable cash subsidy more salient than a tax credit or another mechanism where the transfer results from smaller deductions of income or assets (Thaler 1985). Person N who receives X amount of cash from the state might be likely to say, "The state gave me something I did not have before." Person M who receives a tax credit in the amount of X might instead say, "The state took less from me." Both N and M have X more money in their wallets, but N is more likely to attribute X to a generous state. As a result, disbursements may be more effective in repressive assistance than deductions or waived fees. Social policies that prevent beneficiaries from interacting with one another or society more generally—for example, by generating stigma among recipients, by isolating recipients, or by varying the duration of benefit provision—also are more amenable to repressive assistance because they isolate beneficiaries and prevent them from coordinating or acting collectively.

Finally, repressive assistance may be more likely found when benefits are distributed as part of formal social programs and policies rather than from discretionary accounts. For one thing, formal programs are more likely to facilitate traceable and regular disbursements. Funding from discretionary accounts may be more sporadic. In addition, programmatic policies are more likely attributed to an organization such as a government and a party. If benefits are distributed outside of official social welfare programs, the distribution is more likely to facilitate dyadic ties. In such cases, the target may attribute benefits not to the regime but to the individual who is giving them the benefit. Because Dibao is programmatic, the Zhao family knows that even though block captains and other community cadres helped them obtain Dibao, the benefits they receive would not be possible without the Chinese Communist Party and the government.

5.3 How Repressive Assistance Works

In China, repressive assistance through Dibao provision takes place in the broader context of re-education assistance to targeted populations, who are introduced in Chapter 4. The provision of Dibao to targeted populations is repressive because it raises the cost of contention and deters certain activities such as social mobilization. However, to understand how Dibao represses and raises the costs of contention requires an understanding of re-education, which in turn requires us to examine the ideas and beliefs of the Chinese penal system.

Re-education does not refer to the acquisition of knowledge or skills. It refers to reform. In the Chinese penal context, re-education refers to the transformation of the entire being, from innermost thoughts to outward behavior. Re-education is closely related to "thought reform" (what detractors have labeled brainwashing), used since the revolutionary period by the CCP to win converts to communism (Perry 2017). Although CCP practices of thought reform are influenced by Soviet methods, the Chinese communists, unlike the Soviet, were influenced by the Confucian emphasis on the "malleability and perfectibility" of human beings and believed that human beings could be remade (Lifton 2012; Perry 2002b). Lifton (2012) finds that some who were subjected to thought reform "underwent a profound religious experience. They regarded thought reform as fine and ennobling and felt genuinely reborn" (400). Re-education goes beyond anti-recidivism because it is not simply the prevention of actions of crime (change in behavior) but a change in the underlying thinking and psychology that lead to crime.

Influenced by these underlying beliefs, the Chinese penal system used discipline, deprivation, punishment, and labor in an attempt to completely alter the psychology and cognition of criminals (Dutton 1992; Fu 2005). Physical labor and hardship (what critics have called torture and slavery) were seen as means of engendering cognitive change and psychological engineering. Although political and financial motivations also shape China's penal regime, scholars point to a need to take China's rehabilitative ideology seriously (Fu 2005). We continue to see its influence. "Transformation through education" has been applied to thousands of

Falun Gong followers since 1999 (Tong 2009). Re-education and transformation are core components of China's mass internment of Uyghurs and other Muslims that began in 2018 (Zenz 2019). For critics, re-education as a penal method represents the infringement of human rights to liberty, speech, religion, and assembly; it is synonymous with coercive repressive and human rights abuse.

Whether people within the CCP, within the penal system, within re-education assistance committees, and within society more generally subscribe to some or all of these beliefs about penal reform is unknown. What we know of the Maoist period suggests true believers existed (Lifton 2012; Perry 2002b). Today, many people who work in re-education committees continue to speak in terms of transformation and change. Mrs. Yang describes her work as bringing people "back to shore" and overcoming the brainwashing that cults have imposed (Interview, N2014_939).[3] Another neighborhood administrator described re-education as a way of "helping targeted populations turn to the right path" (Interview, N2013_527).

Re-education assistance work is done in teams. The CCP has used teams for repression since the Maoist period because it recognizes the power of social and peer pressure (Deng and O'Brien 2013; Dutton 1992). Re-education assistance team members often comprise residents committee members, block captains, household registration police, neighborhood watch volunteers, and other community-level party activists and cadres. Similar to Deng and O'Brien's description of relational repression, some re-education team members may themselves be under pressure to participate. For example, re-education team members can include family members of the targeted person, drawing from the long-standing practice of involving family members in "transforming" criminals (Dutton 1992). In addition, re-education team members may include other Dibao recipients who are taking on this "job" because they would lose their Dibao otherwise.[4]

5.3.1 Repeated Interactions

The provision of welfare benefits in the context of re-education increases interactions between the regime and the target, facilitating opportunities for repeated contact. Cash transfers are made monthly, and additional ad hoc benefits as described in Chapter 2 are announced throughout the year. Each time a benefit

3. Although the Chinese regime's own tactics have been labeled brainwashing (洗脑), the regime now frequently uses the term "brainwashing" to refer to the tactics of organizations it has banned.

4. See Chapter 4 for details on the work requirements associated with Dibao.

is disbursed is an opportunity for contact between the regime and the person targeted by repressive assistance.

Provinces, cities, and districts all have autonomy to decide what ad hoc benefits they provide. For example, in Fuzhou, the capital of Fujian Province, ad hoc benefits distributed between 2008 and 2013 included access to low-cost housing for around 4,000 Dibao households, free health check-ups for women of Dibao households, and free public transportation for students belonging to Dibao households. In Hefei, the provincial capital of Anhui, ad hoc benefits during this time period include subsidies for natural gas and water, higher medical reimbursement standards, and waived burial and funeral expenses. In Zhengzhou, the capital of Henan Province, Dibao families with children who are in college could receive up to 8,000 CNY per year in cash subsidies, and Dibao households could receive medical subsidies up to 10,000 CNY per year. In the capital of Hubei Province, Wuhan, Dibao households could receive 10 CNY per month per square meter in housing assistance; Dibao households did not have to pay garbage collection fees and paid reduced fees for water; and children of some Dibao households were selected to participate in free supplemental educational courses for English and other subjects.

I created a data set of ad hoc benefits in 36 cities using online media and government reports (for details on the data set and its creation, see Appendix A.7). The central government requires local governments to make changes related to the Dibao programs public, which includes changes in the Dibao line as well as ad hoc benefits that may be provided to Dibao recipients. Community-specific activities may not be fully captured in this data set because they may not be reported widely. As a result, this data should be regarded as a floor on the number of ad hoc benefits Dibao households could receive. This data serves to provide a better sense of the number and type of interactions facilitated via the Dibao program with targets of repressive assistance.

Figure 5.1 shows the average number of ad hoc benefits announced per city per year between January 1, 2008 and December 31, 2012. There is large variation among cities. Wuxi announced on average less than five ad hoc benefits a year, but Tianjin, Beijing, and Chongqing announced more than 20 per year over this five-year period. This could reflect actual differences in the level of ad hoc benefits or differences in the level of publicity surrounding ad hoc benefits. For cities such as Beijing, roughly one or two ad hoc benefits are distributed each month. If we add this to monthly cash distribution, this means re-education committees can use benefit disbursement as a reason to visit the Dibao household two or three times a month.

The ad hoc benefits in my data set can be grouped into 10 different categories (see Table 5.1). Almost all involved visible and traceable disbursement of

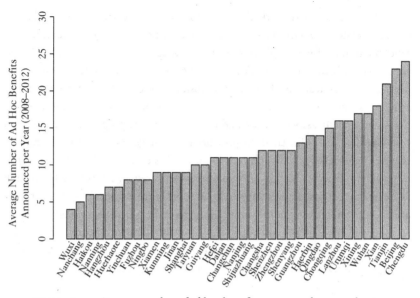

FIGURE 5.1 Average number of ad hoc benefits announced per year by city

benefits—45% were in-kind benefits, 43% were distributions of cash, and the remaining 12% were distribution of services—rather than credits and fee waivers. The largest category was living expenses, primarily cash for food and clothing or

Table 5.1 Ad hoc Dibao benefits by category

Category	Occurrence	
	Number	Percentage
Living expenses	1,033	43%
Medical and health	372	16%
Utilities	284	12%
Housing	243	10%
Education	223	9%
Employment	76	3%
Entertainment	76	3%
Burial and funerary	50	2%
Elderly	22	1%
Transportation	11	0%
Total	2,390	

the distribution of food (pork, rice, oil) and clothing directly. The second largest category related to medical and health expenses, mostly related to medical assistance programs—for example, free health check-ups and screenings, and cash subsidies to cover other out-of-pocket medical expenses. Utilities benefits included heating, gas, water, and trash collection subsidies. Housing benefits refer to access to low-cost housing and housing purchase and rental subsidies. Education benefits were typically associated with education assistance programs that provided cash transfers for children from preschool to college. Benefits in the employment category are typically job training programs and sometimes job openings targeted at Dibao recipients. The entertainment category refers to benefits such as tickets to movies, amusement parks, and other diversions. Burial and funerary benefits refers to subsidies for burial expenses. Benefits in the elderly category include waivers of personal contribution for old age pension programs, access to old persons' homes, and sometimes direct cash subsidies with age limitations. Transportation benefits are subsidies for public transportation.

5.3.2 Facilitating Surveillance

The frequency at which cash transfers and ad hoc benefits associated with Dibao are made facilitates repeated interactions. Through the Dibao program, neighborhood administrators have numerous opportunities to "bring warmth" and "assistance" to targeted populations on Dibao, and the disbursement of benefits serves as a natural starting point for conversations. A block captain with a former prisoner in her building said:

> It was much easier to talk to Duan after he starting getting Dibao. I could ask him about whether he had enough. He could tell me what his needs were, and if he was unhappy, I could learn about why he was dissatisfied (Interview, N2012_831).

Echoing this sentiment, a residents committee member who participated in a re-education assistance committee said:

> Xie was in prison for 10 years, from age 20 to 30. When he was released, he was very uncomfortable and cautious. He would rarely say anything, and when he talked, he was very quiet and would never meet your eyes. He wasn't able to find any jobs because he looked lazy, like he didn't want to do any work. We helped him obtain Dibao so he could have some basic subsistence, and would regularly visit him to see if the assistance was sufficient (Interview, N2013_822).

Surveillance is less noticeable when it is conducted as part of interactions related to the distribution of benefits. When re-education committee members bring news of a Dibao-related benefit, they will often follow up by asking whether the person or family has any additional needs. This discussion of additional needs can easily transition into a discussion of unmet needs. In talking about unmet needs, neighborhood cadres can ask what else the person wants, what s/he is unhappy about, and what s/he is thinking of doing about those needs. Private information is gathered through these conversations about everyday matters.

Neighborhood administrators and block captains also note that if they can give something to the targeted person, that person is more likely to talk and to open up. This is true even if the thing is small in value. A residents committee member said:

> Released prisoners have a hard time when they leave prison. They don't know how things work and how to do things in the real world. It is easy for them to go back to doing the bad things that got them arrested in the first place. The re-education assistance committee emphasizes ideological thought work, which is important, but if we can provide tangible assistance it helps [thought work] be more effective. The people are more willing to listen and to talk to us (Interview, N2013_921).

The distribution of material benefits not only makes information gathering less discernible, it also makes the targets of surveillance more forthcoming.

5.3.3 Obligation and Dependence

The residents committee member quoted above is explaining how tangible assistance enables surveillance. The underlying mechanism that allows this is a sense of obligation. The targeted person feels obligated to speak after receiving something. However, it is not one act of exchange that generates obligation. The sense of obligation is built on repeated interactions where grassroots representatives of the regime have come bearing gifts from the regime. Furthermore, the sense of obligation may be intensified when the re-education committee includes family members, friends, or other preexisting social relations of the target. Because the targeted person has received something (or many small things) from someone s/he has a social relationship with, s/he faces pressure to reciprocate. The strength of obligation may be particularly strong in China because of a Confucian emphasis on reciprocity in interpersonal relationships (Yum 1988), but social influence is an extremely effective means of influence across cultures (Beck et al. 2002; Bond et al. 2012; McClurg 2003). Reciprocation in the form of talking and sharing information enables surveillance, but reciprocation can also involve changes in stated beliefs and in behavior.

Re-education committees often adopt a paternalistic stance, and the authority in this relationship is strengthened by benefit provision. Block captains such as Mrs. Yang take on the role of a concerned elder. They give "advice" to the targeted person with the implication that the targeted person should listen and follow out of deference to and respect for their elders. Re-education committee members are much more likely to use terms such as "guiding," "assisting," and "teaching" than "managing," "controlling," or "forcing." The same residents committee member who talked about the young ex-prisoner Xie also said [emphasis added]:

> If he needed anything else, we could help him get additional benefits. Through these visits, we helped him return to society—to help make his mental state more stable, to *teach* him how to interact with people.

Instead of working through obligation, repressive assistance can also facilitate surveillance and control because targets become completely dependent on the assistance. Material dependence was a core strategy of control in pre-reform China (Walder 1988). Even though market reform and increasing incomes have broken the material dependence of the population on the regime for most of the Chinese population, repressive assistance, because it is targeted at the very poor, continues to work in the same way. In December 2011, the average Dibao line among 36 of China's largest cities was 376 CNY per month. This amount barely supported subsistence living standards, which means that families dependent on it would likely not survive without. Ad hoc benefits, especially benefits in the realm of housing (Hong 2004) such as priority access to subsidies from the Housing Fund (住房公积金), prioritized access to Affordable Housing (经济适用房), and prioritized access to Low-Cost Housing (廉租房) provide shelter to households that might otherwise not be able to access housing. Dibao benefits are not high enough to provide resources that enable recipients to mobilize against the regime. They are just high enough to support basic subsistence and enable dependence.

Dependence often has coercive implications. One local police officer said:

> Li went to prison from 2009 to 2012 for destroying government property [while protesting]. When he was released, he was already 61 years old. He had a 90-year-old mother to support. His wife had cancer. He was under a lot of pressure. Our re-education assistance committee helped Li get Dibao from the sub-district civil affairs office. After he got this living assistance, we visited him regularly to conduct ideological education. We

introduced him to party and government policies that could help him so he would not protest or petition again.... We knew he was thinking of petitioning again. We encouraged him to be brave, to let go of thoughts of revenge. We tried to cheer him up, and help him be self-sufficient (Interview, N2013_841).

"Encouraging" Li to be brave and let go of thoughts of revenge involved talking about the hypothetical provision of additional benefits. The local police officer told Li that if he is in dire need, maybe the community can get him access to some additional measures of relief. However, encouragement also involved references to the potential loss of benefits. Li was told that if he protested, he would go back to prison. How would he be able to provide anything for his family then? What would happen to his mother? What would happen to his sick wife? Li is dependent on these benefits to provide for his family. Because these benefits are provided to him by the regime, Li is trapped in a relationship of dependence with the regime. Li is not making an independent decision to allow himself to be coopted by these benefits. He has no choice because he cannot do without the benefits. Dependence removes alternatives, limits autonomy, and narrows individuals' choices to those demanded by the regime.

Dependence on the regime is exacerbated by the isolation and stigma associated with Dibao. Many Dibao recipients interviewed by Solinger (2011) reported trying to conceal their Dibao status from their acquaintances and described feeling socially detached. Because the names of Dibao recipients are publicly listed in every neighborhood, it is extremely difficult for residents to conceal their status from neighbors. Through interviews conducted with Dibao recipients across China, Han (2012) finds that this leads recipients to feel shame and despair. Isolation and shame hinder communication and contact between Dibao recipients Solinger (2012) and serve to further the dependence of Dibao recipients on the regime.

5.4 *Limitations on Effectiveness*

The above cases show how repressive assistance works to increase costs and deter activities. For the Zhao family, as well as Duan, Xie, and Li, repressive assistance worked. They were all closely watched and managed by their neighborhood-level cadres, subjected to repeated visits, and ultimately deterred from engaging in activities the regime deemed to be problematic. Repressive assistance in theory fulfills two out of four infrastructural mechanisms that Slater and Fenner (2011) argue sustain and stabilize authoritarian regimes—registration (legibility) and dependence. However, how effective is repressive assistance at achieving the regime's goal of maintaining order by controlling targeted populations?

5.4.1 Heuristics in Identification

In almost all of the neighborhoods I visited during my qualitative fieldwork, the targeted populations who received Dibao were released prisoners, released from either prison or re-education through labor camps. I found exceptions in only two neighborhoods. In one neighborhood in Zhengzhou, the block captain identified a Huang as someone who she thought had the capacity to protest over unpaid pensions (Interview, N2013_534). In the other neighborhood in Qingdao, a Wu had been placed into the targeted populations category after he organized other parents to complain about the collection of illegal fees at his daughter's school (Interview, N2012_431).

Most, and perhaps all, of the individuals released from prison I encountered during my fieldwork had no intention of engaging in collective action, and often lacked the resources to organize or carry out protests. Many ex-prisoners had been incarcerated for crimes unrelated to political or social dissent. One man had spent time in prison for fraud, another for burglary, and another for forgery. These released prisoners often lacked the skills to reintegrate into society, much less the ability to organize collective action. For example, Xie, whose situation was described above, lacked basic communication and social skills. He did not want to speak to others, could not make eye contact when he had to speak, and was socially isolated in his neighborhood. These are not the characteristics of someone who is likely to lead or organize collective action. The closest I came to someone released from prison who might have the capabilities required to organize was a man who had been convicted of drug trafficking. He was categorized as a targeted population and local administrators were concerned that he would reconnect with his former associates with ties to organized crime.

For people who have been released from re-education through labor, the story is more mixed. While most had been imprisoned for nonpolitical activities—gambling, prostitution, and drug use—a few had been detained for political activities. One woman, Chen from Zhengzhou (Interview, D2013_51), and one man, Yang from Zibo (Interview, D2012_31), had been imprisoned for practicing Falun Gong. Another man, Li (whose situation is described by a police officer above), had been detained for destroying government property while protesting (Interview, N2013_841). I do not know the future likelihood that any of these three people would engage in some form of protest or collective action, though it seemed unlikely from my interviews. These people, especially the two Falun Gong practitioners, expressed high levels of fear and strong desires to avoid government attention.

Effect of Dibao on Future Collective Action

There is no systematic data on how many Dibao recipients are targeted populations. We cannot ask Dibao recipients themselves if they belong to targeted populations because they do not know. What I do find is that receiving Dibao does not change an average person's stated propensity to participate in collective action. Using data from the China Urban Governance Survey (CUGS) and a fuzzy regression discontinuity design, I examine how Dibao status affects individuals' self-reported plans to participate in future collective action.

The CUGS is a nationally representative survey of urban China with 3,513 respondents (for details on the CUGS, including sampling, see Appendix A.6). The survey includes a question on future plans to participate in collective action:

> Regardless of whether you have done it in the past, is there a possibility you would do the following in the future?

One option presented is "participate in demonstrations/protests/mass incidents" (参与游行/示威/群体性事件). Respondents can choose between "there is a possibility in the future" (将来有可能), "there is no possibility in the future" (今后绝不可能), or "cannot say" (说不清).

Regression discontinuity design is an approach that allows for estimation of causal effects by taking advantage of a cutoff above or below which an intervention (treatment) is assigned. By comparing outcomes close to either side of this cutoff, RDD allows us to estimate average treatment effects without an experimental intervention. Because Dibao is a means-tested program—there is an income threshold above which households are ineligible for Dibao—I can use this income threshold as the cutoff and examine the likelihood of future collective action below and above this cutoff. In the CUGS, household income is assessed in several ways. First, respondents are asked:

> In 2014, what was your total household income (including wages, bonuses, informal income, subsidies and remittances, parents, family, and friends, investment income, and any other income)?

Among 3,513 respondents, 1,112 (32%) provided a numerical answer to this question. Among the remaining respondents, 1,416 (40%) said they did not know, and 985 (28%) refused to answer. If respondents refused to answer or said they did not know, they were presented with a card showing 10 different annual income brackets that ranged from "Less than 15,000 CNY" to "More than 400,000

CNY,"[5] and asked to choose the bracket that includes their total household income. For this second income question, 1,280 of the 2,401 respondents who did not answer the first question provided a response. Overall, 68% of respondents provided information on household income.[6] The CUGS also included a question on whether the respondents' household receives Dibao:

> Does your household receive the Minimum Livelihood Guarantee Scheme? (您家是否有人享受最低生活保障?).

Respondents could answer "Yes" (是) or "No" (否). The income of the respondent and their response to the question of whether or not they receive Dibao benefits is then compared to the locally determined Dibao line. The Ministry of Civil Affairs provides quarterly data on the Dibao line for each county and district in China.[7] I match the Dibao line for each county-level unit included in the CUGS for the time period when the survey was conducted. Among the 50 counties included in the CUGS survey, the minimum monthly Dibao line was 340 CNY per month (USD 50), and the maximum was 800 CNY per month (USD 188). The median Dibao line was 515 CNY per month (USD 76) and the mean was 526 CNY per month (USD 77). I take the 1,099 respondents in the CUGS who provided their annual income and household size, for whom I can directly see which households are eligible for Dibao given their county of residence.

If the Dibao line represents a hard cutoff for Dibao status, then all households with per capita income below the Dibao line should receive Dibao, and no households with income above the Dibao threshold should receive Dibao. We know, however, from previous research that many households with income below the Dibao line do not receive Dibao (exclusion error), and some households with income above the Dibao line do receive Dibao (inclusion error). In the CUGS data, a large number (84%) of respondents whose self-reported income falls below the Dibao line do not receive Dibao. This high exclusion error is roughly in line with estimates that only about 20% to 30% of households eligible for Dibao receive Dibao (Chen, Ravallion, and Wang 2006; Yang 2012). In addition, 4% of respondents who report income above their local Dibao line are Dibao recipients.

---

5. The brackets are less than 15,000 CNY, 15,000-29,900 CNY, 30,000-39,900 CNY, 40,000-49,900 CNY, 50,000-59,900 CNY, 60,000-79,900 CNY, 80,000-99,900 CNY, 100,000-199,900 CNY, 200,000-399,900 CNY, and More than 400,000 CNY.

6. In addition to these questions, enumerators were also asked to make their own, rough assessment of the economic status of the household as "low income," "average income," "middle income," or "high income."

7. See http://www.mca.gov.cn/article/sj/tjjb/bzbz/ (accessed May 2, 2017).

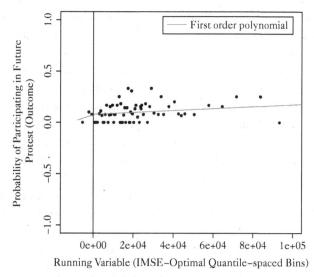

FIGURE 5.2 Dibao and probability of participating in future collective action

This low inclusion error is also within the range of inclusion error from previous studies.

The presence of exclusion and inclusion error means that sharp RDD is not appropriate. However, the CUGS data shows that *probability* of receiving Dibao status is discontinuous depending on whether a household's income falls below or above the local Dibao line (for analysis, see Appendix A.6). This means the main assumption required for fuzzy RDD is met.[8]

Using fuzzy RDD, I find that the provision of Dibao does not influence future plans for protest. Figure 5.2 illustrates that the provision of Dibao does not appear to have an effect on future plans for collective action.[9] The y-axis of Figure 5.2 is the probability of participating in future protest, and the x-axis is the binned difference between CUGS respondents' self-reported income and the local Dibao threshold. Dots to the right of the solid vertical line in Figure 5.2 represent

8. In more technical terms, when a threshold does not perfectly determine treatment exposure, as long as the threshold creates a discontinuity in the probability of treatment exposure, we can use the discontinuity to produce instrumental variable estimators of the effect of the treatment (close to the discontinuity). For Dibao, as long as having income below the Dibao line creates a discontinuity in the probability of receiving Dibao, we can use this discontinuity to produce instrumental variable estimators of the effect of receiving Dibao, close to the discontinuity, on future plans for collective action.

9. Figure 5.2 shows IMSE-optimal quantile-space bins to the left and right of the cutoff (Calonico, Cattaneo, and Titiunik 2014). Using other methods of determining bin size does not change these results.

individuals whose self-reported income falls above the locally set Dibao line, and dots to the left of the solid vertical line are individuals whose self-reported income falls below the Dibao line. Focusing on individuals close to the Dibao threshold, there are no statistically significant differences in plans to engage in future collective action. This result is robust and not due to particularities in the data. Specifically, there is no bunching around the threshold, and the results are not sensitive to the bandwidth range (see Appendix A.6 for details).

One might worry that measuring plans for future collective action—the expected likelihood of participating in "demonstrations/protests/mass incidents" (参与游行/示威/群体性事件) in the future—based on respondents' self reports is problematic. Social desirability bias or preference falsification could lead respondents to mis-report their future plans. We might think that households receiving Dibao might be less likely to report future plans for collective action, for fear of losing their benefits, while households without Dibao might be more likely to report future plans for collective action because they face fewer opportunity costs. If this type of response bias exists, we would observe Dibao having a pacifying effect on individuals' reported plans for future collective action. However, that is not what we find. Dibao does not have a pacifying effect. If we interpret these self-reports as truthful, then we would say that Dibao does not dampen future plans for protest. If we interpret these self-reports as falsified preferences, then we would say that Dibao does not dampen anyone's willingness to say that they will engage in future collective action.

Average Effects of Dibao on Targeted Populations

We do not know for sure whether this null result holds for the subset of Dibao recipients who are receiving the benefit because they are targeted persons. However, there are unlikely to be statistically significant differences in future plans for collective action between targeted populations who fall below and above the Dibao threshold. During my qualitative fieldwork from 2012 to 2013, I gathered details on 23 cases of targeted populations.[10] Five (22%) had previously engaged in socio political contention or intended to do so. This means the large majority of targeted populations have never engaged in protest. As a result, we would not expect Dibao provision to change the overall propensity of future mobilization among this population. We would very likely find that Dibao provision to targeted populations does not, on average, decrease their likelihood of protest or collective action because most targeted populations were never contentious in the first place.

---

10. I encountered the case of the Zhao family after this main fieldwork period, so it is not counted in the 23.

Does this mean using the heuristic of ex-prisoners to identify targeted populations fails? Heuristics are never accurate, but they are appealing because of their simplicity (Tversky and Kahneman 1992). There are two ways in which identification of targeted populations, even though reliant on heuristics, is successful in China. First, political order for the Chinese regime conflates certain expressions of grievances (e.g., collective action) with common crime. Thus, even if the current method of identifying targeted populations does not decrease protests, on average it may serve to suppress a broader class of social ills.

Second, although many individuals whom local governments do not manage to identify as targeted persons may be more likely than those identified as targeted persons to organize protests and collective action, the proportion of individuals who have participated or who intend to participate in contention is likely much higher among targeted populations than in the general population. This is what we observe when comparing my fieldwork results to CUGS, which is representative of China's urban population. In my fieldwork five out of 23 (22%) members of targeted populations had engaged in some form of social mobilization in the past. Among CUGS respondents, only 1.6% (55 out of the 3,415 who answered this question) said they had previously participated in demonstrations, strikes, or mass incidents. If we expand CUGS responses to broader forms of contention, the proportion remains small—only 3% of CUGS respondents said they have petitioned in the past. This echoes the point I made in Chapter 4 that relying on the heuristic of ex-prisoner to identify targeted populations results in good precision (lowers Type I error) but low recall (high Type II error). Many who will engage in the contentious activities the CCP wants to prevent are not identified and incorporated into targeted population lists. As a result, the distribution of Dibao to targeted populations is unlikely to have an effect in limiting overall (average) rates of protest among targeted populations. However, among the targeted persons who have some propensity for contentious protest or mobilization, the program is effective when they are closely monitored.

5.4.2 Variation in Intensity and Timing of Interactions

However, as Chapter 4 showed, not everyone who is identified is closely managed all the time. There is great variation in how repressive assistance is carried out among neighborhoods and over time. Most neighborhoods do not have the manpower—block captains who are deeply penetrated into their communities— to carry out the frequent interactions required for surveillance and control for sustained periods of time. In these instances, local public security officers have to mobilize other community members to fulfill this task. Some of the community members are residents committee members who are already overburdened.

Others are reluctant or unenthusiastic volunteers. There are few repeated inter-actions, and they are not sustained over long periods.

If we look at the CCP's efforts to re-educate Falun Gong adherents, which is admittedly a hard case for re-education, the evidence suggests very limited suc-cess. Noakes and Ford (2015) report that nearly 20 years after the CCP expended all resources at its capacity to stamp out Falun Gong, there still may be millions of Falun Gong followers in China who are connected to the broader organi-zation. Reports from Chinese security agencies detail how re-education and transformation work often fail (Noakes and Ford 2015).

What happens more often is that surveillance and control ramp up in specific times of the year—before political meetings and around national holidays. Gov-ernment officials often believe that collective action and protest are most likely around the time of the Two Meetings or Lianghui (两会)—the local Political Consultative Conference and the local People's Congress—which typically occur within a few days of one another. This phenomenon is captured in the docu-mentary *Petition*, when petitioners amass in Beijing during the Chinese People's Political Consultative Conference and National People's Congress to air their demands (*Petition* 2009).[11] In the study *Unexpected Mass Incidents in China: Causes and Countermeasures* (中国群体性突发事件成因及对策), central and local People's Congresses and Political Consultative Conferences are identified as occasions with high potential for protest (China Administrative Management Association Issue Committee 2009:94). Chen (2009) shows that among peti-tioners in one locality, 20% of petitioning events or threats of petition occurred during special events, in particular Lianghui. The rationale for picking certain times is to "catch the attention of the local leaders who often attend important local events…those events are political rituals that symbolize legitimacy and sta-bility" (Chen 2009:463). King, Pan, and Roberts (2017) show that prior to local political meetings, government astroturfers—so-called 50-cent party members or government commentators—fabricate large volumes of social media posts aimed at distracting the public.

Government documents remind local governments to be on guard prior to and during these sensitive periods. In *Strategies for Preventing and Managing Mass Incidents during the Reform Period*, Zhou writes that in order to prevent protests, officials "need to be diligent during sensitive periods…it is very likely that some people will take the opportunity to organize…and emotions can be easily stirred up again" ("做好敏感时期工作…很可能有一部分人借机扩大事态…会引发群众情绪的重新发作") (Zhou 2008:588). My interviews

---

11. The documentary was filmed from 1996 to 2008; since the 2008 Olympics, this practice has been largely suppressed in Beijing.

with government officials from civil affairs and finance departments, as well as academics involved in the process of determining Dibao policies in Beijing, Wuhan, and Zhengzhou, also reflect this logic. Officials emphasized the distribution of ad hoc benefits for Dibao households before these time periods. According to a department head of a civil affairs bureau in northern China, ad hoc benefits are distributed before Lianghui to prevent social unrest, and to ensure that "these events proceed smoothly…and the masses are passive" (Interview, B2013_112).

Public security documents also emphasize the need to be especially vigilant before and during major festivals such as Chinese New Year and National Day. Monitoring of targeted populations should be intensified before hand. A public security official in west central China noted to me that protests were more likely during holidays because people were not working and had time to organize and participate in collective action (Interview, B2013_946). According to Chen (2009), the "predominant choice" for collective action is the Lianghui meeting, followed by three main holidays: New Year (January 1), Chinese New Year (also known as Spring Festival), and National Day (October 1). Another holiday which serves as a focal point for a potential period of protest is Qingming Festival, or Tomb-sweeping Day, a day when people pay respect to the dead, often visiting the graves of their ancestors. The association between protests and Qingming Festival has historical roots, and for this reason was largely banned during the Maoist era. In recent years, Qingming has become a time to commemorate and protest politically related deaths (Johnson 2016). Central regime and provincial governments have issued notices about the Qingming Festival as a period when local governments need to increase their vigilance to prevent protest.[12]

Using the data set of ad hoc benefits introduced earlier in this chapter, I find that Dibao-related benefits are much more likely to be announced and distributed prior to and during political meetings and national holidays than other times of the year.[13] The left panel of Figure 5.3 shows the difference in the number of online reports of ad hoc benefits for all Lianghui meetings and for Lianghui meetings occurring 20 days away from Chinese New Year. Based on t-tests, it is 38% (18%–58%) more likely that benefits are distributed before or during Lianghui than after. When controlling for Chinese New Year, it is 52% (26%–78%) more likely that benefits are distributed before or during Lianghui than after. To further verify that there is a difference in ad hoc benefits distributed before and after Lianghui, I conduct a permutation test of the difference in ad hoc benefits in all adjacent 10-day periods, not including Lianghui periods and Chinese New Year, for the

12. See http://j.mp/jiangxi and http://j.mp/MinistryCivil (accessed April 10, 2016).

13. Most announcements describe benefits that are being provided, rather than those that will be provided in the future.

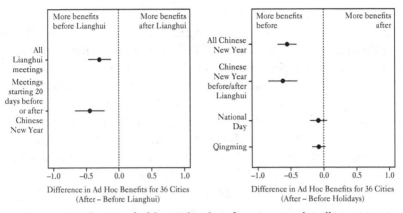

FIGURE 5.3 Distribution of ad hoc Dibao benefits prior to politically sensitive time periods

36 cities. The mean difference in ad hoc benefits before and during Lianghui versus after Lianghui is significantly larger than the mean difference in ad hoc benefits between other time periods of similar duration (p-value 0.004). In addition, the mean number of benefits distributed before and during Lianghui is larger than the mean number of ad hoc benefits distributed in any other 10-day period.

The right panel of Figure 5.3 contains the point estimate and 95% confidence intervals of the difference in the number of online reports of ad hoc benefits for all Chinese New Year holidays, for Chinese New Year holidays occurring 20 days away from Lianghui, for National Day (October 1), and for Qingming Festival, which falls on either April 4 or 5 of each year. This panel shows that there are more ad hoc benefits announced before the start of Chinese New Year than during or after, before the start of National Day than during and after, and before the start of Qingming Festival than during or after.[14] Based on t-tests, the difference in ad hoc benefits is statistically significant at the 5% level for Chinese New Year but not for National Day or Qingming Festival. It is 55% (41%–69%) more likely that benefits are distributed before the Chinese New Year holiday than during or after. Examining only Chinese New Year holidays that fall more than 20 days before or after Lianghui meetings, it is 61% (40%–84%) more likely that benefits are distributed before the Chinese New Year holiday than during or after. For National Day, it is 8% (-5%–20%) more likely that benefits are distributed before

14. Note that this analysis compares the average online reports of ad hoc benefits 10 days before the *starting date* of the holiday and 10 days after the *starting date* of the holiday. Given the duration of these holidays—Chinese New Year holiday lasts for seven days, Qingming Festival lasts for three days, and National Day holiday lasts for seven days—this means that I am comparing benefit distribution before the holiday with benefit distribution during and after the holiday.

the holiday than during or after, and for Qingming Festival, it is 7% (-3%–17%) more likely that benefits are distributed before the holiday than during or after. Even though the results for National Day and Qingming Festival are not statistically significant, the point estimates are in the direction we would expect if local governments used Dibao benefits to mitigate the threat of collective action. Relatively fewer online reports about the Dibao program are made before and after National Day and Qingming Festival, so the lack of statistical significance could be due to lack of power.

These results on the timing of ad hoc Dibao benefit announcements corroborate my fieldwork, which shows that residents committees, block captains, and re-education committees are most active before politically sensitive meetings and key holidays. Neighborhood cadres and volunteers are highly mobilized during these times, and the provision of additional ad hoc benefits facilitates interactions with targets, supports intensified surveillance, and leads to intensified pressure on targeted populations during these times.

Relevant for scope conditions, these temporal patterns of ad hoc benefit distribution do not extend to other social welfare programs in China. Specifically, I compare the timing of announcements related to Dibao with the timing of announcements related to pensions (the Old Age Insurance Program) for all Chinese cities (see Appendix A.7.2 for details) around three major Chinese holidays (Chinese New Year, Qingming, and National Day). While Dibao announcements are much more likely to be made before these holidays (the difference is statistically significant), these time periods made little impact on the timing of announcements related to pensions.

Repressive assistance works because the distribution of material benefits increases interactions between the regime and the target of repression, facilitating surveillance and control with dependence and obligation. Because many who are targeted never intended to protest, repressive assistance may not decrease contentious activity on average among targeted populations. However, repressive assistance is effective in deterring specific activities for individuals when they are closely managed and monitored.

Repressive assistance erases the delineation between repression and concessions. It does so even though Dibao was not designed for repression. At the neighborhood level, the same individuals who facilitate the provision of welfare benefits also conduct surveillance. Residential committee members who process applications for Dibao and other social welfare benefits participate in re-education of targeted populations. Neighborhood block captains visit households to check on receipt of benefits and at the same time gather information for local public security. Repressive assistance sugarcoats repression so that it appears normal, nonthreatening, and benignly paternalistic.

A question I have been asked is whether what I am calling repressive assistance in China is just an anti-recidivism program. To the Chinese regime, the distribution of Dibao to ex-prisoners is absolutely about anti-recidivism, and the distribution of Dibao to targeted populations is about stopping (future) crime. Many people at the neighborhood level who are engaged in the identification and management of targeted populations sincerely believe they are helping to improve lives and shape a better society. Furthermore, many targeted populations are genuinely in need of material assistance. However, to regard the provision of Dibao to preempt disorder as anti-recidivism requires us to subscribe to the Chinese regime's conceptualization of crime, which encompasses expressions of personal grievance, political dissent, religious practices, collective action, and many other forms of expression. It requires us to buy into the regime's tactics of preemptive policing that place stringent limitations on personal autonomy. To equate repressive assistance in China with anti-recidivism requires us to accede to a form of policing and social control that imposes extreme limits on personal expression and liberty.

6

Triggering Backlash

What are the broader implications of prioritizing Dibao to preempt threats to political order? How does the seepage of stability into Dibao distribution affect people who do not receive benefits? How does it affect the relationship between the regime and the public? The bulk of research on the effects of welfare and social policy focus on effects for recipients (Campbell 2012; Pierson 1993; Schneider and Ingram 1993). However, when social assistance is used to enforce political order, examining effects on individuals who do not receive, but want to receive benefits is also of interest.

When the Li family received Dibao, this prompted other residents in the neighborhood of Lagoon Garden to protest. When Mr. Li's neighbors saw his name listed on the bulletin board of Dibao recipients, they went to the residents committee to demand benefits for themselves. Although Mr. Li was not the first person in Lagoon Garden to receive Dibao, other Dibao recipients were elderly, widowed, or disabled. Mr. and Mrs. Li were visibly healthy, and although they were impoverished, other families in the neighborhood believed they faced similar economic circumstances. The neighbors were angry that they did not also receive Dibao. They demanded to know why the Lis had Dibao, and railed against the residents committee for being unfair and incompetent.

This chapter begins by showing how the distribution of Dibao to targeted populations increases contention and low-level, small-scale collective action within neighborhoods. I differentiate between two types of contention with different motivations, goals, and strategies, and I discuss how residents committees try defuse complaints. Finally, this chapter examines how the level of Dibao provision to targeted populations relates to the overall level of collective action events as well as people's general assessment of the government's capabilities and legitimacy.

6.1 Discontent in the Neighborhood

As part of central government efforts to increase transparency in the Dibao program, the names of Dibao recipients are publicized in neighborhoods. Figure 6.1 shows two bulletin boards, one from a neighborhood in Wuhan and one from a neighborhood in Zhenghzhou, that list the names of Dibao recipients and the amount of Dibao subsidy they receive each month. Neighborhood residents can see exactly who is receiving Dibao and can compare the amount of Dibao subsidy to their own monthly earnings. This information prompts some neighborhood residents to approach the residents committee to try to apply for Dibao. However, because of the hard budget constraints on the Dibao program and the general policy of limiting Dibao to people who are not able-bodied, residents committees turn away many would-be applicants. Most are encouraged to find work and told that they should not apply because their application is unlikely to succeed.

Many people are thus discouraged from applying for Dibao. Discouragement is effective in neighborhoods where Dibao is distributed only to those with physical limitations and infirmity. In neighborhoods where Dibao is distributed only to the old, the ill, and the disabled, when individuals who do not fall into these categories approach the residents committee, the residents committee can explain the situation of a few of the Dibao recipients and say, "The people who get Dibao are those who cannot work at all. You can work. Your application is not going to be approved" (Interview, N2013_521). This is usually persuasive because Dibao recipients appear visibly infirm.

In contrast, in neighborhoods where Dibao is also distributed to targeted populations to preempt disorder, residents are more likely to persist in demanding benefits after the initial discouragement. In these neighborhoods, when the residents committee provides examples of infirm Dibao recipients and claims that Dibao goes only to those incapable of work, prospective Dibao applicants may point to names on the bulletin board of individuals they know who are not infirm to invalidate the residents committee's rationale. A woman in charge of Dibao in a

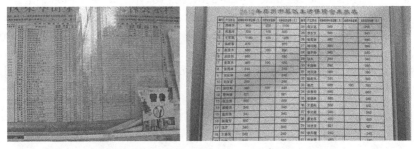

FIGURE 6.1 Bulletin boards listing households receiving Dibao

neighborhood in Wuhan said that residents who want Dibao will repeatedly visit the residents committee (Interview, N2013_622). As a result, she has to spend a great deal of time explaining to them why they cannot obtain the benefit. In another neighborhood in Wuhan, the administrator in charge of Dibao said:

> Dibao work is difficult. The people who are trying to get Dibao are low quality (素质低). Sometimes they will pound tables and chairs, they cry like babies who are being weaned from mother's milk (Interview, N2013_624).

A similar sentiment was echoed by an 11-year administrator of the Dibao programs, who had the following to say:

> People applying for Dibao are those from the bottom rungs of society; sometimes they are too calculating, so you have to have more patience to understand them and to enlighten them (Interview, N2012_524).

The survey of 100 neighborhoods corroborates this difference between neighborhoods where Dibao is and is not distributed to targeted populations. In the neighborhood survey, residents committees were asked an open-ended question about the challenges they encounter in implementing the Dibao program, and then asked to select their most pressing challenge. Four main categories of challenges emerged:[1]

1. Administrative burden of providing Dibao
2. Insufficient resources for Dibao households
3. Individual complaints over Dibao distribution
4. Collective complaints over Dibao distribution

The first category focused on the difficulty of running the Dibao program, including the burden of verifying household income, the complexity of the Dibao application progress, and the tedious reporting requirements. The second category focused on the inadequacy of Dibao benefits. Residents committee members reported that the Dibao line was too low, that cash transfers were too meager, and that Dibao did little to alleviate poverty. The third and fourth categories

---

1. Because open-ended answers could be categorized in different ways, coding rules were developed for each category, and two members of the research team read through the open-ended responses to code replies into these four categories. The average inter-coder agreement for these responses was 93%.

Table 6.1 Main challenges of the Dibao program faced by residents
committees

	Number of Neighborhoods
Administrative burden of providing Dibao	24
Insufficient resources for Dibao households	10
Individual complaints over Dibao distribution	18
Collective action over Dibao distribution	7
Other	5
No challenges	26

related to complaints over Dibao distribution, differentiating between complaints by individuals versus complaints by groups of residents.[2]

Table 6.1 shows how these four categories of challenges are distributed among neighborhoods. Among the 97 neighborhoods responding to the survey, seven residents committees chose not to answer this question, and 26 residents committees did not think they faced any particular challenges related to Dibao.[3] Twenty-four neighborhoods cited administrative burdens as the main challenge to the Dibao program, while 10 neighborhoods thought insufficient resources was the most significant problem plaguing the Dibao program.

Contention over Dibao distribution was described as the main problem associated with the Dibao program among the remaining neighborhoods. In 18 neighborhoods, residents committee members cited individual complaints as the main challenge, while in seven neighborhoods, they cited collective action as the main challenge. Although the number of neighborhoods reporting contention as the main challenge to the Dibao program was not high, reports of contention coincided with the distribution of Dibao to ex-prisoners. Table 6.2 shows logistic regressions of contention on the presence of released prisoners among Dibao recipients. In columns (1) to (3), the dependent variable is contention in the form of individual complaints. In columns (4) to (6), the dependent variable is contention in the form of small-scale collective action. In columns (1) and (4), the

2. Group-based complaints are coded as such when residents committees describe residents complaining together or going to the residents committee together, or when residents committees describe specific disruptive incidents involving more than one resident as the main challenge of running the Dibao program.

3. In roughly half of the neighborhoods where residents committees said they did not face any challenges, there were fewer than 10 Dibao households in the neighborhood.

Table 6.2 Effect of released prisoners receiving Dibao on contention

| | Individual complaints | | | Collective action | | |
	(1)	(2)	(3)	(4)	(5)	(6)
Released prisoners receiving Dibao	2.061***	1.859**	1.510*	1.288	1.946*	0.869
	(0.749)	(0.848)	(0.885)	(0.945)	(1.175)	(1.404)
Intercept	−2.061***	−0.824	−1.354	−2.674***	−21.443	−1,508.992
	(0.413)	(0.630)	(1.053)	(0.517)	(4,458.907)	(6,146.650)
Controls	No	No	Yes	No	No	Yes
City FE	No	Yes	Yes	No	Yes	Yes
Observations	72	72	70	72	72	70

Note: $^*p < 0.1$; $^{**}p < 0.05$; $^{***}p < 0.01$.

only explanatory variable is a dummy variable indicating whether ex-prisoners are among Dibao recipients in the neighborhood. Columns (2) and (5) add in city fixed effects, and columns (3) and (6) add additional control variables for the structural conditions of the neighborhoods such as the age of the neighborhood, and the Hukou status of residents.

Having ex-prisoners among Dibao recipients is predictive of increased individual-level complaints. This result holds across all three specifications shown in Table 6.2. Having released prisoners among Dibao recipients is also correlated with increased probability of collective action. The direction of the coefficient estimates in Table 6.2 columns (4) to (6) are all consistently positive. Only one

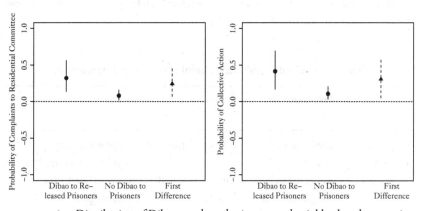

FIGURE 6.2 Distribution of Dibao to released prisoners and neighborhood contention

model reaches statistical significance, but given that collective action was reported by residents committees in only seven neighborhoods, this estimate is likely under-powered.

Using the specifications of columns (2) and (5), the left panel of Figure 6.2 shows the probability that individual complaints are cited by residents committees as the main challenge for the Dibao program with 90% confidence intervals. The right panel of Figure 6.2 shows the probability that collective complaints are cited by residents committees as the main challenge for the Dibao program with 90% confidence intervals. In both cases, in neighborhoods where released prisoners are among Dibao recipients, the level of contention is higher than in neighborhoods where Dibao is not targeted at ex-prisoners. The probability that individual-level complaints are the main challenge facing residents committees in administering the Dibao program is 8% when released prisoners are not among Dibao recipients, while the probability that individual-level complaints are the main challenge is 33% when released prisoners are among Dibao recipients. For collective action over Dibao distribution, the probability that collective action is cited as the main challenge is 10% when released prisoners are not among Dibao recipients, and the probability that collective action is cited as the main challenge is 40% when released prisoners are among Dibao recipients.

6.1.1 Rule-Based Resisters

The motivations, goals, and strategies of neighborhood residents who protest Dibao provision can be separated into two ideal types, whom I will call (1) rule-based resisters and (2) bargainers. These two types of contentious residents have different beliefs and information about how Dibao provision works. They pursue different goals, and they use different strategies to try to obtain Dibao. These distinctions are summarized in Table 6.3.

Table 6.3 Comparison of rightful resisters and bargainers

	Perceptions of Dibao	Goal	Strategy
Rule-based resisters	Implemented unfairly	Obtain Dibao	Deploy existing regulations, commitments
Bargainers	Resource to be bargained over	Obtain material benefits	Cause disturbance, then negotiate

O'Brien and Li (2006) coined the term "rightful resistance" to describe acts of protest that rely on established principles and deploy existing regulations and commitments in claim-making. There is a large debate over whether rightful resistance reflects some type of rights consciousness or if it is simply rules consciousness (Li 2010; O'Brien 2001; Perry 2007, 2009). In the case of Dibao, rule-based resistance is solely about the adherence to pre-existing rules, regulations, and policies governing Dibao, but these types of protesters utilize many of the key strategies of rightful resistance. To avoid the democratic or liberalizing connotation of the term "rights," I use the term *rule-based resisters* to capture this behavior. As shown in Table 6.3, rule-based resisters perceive Dibao as being unfairly implemented when they themselves do not receive it, but other individuals who appear capable of work do. Rule-based resisters believe that if the households listed on the bulletin board are receiving Dibao, then they too deserve Dibao. Often they know something about the people receiving Dibao such as their age range, physical capability, educational background, and type of employment, and know that they themselves are similar to Dibao recipients.

When rule-based resisters protest to the residents committee, they speak of the Dibao program as a commitment made by the Chinese government and the CCP to help the poor. They describe their dire economic circumstances, and they describe their lack of benefits as a failure of the regime to provide for its people. Rule-based resisters point to Dibao regulations that describe eligibility based on means testing. Their claim is that they are being unfairly excluded from the program, and their goal is to obtain Dibao.

To deal with these types of protesters, residents committees rely on their information advantage and the complexity of Dibao policies. For example, in 2013, Henan Province issued "Opinions on Further Improving Urban and Rural Minimum Livelihood Guarantee Scheme" (关于进一步做好城乡居民最低生活保障工作的意见), hereafter Opinion, to elaborate on Dibao's eligibility requirements for the province. The Opinion states that households are eligible for Dibao if family members living together have per capita disposable income below the Dibao line during a stipulated time period, and if the household's assets are in accordance with local provisions. The Opinion defines disposable income to include wages, profits from business and sales transactions, income from assets, and any other value transfers. Assets include all fixed and variable assets of all family members, including cash, savings, securities, collateral, vehicles, boats, housing, debt owed, and other assets. The Opinion also explicitly states that any family owning more than two residences is automatically excluded.[4] In

---

4. For additional details see http://bit.ly/18LSkKt (accessed November 30, 2014).

terms of who constitutes family members, in Zhengzhou, the capital of Henan Province, the Zhengzhou Civil Affairs Department says this can include any combination of spouses, parents, children, paternal grandparents, and maternal grandparents, as well as other individuals designated by the civil affairs agency.[5] This policy is extremely ambiguous and complex, and in addition, there are numerous other local directives and policies related to Dibao. When rule-based resisters approach the residents committee citing laws and policies, the residents committee can respond in kind with numerous other Dibao-related documents that the protesters have likely never seen. The 11-year administrator of the Dibao program quoted above emphasized the importance of guiding those who complain and agitate to trust in the judgment of the government and the CCP by showing them policy documents and guidelines.

In addition, residents committees often argue to rule-based resisters that they know more about the households receiving Dibao than the protesters can ever know. This strategy depends on the information advantage of the residents committee relative to residents. In neighborhoods where residents know relatively little about each other, it is easier for the residents committee to convince rule-based resisters that households receiving Dibao lack some critical assets or exhibit hidden disabilities that explain their Dibao provision. This dynamic resembles game theory models of cheap-talk persuasion, where if the receiver (resident) has an information disadvantage, the sender (residents committee) can always to some extent engage in effective persuasion (Crawford and Sobel 1982). However, in neighborhoods where residents know each other well, it is much more difficult for residents committees to convince rule-based resisters they are ineligible. This suggests that the mutual surveillance among residents, which allows residents committees and local police to better penetrate into neighborhoods and conduct top-down surveillance, also provides the conditions that enable residents to see inequities in benefit distribution that facilitate their protest.

Sometimes, the fact that able-bodied Dibao recipients belong to categories of particular interest to the public security and judicial apparatus becomes known to rule-based resisters demanding Dibao. This can happen because the residents committee, when failing to persuade using other arguments, will tell rule-based resisters that a particular household with able-bodied members is receiving Dibao because someone is an ex-prisoner, former repeat petitioner, or former "cult" member in need of special assistance. Rule-based resisters can also learn this information from neighborhood gossip. Knowing that Dibao is prioritized for ex-prisoners alters rule-based resisters' perceptions of the Dibao program. Instead

---

5. See http://bit.ly/1Cu8Nzq (accessed November 30, 2014).

of perceiving Dibao to be unfairly implemented (problem with rule enforcement), they become opposed to the policy of prioritizing Dibao for ex-prisoners (problem with rule making). In two districts in Qingdao, residents committees gave numerous examples of complaints from other residents wanting Dibao that criminals were being rewarded by the government while ordinary, "good" residents were not (Interviews, N2012_421, N2012_423, N2012_428). In one neighborhood, the residents committee quoted residents as saying that Dibao recipients were hoodlums who did nothing but gamble and play mahjong (Interview, N2012_428). Likewise, a woman in charge of Dibao in a neighborhood in Zhengzhou described how residents were unhappy with the "moral character" of the program's recipients (Interview, N2013_523).

Despite their dissatisfaction, most rule-based resisters are demobilized. When it becomes apparent that residents committees are simply following policies that prioritize Dibao for certain classes of people, most rule-based resisters stop protesting. Residents committees are not engaged in wrong doing, corruption, or other illegal extraction that often lead to successful rightful resistance (O'Brien 1996; O'Brien and Li 2006). Because residents committees can point to higher-level policies and leverage their superior information about Dibao households and Dibao policy, there are limited opportunity structures for rule-based resisters to exploit, and rule-based resisters realize they do not have a good chance of success if they appeal to higher level authorities such as street-level officials. Rule-based resisters lose their anchor for resistance, and most do not exhibit a rights consciousness that leads them to press for policy or institutional changes.

6.1.2 Bargainers

Bargainers disregard the formal rules governing Dibao. As shown in Table 6.3, bargainers see Dibao as a resource to be negotiated over and take the view that obtaining Dibao requires disturbing order. For bargainers, the CCP's preoccupation with stability creates a mechanism through which ordinary citizens can obtain concessions from the regime. Lee and Zhang (2013) describe this phenomenon where local governments distribute cash to buy off those who stage public acts of defiance as "non-zero sum bargaining." They write:

> [D]ishing out cash payments or other material benefits in exchange for compliance has become a patterned and routinized response to popular unrest, summed up in a widely circulated popular jingle: "Big disturbance, big resolution; small disturbance, small resolution; no disturbance, no resolution." The grassroots state has turned into a marketplace where gamesmanship (or *boyi*, meaning strategic game playing) between officials and citizens determines the price tag of stability. (1486)

They note that citizens are "willing and willful players of these legal-bureaucratic games that...motivate them with a real chance of winning material or symbolic compensation" (Lee and Zhang 2013:1481). Chinese academics have referred to bargainers as "professional petitioners" or "professional protesters" (B. Chen 2012).

Although bargainers protest to obtain Dibao, their goal is to obtain some concession from the regime, which can be in the form of Dibao or some other material benefit. Dibao is attractive because many other forms of social welfare benefits are tied to Dibao status, but it is not the only way to obtain material benefits.

Unlike rule-based resisters, bargainers do not deploy rules or regulations to make their claims. Instead, they rely on highly visible tactics of dissent to gain the attention of neighborhood administrators. These strategies may be learned through experience, from observation (either direct or via media), or from the guidance of other activists (Fu 2017). The party secretary of one neighborhood described how a resident approached the residents committee repeatedly and then threatened to commit suicide by jumping off his building because he was denied Dibao (Interview, N2013_511). In another neighborhood, residents banded together to block the entryway into the residents committee and threatened to beat committee members and their families who lived in the neighborhood (Interview, N2013_625). These public disturbances capture the attention of the residents committee, and often that of the local police as well.

Lee and Zhang (2013) argue that grassroots officials are interested in sustaining a certain level of contention because contention justifies demands for bigger budgets and more resources, and because successful management of instability can boost careers. While this may be true for the street- and county-level officials on whom Lee and Zhang (2013) focus, residents committee members have strong incentives to minimize bargaining behavior because these visible disturbances greatly increase their workload, without budgetary or career benefits. Residents committees do not have the resources to accommodate every bargainer who comes their way.

Furthermore, bargaining can escalate in ways that are damaging to the careers of lower-level officials. B. Chen (2012) finds that in one county in Jiangxi Province, veterans collectively petitioned in 2006. In response, the county gave all of the veterans Dibao in the amount of 100 RMB per month. The next year, the veterans collectively petitioned again, and the county increased their Dibao benefits to 200 RMB per month with an automatic rate increase of 15% every year thereafter. Chen's interviews with the veterans showed that this led the veterans to believe that without collectively petitioning, they would never obtain anything. In 2010, thousands of veterans organized to collectively protest in Baiyi Square in the capital of Jiangxi Province, singing revolutionary songs and asking for benefits. Local officials had to go to the capital to retrieve these veterans, and this escalation reflected badly on those local officials.

To defuse bargainers, residents committees use policy justifications and threats. Just as they use the complexity of Dibao policy to discourage rule-based resisters, they do the same to deter bargainers. By referring to policy, residents committees show bargainers that their hands are tied, that they do not have room to maneuver or bargain. Residents committees argue that unlike discretionary stability maintenance funds, Dibao funds are guided by rules that cannot be changed. In neighborhoods where Dibao is distributed to targeted populations and where bargainers know the backgrounds of those receiving Dibao, appealing to policy is often not effective. Bargainers argue that Dibao is already provided to people who caused disturbances in the past and that this is evidence of the Chinese saying "disturbance for resolution." In these instances, residents committees usually threaten bargainers with coercion. Residents committees point out, correctly, that former protesters have been arrested and detained, and tell bargainers that they too may be imprisoned if they persist. Some bargainers, usually those who have organized large groups or successfully amplified their grievance online, do receive accommodation, which can come in the form of Dibao benefits, other types of social assistance, or cash payment from discretionary stability maintenance funds. However, these bargainers often are also placed under surveillance to prevent the continuation or escalation of their protests. Even though bargaining is common, like rule-based resisters, most bargainers are not successful. They do not successfully negotiate for benefits, and although they are subdued, they are resentful and quietly angry at the inequities of how benefits are distributed.

Rule-based resisters and bargainers are two ideal types. In reality, residents who protest the distribution of Dibao may utilize some combination of these strategies. Bargainers can refer to rules to fuel righteous anger. Rule-based resisters may turn to bargaining after they realize the futility of appealing to rules. I differentiate between these two types to acknowledge the variation in how discontent manifests. However, what is most important for our understanding of Dibao and the effects of the CCP's preoccupation with stability on Dibao is that the distribution of Dibao to targeted populations—specifically, to individuals who appear capable of work—generates more contention and protest. Local administrators are largely successful in defusing these protests, by which I mean these protests remain small-scale and localized rather than cross-class or cross-regional. However, subdued protesters are embittered and resentful.

6.2 Higher Levels of Collective Action

The evidence provided thus far is limited to my qualitative interviews and survey of 100 neighborhoods. These neighborhoods are not representative of urban China. Do we see higher levels of protest associated with the distribution of Dibao to targeted populations in general? Based on the previous sections, we would expect more protests—from either rule-based resisters or bargainers—in neighborhoods that distribute Dibao to targeted populations.

Measuring Variation in Dibao Provision to Targeted Populations

Since data on the number of targeted populations receiving Dibao by neighborhood (or even number of targeted populations in general) is not available, I use a proxy to measure the level of Dibao provision to targeted populations. Specifically, I take advantage of variation in whether or not local governments issued city-level policies or launched city-level programs prioritizing Dibao for individuals undergoing re-education as this proxy. While data on targeted populations is secret and classified, information about re-education programs are public. According to the document "Ministry of Public Security Regulations of Targeted Populations," re-education assistance is provided to all targeted populations.[6] Re-education may also be applied more broadly to other elements of society in need of "thought reform" who are not targeted populations, but cities that have policies of providing Dibao to those undergoing re-education are more much likely to be systematically prioritizing Dibao to targeted populations than cities that do not have these city-level policies. In addition, cities with these policies are likely providing Dibao to relatively more targeted populations (as a share of households receiving Dibao) than cities without these policies because of the hard budget constraints local governments face.

All of the cities I visited during my fieldwork contained some neighborhoods that gave Dibao to targeted populations. However, not all cities had city-level policies or campaigns to prioritize Dibao to those undergoing re-education. For example, in July 2008, the Guangzhou city departments of justice and civil affairs jointly issued "Notice on Further Improving Provision of Minimum Living Guarantee for Released Prisoners and Targets of Community Corrections" (关于进一步做好符合低保条件的刑释解教人员及社区矫正对象最低生活保障工作的通知) to emphasize how neighborhoods need to proactively help anyone undergoing re-education who is eligible for Dibao obtain it.[7] This means

---

6. See copy at http://bit.ly/2tAA9F3 (accessed June 1, 2017).

7. See http://www.gdzf.org.cn/gdsgzdt/gz/201209/t20120911_317464.htm (accessed July 24, 2019).

that every subordinate district and neighborhood in Guangzhou is aware of the requirement to ensure that released prisoners who are impoverished have access to Dibao. Similarly, in 2014, the city of Dongying in Shandong launched the *Big Visit* (大走访) campaign to mobilize grassroots administrators to visit the households of every family receiving re-education and to help them obtain Dibao and reduced education expenses, and to facilitate other "charitable works."[8] In contrast, other cities reported anecdotes or local pilots in some neighborhoods of prioritizing Dibao for re-education but no city-level initiative or policy. For example, in the Nankai district of Tianjin, there are news stories describing how Dibao is given to those who are being re-educated for their participation in "cults,"[9] but there does not appear to be a city-level policy in Tianjin. In Jinan, the capitol of Shandong, a news article describes how officials visited the home of someone undergoing re-education, and in providing the backstory, the article describes how the re-education committee helped the household obtain Dibao,[10] but there is no evidence of a city-level policy to prioritize Dibao for those undergoing re-education in Jinan.

This variation allows me to analyze the relationship between the provision of Dibao to targeted populations and public perceptions of the government, as measured in the CUGS, and between such types of Dibao provision and protest, as measured by the CASM-China dataset (Zhang and Pan 2019). To make this analysis consistent, I focus on the 45 cities in the China Urban Governance Survey. In addition, because CUGS data was collected in 2015, I gather data on Dibao provision prior to 2015, and protest data from 2016 onward. I find that 16 cities had city-level initiatives or policies prior to 2015 prioritizing Dibao for those undergoing re-education.[11] Of the remaining 29 cities, some adopted city-wide policies or initiatives after 2015, while in others, there were only neighborhood- or street-level pilots and one-off experiments. While I expect that all cities contained some neighborhoods where Dibao was prioritized for targeted populations, I expect the scale of this activity to be higher in the 16 cities where official policies prioritizing

---

8. See 218.58.213.154:81/art/2014/3/31/art_7941_262895.html (accessed July 25, 2019).

9. See www.bohechashe.org/c/2016-11-01/858583.shtml (accessed July 25, 2019).

10. See https://www.thepaper.cn/newsDetail_forward_2691870 (accessed July 25, 2019).

11. Since such policies would be announced in local party newspapers, the determination of whether or not the 45 cities had city-level intiatives, policy, or program is based on a comprehensive search of the CNKI: China Core Newspapers database, the WiseNews database, Baidu search, and Google search for the name of the city and the name of districts and counties subordinate to the city along with terms for re-education and Dibao in Chinese. Cities with such policies are Chaoyang (Beijing), Datong, Dongying, Fengtai, Foshan, Guangzhou, Huangpu, Huizhou, Nanping, Qingdao, Suizhou, Wuhan, Xi'an, Xuhui, Zhengzhou, and Zhongshan.

Dibao for those undergoing re-education were in place. In the subsequent analysis, cities described as having higher levels of Dibao provision to targeted populations are cities with explicit city-level policies or campaigns of prioritizing Dibao for those undergoing re-education, and cities described as having lower levels of Dibao provision to targeted populations are cities without such policies.

Measuring Collective Action

The main outcome of interest is contentious collective action events that occur in the real world. Measuring protest is extremely important to our understanding of authoritarian regimes in general, but we lack access to independent and reliable measures. Most existing methods of identifying collective action in democratic countries rely on news reporting of these events, but authoritarian regimes often impose strict controls on reporting through state ownership of media outlets, repression and cooptation of private media outlet owners, and the imposition of physical controls on domestic and foreign journalists, (Egorov and Sonin 2011; McMillan and Zoido 2004; Qin, Strömberg, and Wu 2018; Stockmann 2013). This government interference makes it hard to understand even basic factual questions about protest, collective action, and mobilization in authoritarian regimes.

The adoption of digital technologies provides new opportunities to learn about protest and to complement what we already know from traditional media reporting. The internet, social media, and mobile platforms allow individuals to act as broadcasters and to disseminate information on a much larger scale (Diamond 2010; Earl and Kimport 2011; Edmond 2013; Ferdinand 2000). Social media has become an important venue for protesters to speak out and to mobilize, and reflects participants' own accounts of collective action events, which allows researchers to capture how participants describe their motives for mobilization. Social media data are digitized and relatively accessible for large-scale collection. Even with online censorship and propaganda, the digital traces left by protesters, bystanders, and commentators provide us with new ways of identifying collective action events in authoritarian regimes (King, Pan, and Roberts 2013, 2014, 2017).

Along with a larger team, I have created the Collective Action Events from Social Media (CASM) system, which uses deep learning on image and text data from social media to identify collective action events occurring in the real world (see Zhang and Pan 2019 for details). CASM identifies collective action events from social media posts by using keywords related to collective action to extract potentially relevant posts. The system then applies a two-stage deep learning classifier, using image and textual data, to identify posts about collective action events occurring in the real world. Finally, posts discussing the same event are merged to identify unique collective action events (Zhang and Pan 2019). Drawing from

McAdam, Tarrow, and Tilly (2003), collective action is defined as an episodic, collective event among makers of claims where targets are political and economic power holders; where claims, if realized, affect the interests of at least one of the claimants; and where the action of claimants is a contentious event with public physical presence involving at least three participants.

We implemented CASM for China (CASM-China) using social media data from Sina Weibo. CASM-China does extremely well in identifying posts related to collective action events, as assessed through cross-validation and out-of-sample validation, and also does well in identifying unique collective action events (Zhang and Pan 2019). Despite the fact that online censorship in China focuses on suppressing discussions of collective action in social media, censorship does not have a large impact on the number of collective action events identified through CASM-China. This is because online censorship in China focuses on removing discussions of collective action that have captured the public's attention (are viral or bursty), but most social media posts about collective action do not receive much attention (are not viral or bursty). In addition, censorship of bursts is often incomplete (Roberts 2018). In assessing the external validity of CASM-China, we find that the system will miss collective action events taking places in minority regions, such as Tibet and Xinjiang, where social media penetration is lower and more stringent internet controls (e.g., internet blackouts) are in place.

CASM provides information on the timing and location of the collective action event. The day the social media post is made is taken as the time of the collective action event. Protesters use social media to call attention to their activities, so online reports of real-world collective action events are generally contemporaneous with the event itself. The location of the collective action event is taken from the geolocation metadata associated with the social media post when it is available, and when it is not, location information is extracted from the text of the social media post.

To make this analysis comparable to the analysis of government perceptions described in the next section, I focus on collective action events taking place in the cities sampled as part of the CUGS survey. A total of 38 cities in provinces and seven districts in province-level municipalities were sampled in the 2015 CUGS. I focus on the 38 cities because the CASM-China event-level data is not directly comparable between cities located in provinces and districts located in municipalities.

The CASM-China data set identifies 4,865 collective action events in the 38 CUGS cities for the 18-month period between January 2016 and June 2017.[12] Among these, 1,418 events (29%) related to protest over social welfare issues,

---

12. Substantive results do not change if I use protest data that extends into 2015. June 2017 is when CASM-China data ends.

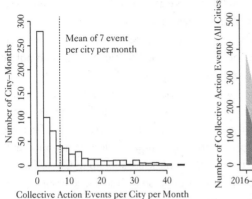
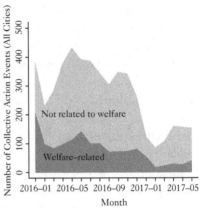

FIGURE 6.3 Collective action events

which includes protests about Dibao, social insurance, unemployment benefits, other welfare benefits, and wages.

The left panel of Figure 6.3 is a histogram of the number of collective action events per city per month. This distribution has a very long right tail. The mean number of collective action events per city is seven, and the median is four. There are 123 city-months where CASM-China did not capture any collective action events. There are four city-months where there were 40 or more collective action events.

The right panel of Figure 6.3 shows the total number of collective action events in all 38 cities by month. The total number of events declines in 2017. As discussed in Zhang and Pan (2019), there is an overall decline in the number of collective action events from 2013 onward. This decline remains even after controlling for the decreased popularity of the Weibo platform where data is collected. This decline does not disproportionately affect protests related to social welfare. We also have no reason to think that Weibo usage differs between cities with and without explicit policies prioritizing Dibao for targeted populations, nor is it likely that Weibo censorship varies between these two types of cities, because Weibo censorship is overseen by Beijing, where Sina is registered.

Control Variables

The overall number of protests and the number of protests captured by CASM-China may be influenced by a host of other factors. We might expect there to be more collective action events in cities with larger populations or in cities where the government is more fiscally constrained. We might expect there to be more reports of protests in cities that have more Sina Weibo users or that are wealth-ier. To account for these confounding factors, I control for logged population,[13] logged GDP per capita, and logged government expenditures.[14] In addition, since the main explanatory variable is the prioritization of Dibao for targeted popula-tions, I also include as controls the overall city-level expenditure on Dibao and the number of Dibao households in that city.[15]

Table 6.4 shows the results of OLS regression where the outcome is the aver-age number of collective action events per month per city from January 2016 to June 2017.[16] The unit of analysis is the city. Columns (1) and (2) of Table 6.4 focus on all collective action events, while (3) and (4) focus only on social welfare-related events. Cities that have a higher level of Dibao provision to targeted populations are more likely to have higher levels of collective action events than cities that have lower levels of Dibao provision to targeted populations (column 1), and the effect is statistically significant. The effect remains positive but loses statistical significance after control variables are included (column 2). Cities that have a higher level of Dibao provision to targeted populations are also more likely to have higher levels of welfare-related collective action events (column 3), and this result is statistically significant and remains so after the inclusion of controls (column 4).

Figure 6.4 plots the quantities of interest—specifically, the mean expected value of the average number of collective action events per city per month for cities that have higher (black squares) and lower (black circles) levels of Dibao provi-sion to targeted populations from January 2016 to June 2017—based on the model with controls shown in column 4 of Table 6.4. Figure 6.4 shows that there were on average 8.7 collective action events per city per month in cities with higher levels of Dibao provision for targeted populations, and 6.4 collective action events per city per month in cities with lower levels of Dibao provision for targeted popula-tions. There were on average 2.8 collective action events related to social welfare

13. Population is also used to account for variation in Sina Weibo usage. Population is used as a proxy because the CUGS survey sampled urban areas where the difference between the overall city population and the population using Weibo is unlikely to be drastically different between cities.

14. Data is based on 2013 numbers from the National Bureau of Statistics via EPA China Data. Population is based on total population at the end of 2013, and expenditures refer to general budgetary expenditures.

15. City-level Dibao data from the Ministry of Civil Affairs, http://cws.mca.gov.cn/article/tjsj/dbsj/ (accessed April 27, 2017).

16. Substantive results do not change if event count models, such as negative binomial regres-sion, are used.

Table 6.4 Relationship between providing Dibao to targeted populations and collective action

| | Number of events per month per city | | | |
| | All protests | | Welfare-related protests | |
	(1)	(2)	(3)	(4)
More Dibao for targeted populations	5.093** (2.463)	2.128 (1.777)	1.835** (0.680)	1.004** (0.460)
Log GDP per capita		1.080 (2.277)		0.139 (0.589)
Log govt. expenditure		4.947 (3.843)		1.545 (0.994)
Log population		2.170 (3.590)		0.699 (0.929)
Log Dibao expenditure		1.194 (1.081)		0.428 (0.280)
Log Dibao households		−0.029 (1.549)		−0.264 (0.401)
Intercept	5.504*** (1.384)	−28.015 (27.618)	1.494*** (0.382)	−4.465 (7.145)
Observations	38	36	38	36

Note: *$p < 0.1$; **$p < 0.05$; ***$p < 0.01$

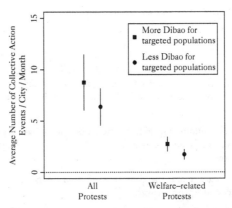

FIGURE 6.4 Distribution of Dibao to targeted populations and collective action

per city per month in cities with higher levels of Dibao provision for targeted populations, and 1.8 per city per month in cities with lower levels of Dibao provision for targeted populations. This analysis suggests that cities with a higher level of Dibao provision for targeted populations are more likely to have a higher number of collective action events, and especially a higher number of social welfare-related protests, than cities with lower levels of Dibao provision to targeted populations.

6.3 *Worsening Perceptions of Government Performance and Legitimacy*

Does the prioritization of Dibao for targeted populations change how the public perceives the government? Does it change the public's satisfaction and trust in the government? I can answer these questions using data from CUGS, which measures respondents' trust in (信任) and satisfaction with (满意) central- and city levels of government. These questions are often used to gauge government legitimacy (Shi 2001). In addition, the CUGS asks respondents to assess government capabilities in several areas, including (1) "our government's ability to preserve social stability" (我国政府维护社会稳定的能力), (2) "our government's ability to provide social welfare" (我国政府提供社会福利的能力), (3) "our government's ability to listen and to respond to opinions of the public" (我国政府听取和回应社会大众意见的能力), and (4) "our government's ability to restrain the behavior of party and government officials" (我国政府约束党政官员行为的能力). Responses are coded to range from -1 (very weak) to 1 (very strong). With government trust and satisfaction, as well as the four capabilities described above as the outcome variables, I use OLS regression to estimate differences between cities with higher versus lower levels of Dibao provision for targeted populations.

Several alternative explanations may influence the assessments of government capabilities and government legitimacy. First, it could be that the proxy for higher levels of Dibao provision to targeted populations—cities with explicit city-wide policies or campaigns prioritizing Dibao for persons undergoing re-education—are also cities with larger ex-prisoner populations or higher levels of crime. This could lead CUGS respondents living in those cities to hold more negative assessments of the local government. Since the level of crime is related to the overall size of the population, population is included as a control. The size of the ex-prisoner population may also be related to the wealth of a city. Ex-prisoners may be attracted to wealthier cities where there is more opportunity, but ex-prisoners may also be purposefully kept out of wealthy cities as a method of

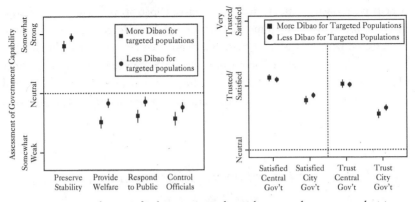

FIGURE 6.5   Distribution of Dibao to targeted populations and government legitimacy

governmental control.[17] These two forces may cancel each other out, but regardless, wealth—per capita GDP and government fiscal expenditures—are included as controls. Second, it could be that cities with higher levels of Dibao provision for targeted populations have higher levels of Dibao provision in general, which may alter respondents' perceptions of the government (Huang and Gao 2018, 2019). To account for this, I include the level of Dibao expenditures and the number of Dibao households as controls. Finally, we may expect individual-level characteristics such as age, level of income, education, and CCP membership to influence perceptions of Dibao as well as perceptions of the government. These respondent-level characteristics are also included as controls.

The left panel of Figure 6.5 shows the mean expected values (with 95% confidence intervals) of respondents' assessments of government capabilities in four areas based on CUGS data for respondents in cities with higher levels of Dibao provision for targeted populations (solid black squares) and cities with lower levels (solid black circles). The only area where respondents assess government capabilities as strong (rather than weak) is stability preservation. However, respondents in cities with higher levels of Dibao provision for targeted populations have a lower assessment of government ability in preserving stability (0.27) than respondents in other cities (0.32); this difference is statistically significant after including individual-level and city-level controls (see Appendix A.6 for regression table). Respondents in general believe government capabilities in the three other areas are weak, and respondents in cities with higher levels of

_____

17. See Wang (2005) discussion of how released prisoners are relegated to remote regions to keep them from urban centers.

Dibao provision to targeted populations even more so. Respondents in cities with higher levels of Dibao for targeted populations policies think the government as a whole is much weaker in providing social welfare (-0.16) than respondents in other cities (-0.06), weaker in listening and responding to the voices of the public (-0.13 vs. -0.05), and weaker in controlling corruption among government and party officials (-0.14 vs. -0.08). All of these differences between respondents in cities with higher and lower levels of Dibao provision for targeted populations are statistically significant.

The right panel of Figure 6.5 shows the mean expected values (with 95% confidence intervals) of respondents' satisfaction with and trust in central- and city levels of government. Respondents are generally trusting of and satisfied with central- and city levels of government. On a scale where 1 is very trustworthy and -1 is very untrustworthy (very satisfied to very unsatisfied), the mean response overall is between neutral and very trustworthy/satisfied. This is in line with other public opinion surveys in China, including those using experimental methods, which consistently show high levels of government legitimacy (Dickson et al. 2016; Jiang and Yang 2016; Li 2004; Manion 2006; Shi 2001; Tang 2016).

The mean response of respondents in cities with higher levels of Dibao provision for targeted populations are shown with solid black squares, and respondents in cities with lower levels in solid black circles.[18] The level of trust in and satisfaction with central-level government does not change between cities with higher and lower levels of Dibao provision for targeted populations. However, trust in and satisfaction with city-level governments is lower in cities that have higher levels of Dibao provision for targeted populations than those with lower levels. Trust in city-level governments is lower (0.28) among respondents in cities with higher levels of Dibao provision to targeted populations than respondents in cities with lower levels (0.33). Satisfaction with city-level government is also lower among respondents from cities with higher levels of Dibao for targeted populations (0.38) than those with lower levels (0.42). These differences in the levels of trust in and satisfaction with city-level governments are statistically significant after controlling for individual-level characteristics and city-level covariates (see Appendix A.6 for regression results).

In this analysis, cities considered to have higher levels of Dibao provision to targeted populations are cities with explicit policies prioritizing Dibao for

---

18. These estimates are based on OLS regression with controls for age, gender, household income, level of education, CCP membership, and the city's logged GDP per capita in 2013, logged government expenditure in 2013, logged total population in 2013, logged Dibao expenditures, and logged number of Dibao households. See Appendix A.6 for regression tables.

re-education, and cities considered to have lower levels of this type of Dibao provision are cities without such policies. We may be concerned that some cities, which actually have city-level policies or programs prioritizing Dibao for re-education, have not made their policies easily accessible, and so they are miscategorized as not having such policies in the analysis of collective action and government perceptions. If this is true, then the result we observe should be interpreted as follows: cities which have publicized their prioritization of Dibao for targeted populations and others undergoing re-education are more likely to have a higher number of collective action events and more negative perceptions of the government than other cities which have not publicized these policies or do not have these policies. This is not at odds with the results of my fieldwork.

Visibility of able-bodied Dibao recipients is what sustains protest. Visibility of policies prioritizing Dibao for re-education could generate the results we see, especially if the Chinese public, regardless of whether or not they are eligible for Dibao, are generally opposed to any program that they perceive to be aiding individuals with "criminal" associations, regardless of the type of crime. In other words, the mechanism motivating protest and negative government perceptions could be unrelated to the characteristics of who is already receiving Dibao. Here, would-be applicants simply want the benefit and are more likely turned away because of hard budget constraints because relatively more targeted populations are on Dibao, and that is why we observe more protest and negative perceptions. Or, the outcomes we observe could be driven by the characteristics of Dibao recipients. Here, would-be applicants want benefits and do not see current recipients as deserving, and that is why we observe more protest and more negative assessments of the government. Both interpretations are supported by my fieldwork. For example, when the rule-based resisters described in Section 6.1.1 find out that Dibao is given to able-bodied ex-prisoners as part of government policy, they are angry at the policy and the government that makes this policy, but other rule-based resisters who are unaware why able-bodied individuals receive Dibao simply protest because they too want the benefit. Both mechanisms through which the provision of Dibao to targeted populations stirs discontent are likely operating. While these mechanisms deserve to be disentangled in future research, the key point here is that there is an association between the use of Dibao to preempt disorder and public discontent.

To go one step further, we need to ask whether this discontent is problematic for the Chinese regime, and to do that, we have to think about the counterfactual. When Dibao is prioritized for targeted populations, there are higher levels of contention and small-scale protest at the neighborhood level, as well as higher levels of protest related to social welfare at the city level. However, we can easily imagine that if there were no Dibao policy, people who share in poverty would come together in large-scale collective action to protest fundamental social inequalities. Some might say that the Dibao program creates cleavages and conflicts among the poor that undermine political mobilization and transform political discontent, which has the possibility of manifesting as cross-regional protests into localized haggling over implementation and administrative rules.

However, an alternative counterfactual is not a China without Dibao; it is a country where social welfare programs such as Dibao are implemented according to a logic that is readily apparent and agreed upon by all. In China today, national-level Dibao policies discussed in Chapters 2 and 4 describe a means-tested program with stipulations for work. Based on this logic, Dibao would be distributed only to households with income below the locally set Dibao line whose members had no ability to engage in labor. An alternate logic of distribution is a fully funded Dibao program where everyone under a locally determined income obtains the benefit, and income is assessed in a simple and transparent manner (e.g., based on wages from formal employment). In both scenarios, there would likely be lower levels of contention and protests over Dibao provision. Bargainers would no longer regard Dibao as a site for negotiation, and there would be no discrepancy between the rules and the reality for rule-based resisters to anchor their contention. This decrease in contention and the sources of dissatisfaction would perhaps lead to better evaluations of government capabilities and legitimacy.

The reality is that Dibao is distributed according to two logics—maximizing work and preserving political order. From the perspective of the regime, both logics are guided by policy. The logic of maximizing work appears in the country's main Dibao policy documents. The logic of using Dibao to preserve order is a way of implementing Comprehensive Management of Public Security and appears in documents issued by the justice and public security departments. By appealing to these policy documents, residents committees are largely capable of defusing contention. Protests remain small in scale and localized. Complex policies, information advantages, and threats of coercion are often effectively used to defuse both rule-based resisters and bargainers.

Contention over Dibao is reduced to haggling over administrative rules, but haggling leaves people resentful and unsatisfied. From the perspective of people who experience the Dibao programs as would-be applicants, Dibao is supposed to be a programmatic concession made by the Chinese government to address extreme poverty, but the ways in which Dibao is distributed and the complexity of rules cited by Dibao administrators make the program appear arbitrary and restrictive. Research in the United States has shown how perceptions of the administration of social policies as either rational or arbitrary influence recipients' perceptions of the policy as well as the government behind the policy (Soss 1999;

Tyler 1998). In the case of Dibao, the spirit of the Dibao program is violated, and would-be applicants either become disillusioned with the policy or stop believing that its rules have any real meaning. They are left unsatisfied and resentful with the program, and this dissatisfaction and bitterness may spill over into their perceptions of the government more generally.

The Dibao policy was intended to programmatically address issues of social instability, but as the goal of political order has seeped into the program, the program and by extension the government behind it becomes arbitrary and capricious in the eyes of would-be applicants. Although this discontent has not generated any large-scale, cross-class, or cross-regional mobilization that poses any real threat to the CCP, the regime's preoccupation with political order produces simmering dissatisfaction as it undermines the programmatic initiatives of the government.

7

Becoming a Digital Dictatorship

In this book, I have employed novel data sets and diverse methodological approaches to show how China's pursuit of political order seeps into the Dibao program, and its consequences for both beneficiaries and those who are denied benefits. The Dibao program was first adopted to alleviate urban poverty and its attendant discontent, but as the CCP's conceptualization of stability and the regime's strategy to pursue political order changed, Dibao became, over time, a tool to strengthen control over specific individuals suspected of threatening social stability. The fear of disorder motivates the government to be more responsive and helpful to Dibao applicants. The fear of disorder leads to two logics of Dibao distribution. Dibao is not only prioritized to the elderly, disabled, and infirm, as mandated by government documents focused on Dibao, but also prioritized for targeted populations, individuals suspected of potentially threatening social order in the future, as a result of government policies related to security and stability that seek to bring various resources of the regime to bear on controlling these populations. The seepage of political order into Dibao changes the allocation of Dibao resources and the composition of Dibao recipients. For those who receive Dibao because they are targets of repression, Dibao provision serves as a form of repressive assistance that constrains recipients' autonomy and choices through surveillance, obligation, and dependence. For those who are denied Dibao because they are neither infirm nor targets of repression, the contradictory logics of Dibao distribution increase contention and protests while worsening perceptions of government performance and legitimacy.

The distribution of Dibao to targeted populations is aimed at strengthening the regime's ability to preempt threats to political order. It is contingent on surveillance. This book shows how neighborhood-level networks of mutual surveillance are used to determine who receives Dibao, and how the distribution of benefits in turn intensifies surveillance. However, mutual surveillance at the neighborhood level also fuels contention because it reveals the disparities of Dibao distribution. We are at the beginning of a new digital era characterized by explosive growth in individualized, digitized information, and fast-paced advances in computing power and machine learning. What are the consequences of digitization for surveillance, preemptive control, and China's preoccupation with political order?

7.1 *Role of the Public in Mass Surveillance*

All types of regimes invest in surveillance capabilities in order to identify potential threats to their rule, but autocrats face a particular imperative to understand their subjects' private preferences and the activities of regime agents to restrain mass and elite threats (Svolik 2012). Despite this imperative, autocrats often lack access to reliable sources of information (Kuran 1997; Wintrobe 1998). Authoritarian regimes have traditionally relied upon monitoring agencies (e.g., secret police, oversight committees) to gather information on regime agents and the public; however, monitoring agencies are vulnerable to manipulation by those they are intended to monitor because regime agents—bureaucrats, lower-tier officials—have incentives to bribe monitors to suppress information such as public grievances that might reflect badly on themselves (Pan and Chen 2019).

To obtain more reliable information, autocrats can implement elections and free the media. Freeing the media is generally thought to produce reliable information because in a competitive media market, media outlets have little incentive to collude with local officials for monetary gain. However, free media often is not desirable for autocrats because it can generate common knowledge of the regime's failures and improve coordination against the regime (Chwe 2013; Egorov, Guriev, and Sonin 2009; Persson and Tabellini 2006; Tilly 1978). Adopting electoral institutions also is risky because it carries the possibility of more robust political liberalization and regime change (Howard and Roessler 2006; Teorell and Hadenius 2007). In China, elections are limited to the village and neighborhood levels (O'Brien and Li 2000), and delegates to China's legislative institutions at provincial and national levels are elected by legislatures at the next lower level (Manion 2016; Truex 2016). Chinese media is commercialized, and some forms of investigative journalism are allowed (Lorentzen 2013; Repnikova 2017; Stockmann 2013), but media outlets remain tightly state-controlled (Jaros and Pan 2018; Qin, Strömberg, and Wu 2018).

An alternative for authoritarian regimes to gather information is so-called bottom-up participation channels, where information voluntarily provided by the public is used for government surveillance. The public can (1) provide information about themselves and (2) provide information about others they know, such as family members, friends, neighbors, and coworkers.

Information about Oneself

Individuals reveal information about themselves when they complain to the government. Complaints provide a reliable source of information for autocrats because when citizens complain to the government, they are looking to the government to solve their problems, and as a result, they have little incentive to hide or falsify information. In communist Bulgaria, citizen complaints were transmitted to top leaders as a way of gauging public support (Dimitrov 2014c). In the Soviet Union under Brezhnev, citizen complaints were used to gather information on the public's redistributive preferences (Dimitrov 2014b). In China, the Bureau of Letters and Visits (信访局) is responsible for managing complaint letters and in-person petitions (Chen 2009; Dimitrov 2014a). Each level of government, as well as party-state agencies at various levels, have Letters and Visits offices. Bureaucrats working in these offices prepare summary reports for government and CCP superiors on general trends and key cases. These reports are reviewed by local officials and sent up the administrative hierarchy until they are centrally aggregated at the State Bureau for Letters and Visits in Beijing. Dimitrov (2014a) finds that petitions sent through the system of letters and visits provide the regime with information on popular dissatisfaction with policy implementation, corruption, and general levels of regime support.

The growth of information communication technologies has increased channels for public complaints. In China, citizens can share their complaints through telephone hotlines (*Economist* 2017), government-managed websites (Chen, Pan, and Xu 2016; Distelhorst and Hou 2017), commercial social media sites (King, Pan, and Roberts 2013, 2014), web and mobile apps (*China Daily* 2015), and online anti-corruption campaigns (*Xinhua* 2012; Qin, Stromberg, and Wu (2017)). Scholars argue that autocrats effectively glean information on the misconduct of regime agents from posts shared on social media and punish these officials based on this information (Dimitrov 2014a; Nathan 2003; Qin, Stromberg, and Wu 2017). Some research even suggests that these online channels may increase authoritarian accountability (Gunitsky 2015; Noesselt 2014; Qiang 2011; Yong 2005). The CCP propaganda department (宣传部) is the primary agency responsible for monitoring public opinion and sentiment through citizen complaints (Central Propaganda Department 2009; National Grassroots Party Work Key Textbook 2013).[1] Approximately half of the areas on which CCP propaganda

---

1. Government bureaus and offices (e.g., Bureau of Letters and Visits, Public Security Bureau), and China's Cyberspace Administration (CAC) also deal with citizen complaints. However, instead of monitoring, government bureaus are tasked with collecting, investigating, and ultimately resolving complaints related to their areas of work in their geographic jurisdictions. CAC, also known at the central level as the Office of the Central Leading Group for Cyberspace Affairs, is tasked with governing the internet. CAC, located at the central and provincial levels

departments are evaluated relate to monitoring public sentiment and reporting this information to upper-level superiors (Pan and Chen 2018).

China is not the only authoritarian regime that proactively seeks citizen complaints. Egypt, Pakistan, Russia, Saudi Arabia, Singapore, and Vietnam all have adopted online platforms where citizens can express their grievances. In Egypt, citizens can complain through ministry and other government websites (OECD 2013). Khyber Pakhtunkhwa Province in Pakistan created the KP Citizens Portal (http://smart.pmru.gkp.pk/) to gather complaints. In Russia, ministries have federal and regional websites where citizens can submit complaints, such as 36.mvd.ru/ for the police department and 36.mchs.gov.ru/ for the Ministry of Emergency Services in the Voronezh region. The Saudi Arabian website shakwa.net works with officials to gather citizen complaints. In Singapore, citizen complaints are gathered through various online channels (Rodan and Jaya-suriya 2007). Various cities in Vietnam have set up online complaint sites (e.g., http://egov.danang.gov.vn/gop-y).

Information about Others

The public also can provide information to the government about those around them. Although individuals may be truthful when they complain to the government, not all grievances will be voiced, especially if the individual believes that voicing grievances through officially sanctioned channels is ineffective or likely to result in sanctions. However, the regime would like to uncover these private sentiments that have the potential to coalesce and escalate into social mobilization.

To gather this information, authoritarian regimes around the world have a long history of using grassroots informants (Bruce 2003; Fijnaut and Marx 1995; Shearer 2014; Weiner and Rahi-Tamm 2012; Weyrauch 1985). In China, the regime has used peers for surveillance, rather than rely solely on superiors or authority figures, since the Maoist era (Yang 1989). The regime employs local activist-informants and social eyes and ears (社会耳目) to gather information at the grassroots level (Dutton 2005; Schoenhals 2013). More broadly, there often has been an expectation of mutual surveillance in China, where everyone is required to watch over everyone else (Shirk 1982). Starting in the 2000s during Zhou Yongkang's tenure as head of public security, the CCP placed a renewed emphasis on long-standing modes of neighborhood-level grassroots surveillance.

---

of government, regulates the activities of internet content providers, from news portals to social media platforms, and penalizes companies and individuals that fail to comply with government regulations (Cyberspace Administration of China 2017).

Mutual surveillance is not limited to China. Informal forms of mutual surveillance exist in neighborhoods around the world, where neighborhood watches and other resident groups form to combat crime by keeping an eye on each other (Zurawski 2004). Mutual surveillance imposed by the government or other authorities also has been identified historically and around the world.[2] State-sponsored forms of mutual surveillance differ from informal forms, because they aim not only to have "eyes on the street" in a particular neighborhood (Jacobs 1961) but to systematically aggregate and track information generated by eyes on the street on a mass level.

The identification of targeted populations in China derives from both channels of bottom-up surveillance. Some people complain, and because of the nature of their complaint or their history of complaints, they are placed onto targeted population lists. One official who worked in a Letters and Petition Bureau told me that if a person visits the office even one time, they will be flagged for more intensive monitoring (Interview, N2014_721). While this monitoring is not at the level of being listed as a targeted population, it illustrates the direct linkage between voluntarily providing information about oneself and state surveillance. Other targeted persons are identified through mutual surveillance conducted by block captains and other residents who are tasked with gathering information about their peers and passing it along to representatives of the regime.

7.2 Mass Surveillance in the Digital Age

Some argue that surveillance in the digital age is *predictive* while traditional surveillance was *reactive* (Andrejevic and Gates 2014; Liang et al. 2018; Lyon 2016). This is not the case in China. The targeted population program is a strategy of preemptive control that has been in place since the 1950s. It is premised on the belief that the regime could, with some degree of certainty, predict who is more or less likely to take action the regime wants to suppress, and that the regime should systematically identify these individuals from the entire population and intervene in their behavior. The task for surveillance in the Chinese regime has always included the objective of identifying individuals who might take future actions the regime deems objectionable, and thus this surveillance is not concerned only with monitoring current behavior but also with being able to see into the future. In addition, because targeted populations are a subset of the entire population, to identify the few individuals who might make objectionable future actions, the Chinese surveillance apparatus has always been responsible for population-level surveillance.

---

2. Examples range from Edo-era Japan (Lyon 2006) to Nazi Germany (Los 2004).

Traditional surveillance relied on heuristics to implement preemptive control. Many citizens do not complain and volunteer information about their opinions, preferences, and behaviors that give the regime useful information about their future behavior. Neighborhood block captains and other grassroots informants, no matter how knowledgeable and experienced they are, cannot know the future actions of everyone they are tasked with monitoring. Instead, concrete past behaviors such as repeated petitioning and past characteristics such as imprisonment are used as heuristics to identify targeted populations. If we adopt the perspective of the CCP regime, and put aside the extensive limits on personal freedom and autonomy this form of surveillance and preemptive control entails, what are the implications of the use of heuristics to identify targeted populations? From one perspective, these heuristics fail because they fail to capture many people who take actions objectionable to the regime but had not done so, or had not done so in a detectable manner, in the past. From another perspective, these heuristics succeed because those who are monitored are, on average, more likely to disturb order than the general population. Furthermore, it may not matter to local police and administrators of the targeted population program that many who are listed as targeted persons are extremely unlikely to threaten the regime. They can justify to their superiors the inclusion of these individuals because these individuals exhibit certain past characteristics, and they can fulfill quotas for the number of individuals they are tasked with monitoring and justify their budgets.

Does any of this change in the digital age? More and more of our everyday interactions take place on digital devices and platforms. We use our smartphones, laptops, and other devices to conduct business, to keep up with family, friends, and other social connections, to find and share information, to manage financial transactions, and to facilitate mundane daily tasks such as commuting, ordering food, and buying basic necessities. Because these interactions take place on digital devices, they are recorded in digital, machine-readable formats. Each of us generates huge amounts of detailed, individual-level information that is becoming cheaper to store and process. For example, because we often carry our phones with us, our location data reveals information about where we go, how quickly we move, and whom we are with. Separate streams of data—for example GPS location, content consumed on a social networking app, or financial transactions on an e-commerce app—often are joined together to create extremely detailed and fine-grained portraits of our behavior. These data can allow everything about everyone to be tracked all the time. Digital technologies enable governments to have much more data, about more people, than ever before.

Digital technologies alter bottom-up forms of surveillance, both in how people reveal information about themselves and in how they reveal information about others around them. In the past, if a person were to reveal information about themselves by complaining to the government, they would do it knowingly. When they go to a petition office to complain, they know and expect the information to reach the government.[3] In the digital age, most people have little idea of the extent of information they are constantly generating that is bought and sold. Scholars have studied how these involuntarily provided data are commercialized and commodified by companies who profit from them (Schneier 2015; Zuboff 2015). But these data are not useful only for profit-making but also for government surveillance.

Not only are people providing more information about themselves, digital technologies also facilitate mutual surveillance, and a type of mutual surveillance that does not rely on willing (or unwilling) informants. Digital technology enables involuntary forms of mutual surveillance on which governments can capitalize. For example, examining the data of one individual on a social networking site—or any platform that creates linkage between individuals, such as email and messaging apps—can reveal a great deal about their social contacts at the individual, group, and network levels (Huisman 2014; Kim and Leskovec 2011). Suppose Person A is a target of interest to a government, but to avoid the government they do not have an online presence. If Person A has friends B, C, and D, who are on online, governments can learn about Person A by examining the online social data of B, C, and D. In this case, B, C, and D have facilitated mutual surveillance unknowingly and involuntarily.

Much of the digital information we generate is directly collected by companies rather than the government. The extent to which governments can access this information varies greatly. In some countries, governments are limited in what they can obtain by law. In others, governments are limited by their own technical and extractive capacity. Compared to other countries, China is relatively unlimited in accessing such data—the Communist Party is above the law, the government has invested extensively in expanding its technical capacity, and Chinese companies collecting data of interest to the regime have strong incentives to comply when the regime demands this information.[4]

Digital technologies help countries like China to collect much more information about their entire population than previously, and to do so in a way that is less detectable to the public. This book showed that mutual surveillance facilitates government surveillance but also enables residents to contest the distributive decisions of the state. This happened because mutual surveillance lessens

---

3. People can be coerced to provide information about themselves, but the truthfulness of such information differs from voluntarily provided information.

4. This is not to say that companies comply all the time with government directives, but if the regime makes strong demands, it is difficult for firms to resist.

the information advantage of the regime vis-a-vis the population. Mutual surveillance is more effective when those engaged in it know each other well. But when neighbors know each other well, they are more likely to see inequities in welfare distribution and more likely to contest these decisions.

When mutual surveillance is involuntary, this will no longer be the case. The information advantage of actors who can aggregate data becomes much greater because individuals cannot see the data in aggregate. The residents committee members interviewed for this book already use their information advantage to defuse Dibao protests. This will only become easier to do as representatives of the regime have access to more aggregated data. The original hope of information communication technologies, such as the internet and social media, was that they would give individuals, especially those living under repressive regimes, access to more information to improve coordination and collective action (Diamond 2010; Earl and Kimport 2011; Ferdinand 2000; Howard et al. 2011). Perhaps these technologies enabled this at the onset (Steinert-Threlkeld et al. 2015; Steinert-Threlkeld et al. 2017; Tufekci and Wilson 2012), but as powerful actors such as governments perceived danger in these technologies, they brought extensive resources to bear to reassert their information advantage (Kalathil and Boas 2010; MacKinnon 2012; Morozov 2012). Computational technologies are likely to continue tipping the information advantage in favor of governments.

However, the question remains—does this information advantage strengthen an authoritarian regime's ability to impose preemptive control? Surveillance requires data, which digital technologies generate. Data combined with advances in machine learning—for example, in the area of deep learning—and rapid increases in computing power have transformed the private sector. Businesses use these assets to predict consumer behavior with the aim of intervening in such behavior to generate revenue. Presumably this same combination of factors can be used to predict the behavior of a government's subjects with the aim of intervening in their behavior to pursue goals such as political order.

For the past few years, China has been investing heavily in AI for surveillance and preemptive control. China is the world's biggest market for security and surveillance technology, and by 2020 China aims to have nearly 300 million cameras installed to enable surveillance of its entire population of 1.4 billion people.[5] Meng Jianzhu, former secretary of the Central Political and Legal Affairs Commission, told the news outlet *The Paper* (澎湃) in 2017 that "AI will drastically improve the predictability, accuracy and efficiency of social management."[6]

---

5. See https://s.nikkei.com/2QNbWoS and https://nyti.ms/2ufnkiB (accessed July 20, 2019).

6. See https://www.thepaper.cn/newsDetail_forward_1801222 (accessed May 5, 2018).

In 2015, the Ministry of Public Security issued "Regulations on Public Security Agency Information Sharing" (公安机关信息共享规定), which asked lower levels of government to aggregate data in order to facilitate predictive policing.[7] This document, along with other policies, has encouraged the adoption of "Police Cloud" systems that are focused on improving the identification and monitoring of targeted populations. Data centers that collect and analyze these data in close to real time have been set up in Beijing and Zhejiang. In Tianjin, the local government uses these data to track the movements of targeted populations and to enable fast police response to prevent objectionable behavior. In 2016, Baidu announced it had developed a gradient boosting algorithm that used Baidu maps query data and mobile GPS data to predict "anomalous" crowd formation one to three hours before such a crowd could form.[8] In 2017, Li Xuewen, a political dissident who was wanted by the CCP for organizing a memorial to commemorate Nobel Peace Prize laureate Liu Xiaobo, believes that he was immediately arrested upon exiting the Guangzhou railway metro stop because of the use of facial recognition technology by police.[9] In early 2019, Victor Gevers, a security expert, disclosed an unsecured MongoDB database owned by SenseTime, a private Chinese AI company, that tracked the personal information of 2.6 million people in Xinjiang by collecting their location data via cameras and locations where IDs are scanned (e.g., hotels, train stations).[10] Shortly thereafter, Gevers reported another unsecured Chinese database tracking pedestrians and cars, where cameras were triggered to take photos after automatically detecting traffic violations.[11]

China's best-known effort at population-level predictive surveillance is its social credit system. In 2014, China's State Council issued the "Planning Outline for the Construction of a Social Credit System (2014–2020)" (社会信用体系建设规划纲要[2014—2020年]), hereafter Planning Outline, which laid out the goal of creating a broad and encompassing social credit system to monitor not only financial and commercial activities but also social behaviors by 2020 (Liang et al. 2018; Meissner and Wübbeke 2016).[12] Forty-seven ministerial departments have collaborated on the project, and several of China's leading private tech firms

---

7. See http://www.gov.cn/xinwen/2016-03/01/content_5047882.htm (accessed January 26, 2018).

8. See paper at https://arxiv.org/pdf/1603.06780v1.pdf (accessed May 5, 2018).

9. See https://bit.ly/2KpwIrX (accessed May 5, 2018).

10. See https://bit.ly/2GMomtf (accessed July 17, 2019).

11. See https://bit.ly/2UhD3cs (accessed July 17, 2019).

12. For policy document, see http://www.gov.cn/zhengce/content/2014-06/27/content_8913.htm (accessed July 5, 2019).

initially joined the partnership (e.g., Alibaba, Tencent, Baidu). Liang et al. (2018) find that the government's current social credit data platform has aggregated 400 central and local government data sets containing at least 537 variables pertaining to individuals, firms, and other organizations. It is unclear to what extent the government has been able to successfully obtain and integrate data from private companies. In 2015, the central government issued licenses to eight tech companies to develop pilot consumer social credit programs, but revoked these licenses in 2017 due to conflicts over data sharing. Currently, government and private social credit scoring systems are developing in parallel. The next phase of the government's social credit system, which starts in 2020, aims to assess credit of individuals, firms, government offices, and other organizations using the amassed data. The beginnings of this can be seen in the "Reward and Punishment Mechanism" that counties and higher levels of governments have already begun to implement, which comprise red lists (rewards) and black lists (punishment) of individuals, firms, government agencies, and other organizations.

7.3 Perils of Prediction

When news reports cover China's social credit system and digital surveillance systems (and there has been a great deal of coverage), what is emphasized is the scope and depth of the efforts. What has received much less attention is whether and how these technologies change the Chinese regime's control of its population. More specifically, will the incredible growth in data, computation, and machine learning allow the regime to better predict who will disturb political order in the future?

The vast majority of machine learning algorithms being used for predictive analytics are probabilistic, not deterministic. While they are constantly being improved, they are never right 100% of the time. Let's take the example of detecting crowd formation, which is of interest to the Chinese regime because it would like to prevent large-scale collective action. Sabokrou et al. (2018) use cutting-edge deep learning techniques (convolutional neural networks) to detect crowd anomalies, which are defined as rare or unexpected events, from video. These techniques outperform most existing methods, but the equal error rate of the best system is still 10% to 15%. This means that for a binary classification problem (e.g., there is an anomaly or not in the frame), the system is wrong 10% to 15% of the time. Most of the errors are due to false positives, non-anomalies being classified as anomalies.

Most English-language publications on crowd detection use the same data sets—for example, the UCSD Anomaly Detection Dataset—for training classifiers.[13] Some have argued that China will "win" the "war" on AI because it has access to unparalleled amounts of data, which could be used to train better classifiers and algorithms (Lee 2018). However, large amounts of data may not be good data. Deep learning systems are supervised machine learning methods that rely on training data, often generated by humans and often requiring human validation. As human beings rely on heuristics to make difficult judgments, these biases will carry over into machine models and machine systems (Caliskan, Bryson, and Narayanan 2017).

Looking at Baidu's crowd anomaly detection algorithm, it is not readily apparent that more data is the answer. Baidu uses its proprietary, and presumably very large-scale, data to train its classifier to detect crowd anomalies. At the maximum F1-score, which is one way of balancing the trade off between detecting false positive and false negatives,[14] the precision and recall of the system are both around 0.7. Precision and recall are calculated by:

$$precision = \frac{true\ positive}{true\ positive + false\ positive}$$

$$recall = \frac{true\ positive}{true\ positive + false\ negative}$$

This means that approximately 30% of the time, the Baidu classifier identifies an anomalous crowd when one does not exist (false positive), and approximately 30% of the time, the classifier fails to detect actual anomalies (false negative). I have no doubt that if Baidu continued to work on this algorithm after the paper was published in 2016, the system will have improved significantly. However, no system can achieve perfect precision and recall. There is always a trade off.

Assuming the CCP has access to unparalleled amounts of data, computing power, and the most cutting-edge machine learning methods, it would still need to make a decision about how to trade off precision and recall. To what extent would it care about precision (minimizing false positives) versus recall (minimizing false negatives) given its preoccupation with political order? If we assume that local officials, who are tasked with implementing systems of preemptive control, want to avoid serious mistakes (namely to avoid large-scale collective action) while continuing to justify their budgets (to make it appear as if there is a need to fight against disorder, and they are actively trying to enforce order), then recall would be prioritized over precision. Precision matters less because false positives—people who do not pose a threat to political order but are deemed as threats—are not problematic to local officials as long as false positives do not

---

13. See http://www.svcl.ucsd.edu/projects/anomaly/dataset.htm (accessed July 8, 2019).

14. The F1-score is the harmonic average of precision and recall.

overwhelm true positives. This is what we see in the management of targeted populations described in this book. It does not matter if some of the people who are listed pose no threat, as long as those who are listed pose, on average, a larger threat than those who are not listed as targeted populations. On the other hand, recall matters a great deal because false negatives—people who do pose a threat to order but are missed by the system—could generate negative consequences for local officials. What is the consequence of prioritizing recall over precision? If we look at the Baidu algorithm described in Zhou, Pei, and Wu (2018), in order to achieve perfect recall, precision falls below 0.3, meaning that more than 70% of anomalies identified are not actual anomalies. The consequence of prioritizing recall is that many who pose no threat to the regime will be classified as threats.

Is this realistic? Would the CCP be willing to trade off low precision (high levels of people incorrectly identified as threats to political order) in order to maximize recall (low levels of people who threaten political order but are not identified as such)? When we look at what is happening today in Xinjiang, the answer seems to be yes. Xinjiang has implemented a machine-supported digital surveillance system at scale, and several hundred thousand to over a million Muslim minorities have been interned for re-education in Xinjiang (Zenz 2019). News reports and human rights reports provide many examples of detainees who do not appear to have done anything remotely threatening to the regime. This is exactly what we would expect to see if a massive machine-guided system for surveillance and preemptive control maximized recall at the expense of precision to ensure that no real threats escape. Imprisoning large numbers of people boosts security-related budgets, which benefits those implementing these systems, and this large-scale imprisonment makes it much more likely that individuals who threaten China (whether defined as terrorists based on international definitions or on China's own definitions) are under government control.

China is under increased international pressure to release Muslim prisoners, but it is unlikely that the regime will give up on political order even if it shuts down these camps and never re-opens them. The regime might turn to less overt forms of control such as the neighborhood-based repression of targeted populations and repressive assistance described in this book. These methods are already in use, and in a world of increasing data, computing power, and advances with machine learning, they may well expand. Digital technologies are unlikely to fundamentally alter the Chinese regime's use of preemptive surveillance and control to pursue political order, but they will expand the scope and increase the human cost. The CCP will have more data about more people at more fine-grained time intervals, and these data will likely expand the number of individuals who are under more intensive surveillance and control.

7.4 Call for Future Research

A number of empirical questions arise from this book, and a common theme is a need to bridge theories and concepts from different literatures. Many of the phenomena I have examined in this book—seepage, repressive assistance, and surveillance—speak to a need for future research to traverse different areas of social science research.

Thelen (2003) notes that many researchers are drawn to the study of institutions because institutions can be resilient and resistant in the face of exogenous shocks, yet transform substantially in the absence of shocks. The field of historical institutionalism has greatly advanced our understanding of how institutions change gradually over time, but the vast majority of this work has focused on established, democratic contexts. Institutions do not change gradually only in consolidated democracies with high levels of economic development. They can also evolve gradually in longer-lasting authoritarian regimes, such as monarchies and single-party regimes. But we know little about how they do so. Institutions play a central role in theories of authoritarian politics, but research on authoritarian institutions has been focused on their emergence and their effects rather than on their evolution. Seepage, as conceptualized and illustrated in this book, is a move in the direction of bringing institutional evolution to the study of authoritarian institutions. Many unanswered questions remain. Do we observe seepage in other policy areas and institutions in China? Do we see seepage beyond China? If so, when and where? Most importantly, in what other ways do authoritarian institutions change, and what are the implications of institutional change on authoritarian politics and outcomes such as competition among elites, state–society interactions, economic development, and social mobilization?

Scholars of repression have greatly expanded our understanding of the array of tactics governments use to suppress social mobilization and other activities they deem objectionable (Blaydes 2018; Davenport 2015; Davenport, Armstrong, and Zeitzoff 2019; Davenport and Inman 2012; Earl and Soule 2010; Goldstone and Tilly 2001; Opp and Gern 1993; Sullivan and Davenport 2017; Tilly 2005). There is also a large literature on how governments coopt opposition, including through the use of social welfare.[15] These literatures are largely separate, yet the phenomenon of repressive assistance shows that repression need not be coercive, and strategies we typically consider cooptive may, in some cases, act as tools of repression. Where else might repressive assistance be found? When else does benefit distribution serve repressive ends? What other tactics do governments use to

---

15. See Chapter 1 and Chapter 5 for discussion.

repress that are not coercive, difficult to detect, and unlikely on the surface to spur anger or outrage?

As digital technologies develop, there is increasing concern that these technologies will give more power to authoritarian regimes, enabling them to better control their population and to suppress dissent and autonomy. These concerns are warranted, and we should closely examine how these technologies are used by states, corporations, and other actors. At the same time, however, we have to understand these digital technologies in order to understand to what extent they change or do not change the nature of authoritarian rule and the dynamics of authoritarian politics, and we have to understand authoritarian politics in order to understand their role. If we believe everything we read in the news, we might believe that our world is on the verge of a dramatic and possibly terrible change because of artifical intelligence and new computational technologies. If we read political science research, aside from research on social media, computational technologies might as well not matter. The reality is likely somewhere in between, and likely hidden in the nuances of how politics work. As social scientists are increasingly trained in computational methods, there is an opportunity not only to apply these methods as methods (shaping how research is done) but to apply deep, technical understanding of these computational methods to understand their effects on politics and society. Will these technologies change political competition and political outcomes? Where? When? How?

To answer these questions will not be easy. This book suggests that research may need to utilize a broad array of methodological approaches, which cannot be simply broken down into qualitative and quantitative methods. For this book, field interviews and close analysis of government documents were crucial in generating the insights and intuitions underlying the main argument. Computational methods and machine learning, along with survey-based research, were needed to generate novel data sets to test my theories, and randomized experiments were essential to obtaining causal inference. Altogether, interview-based methods, survey-based methods, computational methods, and experimental methods were needed to uncover and to scientifically validate the findings of this book.

Finally, for any book on China, there is the inevitable question of, what does this mean for the durability and survival of the Chinese regime? The results of this book do not predict the imminent collapse of the Chinese regime or any other party autocracy. However, the book calls into question the extent to which China is resilient to contention in the long run. It raises the question of whether, despite China's institutional arrangements and high level of state capacity, its fixation on political order undermines programmatic attempts to gain political trust and legitimacy for the CCP. It appears unlikely that China will loosen its grip on social control and turn away from its pursuit of order. Instead of de-emphasizing the need for political order, China appears to be well on its way to tightening social control in order to try to mitigate the problems produced by its quest for political order. We need to continue to examine these strategies to understand their effects, but what we have learned suggests that many casualties will result from China's quest for political order, perhaps even order itself.

Appendix

A.5 100-Neighborhood Survey

I conducted a survey of 100 neighborhoods in four cities in Eastern (Hangzhou), Central (Wuhan, Zhengzhou), and Western (Xian) China from March to June 2013. A total of 21 central urban districts in these four cities were randomly selected, and three to five neighborhoods in each district were selected for enumerator visits. Selected districts include:

- Hangzhou: Shangcheng, Xihu, Gongshu, Jianggan
- Wuhan: Wuchang, Hanyang, Jiangan, Jianghan, Hongshan, Qiaokou
- Zhengzhou: Zhongyuan, Erqi, Guancheng, Jinshui, Huiji
- Xian: Weiyang, Xincheng, Baqiao, Lianhu, Beilin, Yanta

Enumerators were college students from local universities where I was based for my fieldwork who were residents of the cities in which the research was being conducted. Enumerators were recommended by local university professors for their experience in conducting field research, and all were trained prior to survey implementation. Local enumerators were selected so that local dialect would not be a hindrance in conducting interviews. Enumerators asked to speak with either the residents committee party secretary, the residents committee director, or the residents committee member in charge of Dibao. If none of these people was available, enumerators would wait until one of them returned, or try again on another day. Enumerators had letters of introduction from local universities explaining the goals of the research, and only three residents committees opted not to participate. Interviews took place during the working hours of the residents committee, typically between 9–11a.m. and 2–4p.m. from Monday through Friday.

Table A.1 shows the number of neighborhoods, residents committee members, and residents surveyed by city, as well as percentages for each city. Roughly one-quarter of neighborhoods were located in Wuhan and Zhengzhou.

Table A.1   **Neighborhoods and respondents by city**

	Neighborhoods		RC members		Residents	
Hangzhou	18	18.6%	18	17.5%	55	18.0%
Wuhan	24	24.7%	27	26.2%	74	24.2%
Zhengzhou	25	25.8%	28	27.2%	81	26.5%
Xian	30	30.9%	30	29.1%	96	31.4%
Total	97		103		283	

Hangzhou represents a smaller proportion (18.6%) of neighborhoods surveyed, and Xian slightly more (30.9%). One residents committee member was surveyed for each neighborhood in Hangzhou and Xian, while in a few neighborhoods in Wuhan and Zhengzhou more than one residents committee member participated in the survey. Where possible, at least three residents were surveyed in each neighborhood.[16]

A.5.1 Neighborhood Characteristics

I also collect data on the structural and demographic conditions of the neighborhood, including the age of buildings in the neighborhood as reported by the residents committee,[17] the proportion of residents with rural, or what is officially called agricultural, *Hukou* as reported by the residents committee, and the existence of rental advertisements in the neighborhood's public spaces.

The distribution of the age of the neighborhood is shown in Table A.2. Nearly 35% of neighborhoods contain buildings constructed within the past 10 to 15 years (in the 2000s), fewer than 20% contain buildings constructed in the 1990s, and nearly 50% of neighborhoods were built in the 1980s or before.[18] Among 97 neighborhoods surveyed, 11 (11%) included residents with rural residential permits. Eighteen neighborhoods (19%) had apartments for rent.

---

16. In one neighborhood, no residents were available for interview; in one neighborhood only one resident was available for interview; and in three neighborhoods only two residents were available for interview. Excluding neighborhoods with fewer than three resident interviews does not change substantive results.

17. If the ages of the buildings in the neighborhood vary, I take as age the age of buildings that are most common in the neighborhood.

18. Two of the older neighborhoods surveyed, one in Wuhan and one in Hangzhou, date back to the 1940s.

Table A.2 Age of neighborhoods surveyed

Neighborhood age	Number of neighborhoods	Percentage of neighborhoods
Pre-1980s	18	21.7
1980s	21	25.3
1990s	15	18.1
2000s	29	34.9

Table A.3 Surveillance capacity and identification of released prisoners

	(1)	(2)	(3)
High surveillance capacity	1.531*	1.694*	1.804*
	(0.884)	(0.948)	(1.032)
Neighborhood age		0.0003**	0.0002*
		(0.0001)	(0.0001)
Rental apartments		−0.748	−1.625
		(0.954)	(1.118)
Rural Hukou		0.168	1.204
		(1.561)	(1.666)
Social capital			−2.915**
			(1.472)
Intercept	−0.693	−1.639	1.467
	(0.548)	(1.098)	(1.893)
City FE	Yes	Yes	Yes
Observations	80	78	78

Note: $^*p < 0.1$; $^{**}p < 0.05$; $^{***}p < 0.01$.

A.5.2 Surveillance, Released Prisoners, and Dibao

Table A.3 shows the predictive effect of neighborhood surveillance capacity on the reported presence of ex-prisoners based on logistic regression. In column (1), only neighborhood surveillance capacity is included. In column (2), control variables include age of the neighborhood, presence of rental apartments, and presence of rural residents. In column (3), social capital is added to the regression. In all specifications, surveillance capacity predicts the identification of released prisoners, and all results are statistically significant at the 0.1 level. In addition,

Table A.4 Surveillance capacity and Dibao for released prisoners

	(1)	(2)	(3)
High surveillance capacity	1.531*	1.648*	1.822*
	(0.884)	(0.942)	(1.034)
Neighborhood age		0.0002	0.0002
		(0.0001)	(0.0001)
Rental apartments		−0.435	−1.336
		(0.929)	(1.102)
Rural Hukou		0.503	1.593
		(1.515)	(1.636)
Social capital			−2.954**
			(1.453)
Intercept	−0.916	−1.834	1.274
	(0.592)	(1.134)	(1.888)
City FE	Yes	Yes	Yes
Observations	72	70	70

Note: $^*p < 0.1$; $^{**}p < 0.05$; $^{***}p < 0.01$.

the results of Table A.3 show that older neighborhoods are more likely to have released prisoners, but this result does not dampen the relationship between surveillance capacity and presence of released prisoners. These results demonstrate the relationship between surveillance capacity and the identification of released prisoners.[19]

When neighborhoods have stronger surveillance capabilities, Dibao benefits are more likely to be given to ex-prisoners. Table A.4 shows logistics regressions of the predictive effect of neighborhood surveillance capacity on the provision of Dibao to released prisoners. In column (1), only neighborhood surveillance capacity is included. In column (2), control variables including the age of the neighborhood, presence of rental apartments, and presence of rural residents are added and in column (3), social capital is added. In all three specifications, as we would expect, surveillance capacity is predictive of the provision of Dibao to released prisoners, and the results are statistically significant at the 0.1 level. In Table A.4, we also see that the level of social capital in a neighborhood is negatively associated with the presence of released prisoners among Dibao recipients;

19. When multiple imputation is used to impute missing data, the substantive results do not change.

Table A.5 Surveillance capacity and Dibao for the disabled

	(1)	(2)	(3)
High surveillance capacity	−1.564**	−2.634***	−2.814***
	(0.786)	(1.011)	(1.071)
Neighborhood age		0.00003	0.00005
		(0.0001)	(0.0001)
Rental apartments		2.659**	2.937**
		(1.225)	(1.270)
Rural Hukou		−0.079	−0.456
		(1.518)	(1.596)
Social capital			1.226
			(1.361)
Intercept	−0.588	−2.507*	−3.794*
	(0.558)	(1.378)	(2.007)
City FE	Yes	Yes	Yes
Observations	72	70	70

Note: *p < 0.1; **p < 0.05; ***p < 0.01.

however, the level of social capital does not diminish the relationship between surveillance and provision of Dibao to released prisoners.

Although the rate of providing Dibao to the disabled is high across neighborhoods, neighborhoods with high surveillance are less likely to provide Dibao to the disabled. Table A.5 shows three logistics regressions of the predictive effect of neighborhood surveillance capacity on the provision of Dibao to the disabled. In column (1), only neighborhood surveillance capacity is included. In column (2), control variables include age of the neighborhood, presence of rental apartments, and presence of rural residents, and column (3) adds the social capital variable. In all three specifications, surveillance capacity is predictive of decreased provision of Dibao to the disabled, and these results are statistically significant at the 0.05 and 0.001 levels.

A.6 China Urban Governance Survey (CUGS)

From June 19 to August 28, 2015, the China Urban Governance Survey (CUGS) was conducted by the Research Center on Data and Governance at Tsinghua University. Questions pertaining to social welfare, as well as plans for future collective action, were included in this survey.[20] The target populations for the survey were Chinese urban residents aged 18 and above who had lived in the sampled communities for at least a month. Given the focus of this book on urban Dibao, the sample of the survey exactly matches the population of interest.

A.6.1 Sample

Sampling for the CUGS is conducted using GPS Assisted Area Sampling (Landry and Shen 2005). The GPS Assisted Area Sampling uses four strata. The primary sampling units are county-level cities and urban districts, whose names are taken from the *National Sub-county Population Statistics 2010* (Ministry of Public Security 2011). Fifty county-level cities and urban districts were selected through probabilities of selection proportional to measures of size (PPS). Specifically, all county-level cities and urban districts were ordered by population as recorded in the 2010 census, and 50 county-level cities and urban districts were randomly sampled from this sorted list to ensure a mix of low-, medium-, and high-population areas. For each selected county-level city and urban district, two street offices were drawn by PPS. Street offices are then divided by 30sec by 30sec half-square minutes (HSMs), which were ordered by population density based on high resolution image data, and two HSMs were drawn by PPS from each street office. Within the HMS, a 90m by 90m surface was randomly drawn, and samplers equipped with GPS receivers were sent onsite to enumerate all the residential addresses within the selected area. If the number of addresses within a selected area exceeded 30, system sampling would be deployed to draw 30 addresses. Within each listed address (household), residents aged 18 and above who had lived in the district/county for at least one month were identified as candidates. Among candidates, the respondent was chosen according to the Kish grid (Kish 1965). This method of sampling overcomes the inability of sampling procedures based on household lists to reach mobile populations and avoids problems generated by inconsistency between registered households and residential addresses. Using this sampling procedure, 5,807 residential units were identified. Among them, 5,526 were deemed eligible; 281 residential units were excluded because they did not fulfill the one-month residency requirement or because the unit was empty. In all, 3,513 interviews (63.6%) were completed and validated.

Survey respondents are representative of China's urban population. The left panel of Figure A.1 shows the age distribution of respondents, who are between

---

20. The survey covered a wide range of topics, including assessments of the quality of governance, political participation, internet usage, and public attitudes toward political and economic policies, as well as demographic information about the respondents.

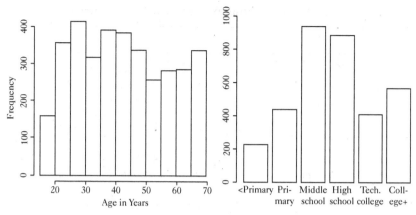

FIGURE A.1 Age and education of respondents

18 and 70, and the right panel of Figure A.1 shows the educational attainment of respondents. The modal educational achievement of respondents is middle school (27% of respondents), followed by high school (26%), college and above (16%), primary school and technical/community college (12%), and less than primary school (7%). Half of respondents are male (50%), roughly two-thirds (67%) have urban *Hukou*, 63% are currently employed, 12% are Communist Party members, and 17% have been outside of mainland China. The distribution of age, educational attainment, gender, urban *Hukou* status, and employment in our sample is very similar to that of the 2010 Chinese Population Census.[21]

A.6.2 Fuzzy RDD

Discontinuity in Probability of Treatment

The treatment (D) is Dibao status (1 or 0). Z refers to whether a respondent's household income is below or above the local Dibao line, where X is household income, and c is the local Dibao line:[22]

$$Z_i = \begin{cases} Z_i = 1 & \text{if } X_i < c \\ Z_i = 0 & \text{if } X_i > c \end{cases}$$

These equations mean that if household i has income X_i below the local Dibao line c, then Z is equal to 1 because the household's income is below the local Dibao line; and if household i has income X_i above the local Dibao line, then Z is equal

---

21. See http://www.stats.gov.cn/tjsj/pcsj/rkpc/6rp/indexce.htm for details.

22. $(X - c)$ is also known as the running variable.

Table A.6 Discontinuity in probability of treatment

	(1)
Z	0.1763**
	(0.087)
$X - c$	-3.338×10^{-6}***
	(1.032×10^{-6})
$Z \cdot (X - c)$	8.586×10^{-5}*
	(4.741×10^{-5})
Intercept	0.096***
	(0.017)
Observations	792

Note: *p < 0.1; **p < 0.05; ***p < 0.01.

to 0 because the household's income is below the local Dibao line. In order to use fuzzy RDD, we are looking for discontinuity in $E[D|X]$ such that:

$$E[D|Z = 1] \neq E[D|Z = 0]$$

Table A.6 shows that among CUGS respondents, there is a discontinuity in the probability of receiving Dibao at an income threshold because the coefficient estimate for Z is positive and statistically significant. In plain terms, a respondent's household income being below the local Dibao line is a statistically significant predictor of whether the household receives Dibao. We can also observe this treatment discontinuity in Figure A.2. Individuals reporting household income below the cutoff are more likely to receive Dibao than individuals reporting household income above the cutoff. Figure A.2 shows IMSE-optimal quantile-space bins to the left and right of the cutoff (Calonico, Cattaneo, and Titiunik 2014).[23] Respondents reporting household income below the cutoff are more likely to receive Dibao than those reporting household income above the cutoff.

Effect of Dibao on Future Collective Action

Table A.7 shows estimates of the effect of Dibao status on future collective action, using five different specifications.[24] These five specifications include different

---

23. Using other methods of determining bin size does not change these results.

24. This is the result of $Y = \beta_0 + \beta_1(X - c) + \beta_2(Z \cdot (X - c)) + \alpha D$, where D is instrumented with Z and where Y refers to future collective action; in some specifications, polynomials have been added.

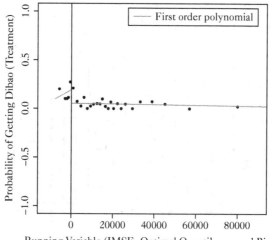

FIGURE A.2 Treatment discontinuity

Table A.7 Effect of Dibao on future plans for collective action

	(1)	(2)	(3)	(4)	(5)
Dibao Status	0.1134	−0.2358	−0.3746	0.0143	0.0272
	(0.9139)	(0.7922)	(0.8867)	(0.3134)	(0.1471)
Polynomial order	1	2	4	4	4
Bandwidth type	mserd	mserd	mserd	msetwo	cercomb2
Observations left	28	31	31	32	26
Observations right	54	93	86	711	53

Note: *p < 0.1; **p < 0.05; ***p < 0.01.

orders of the local-polynomial used to construct the point-estimator, from $p = 1$ to $p = 4$, and shows three different bandwidth selection procedures, which produces different bandwidths used to construct the regression discontinuity point estimator.[25] Across specifications, Dibao status does not increase or decrease the likelihood of future collective action.

---

25. mserd is a MSE-optimal bandwidth selector for the RD treatment effect estimator; msetwo uses two different MSE-optimal bandwidth selectors (below and above the cutoff) for the RD treatment effect estimator, and cercomb2 uses the median of three different CER-optimal bandwidth selectors for each side of the cutoff separately (Calonico, Cattaneo, and Titiunik 2014).

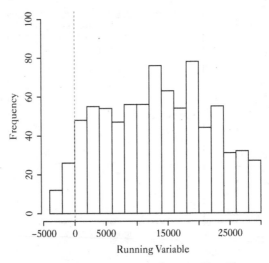

FIGURE A.3 Histogram of running variable

Robustness of Results

To ensure that this result is robust and not due to particularities in the data, which could make the use of fuzzy RDD inappropriate, I conduct several additional analyses. First, I examine whether there is bunching around the threshold and whether my results are sensitive to bandwidth range. Figure A.3 is a histogram of the running variable, $(X - c)$. We do not observe bunching around the cutoff (c), which is shown as the dotted vertical line in Figure A.3. A Wald test corroborates this visual inspection. We cannot reject the null hypothesis of no discontinuity in the running variable (p-value = 0.117). What this shows is that households are not working to ensure that their household income falls just below the Dibao threshold, for example by working fewer hours, bringing home slightly less money. This result is not surprising given how low local Dibao lines are, and the unpredictability of income for many impoverished households. It would be extremely difficult to manipulate household income so that income falls just under the local Dibao line. In addition, given the level of exclusion error, having income below the Dibao line is no guarantee of Dibao, and incentives to manipulate (lower) income in order to qualify are likely low. In sum, at the threshold, we can assume continuity and random assignment.

Second, I examine whether these results are sensitive to bandwidth range. I estimate the effect of Dibao status on future collective action with differing numbers of observations to the left and right of the cutoff.[26] Figure A.4 shows two

---

26. I estimate $Y = \beta_0 + \beta_1(X - c) + \beta_2(Z \cdot (X - c)) + \alpha D$, where D is instrumented with Z without the addition of polynomials.

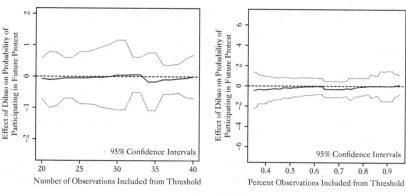

FIGURE A.4 Changes to bandwidth

ways in which bandwidth range varies. In the left panel of Figure A.4, bandwidth is changed based on the number of observations—from 20 to 40—included in the RD point estimate, to the left and right of the threshold. In this analysis, equal numbers of observations are included to the left and right of the threshold. Across these different bandwidth ranges, the effect of Dibao status on future collective action is 0. In the right panel of Figure A.4, bandwidth is changed based on the percentage of observations—from 35% to 95%—included to the left and right of the threshold. By using percentage, the numbers of observations to the left and right of the threshold are unequal (since there are many more observations to the right of the threshold than to the left). Again, across these different bandwidth ranges, the effect of Dibao status on future collective action is 0.

A.6.3 Dibao for Targeted Populations and Perceptions of Government

Table A.8 shows the OLS regression of the relationship between higher and lower levels of Dibao provision for targeted populations by city and CUGS respondents' assessments of government capabilities. Table A.9 shows the relationship between Dibao provision to targeted populations and CUGS respondents' assessments of government legitimacy.

Table A.8 Relationship between providing Dibao to targeted populations and assessment of government capabilities

	Government Ability to:			
	Preserve Stability (1)	Provide Welfare (2)	Be Responsive to Public (3)	Rein in Officials (4)
More Dibao for Targeted Populations	−0.049*** (0.019)	−0.106*** (0.022)	−0.080*** (0.022)	−0.063*** (0.024)
Age	0.004*** (0.001)	0.004*** (0.001)	0.004*** (0.001)	0.005*** (0.001)
Male	−0.024 (0.017)	−0.048** (0.019)	−0.055*** (0.020)	−0.072*** (0.021)
Log HH Income	−0.002 (0.002)	−0.004* (0.002)	−0.005** (0.002)	−0.007*** (0.003)
CCP Member	−0.020 (0.026)	−0.018 (0.030)	−0.040 (0.031)	−0.036 (0.033)
Level of Education	0.028*** (0.007)	−0.010 (0.008)	−0.019** (0.008)	0.008 (0.009)
Log 2013 GDP per capita	0.030 (0.021)	−0.010 (0.024)	0.003 (0.024)	0.017 (0.026)
Log 2013 Govt. Expenditure	−0.029 (0.038)	0.021 (0.044)	0.013 (0.045)	−0.036 (0.048)
Log Total Population	−0.008 (0.041)	−0.055 (0.047)	−0.067 (0.049)	−0.049 (0.052)
Log Dibao Expenditures	−0.024*** (0.009)	−0.007 (0.010)	−0.021** (0.011)	0.001 (0.011)
Log Dibao Households	0.020 (0.016)	0.015 (0.018)	0.022 (0.019)	0.022 (0.020)
Intercept	−0.320 (0.280)	−0.152 (0.323)	−0.236 (0.333)	−0.457 (0.354)
Observations	2,943	2,859	2,806	2,790

Note: *p < 0.1; **p < 0.05; ***p < 0.01.

Table A.9 Relationship between providing Dibao to targeted populations and perceptions of government legitimacy

	Satisfaction in Central Gov't (1)	Satisfaction in City Gov't (2)	Trust in Central Gov't (3)	Trust in City Gov't (4)
More Dibao for	0.015	−0.039**	0.006	−0.047**
Targeted Populations	(0.016)	(0.018)	(0.017)	(0.020)
Age	0.005***	0.005***	0.006***	0.006***
	(0.001)	(0.001)	(0.001)	(0.001)
Male	−0.018	−0.035**	−0.007	−0.076***
	(0.014)	(0.016)	(0.015)	(0.018)
Log HH Income	−0.002	−0.005**	0.001	−0.006**
	(0.002)	(0.002)	(0.002)	(0.002)
CCP Member	0.043*	0.004	0.049**	−0.014
	(0.023)	(0.026)	(0.024)	(0.029)
Level of Education	0.003	0.001	0.007	0.012
	(0.006)	(0.007)	(0.006)	(0.008)
Log 2013 GDP per	−0.051***	0.003	0.007	0.072***
capita	(0.017)	(0.019)	(0.018)	(0.022)
Log 2013 Govt.	0.074**	0.086**	−0.088***	−0.068*
Expenditure	(0.031)	(0.035)	(0.032)	(0.039)
Log Total Population	−0.054	−0.095**	0.073**	0.009
	(0.033)	(0.038)	(0.035)	(0.042)
Log Dibao Expenditure	0.011	0.0003	−0.001	−0.006
	(0.007)	(0.008)	(0.008)	(0.009)
Log Dibao Households	−0.040***	−0.009	0.003	0.005
	(0.013)	(0.015)	(0.014)	(0.017)
Intercept	1.078***	0.151	0.280	−0.540*
	(0.233)	(0.263)	(0.246)	(0.293)
Observations	3,104	3,106	3,104	3,091

Note: $^{*}p < 0.1$; $^{**}p < 0.05$; $^{***}p < 0.01$.

A.7 *Ad Hoc Dibao Announcements*

I collected all online reports mentioning Dibao from January 2008 to June 2013 for 36 cities,[27] which include all of China's provincial-level cities and provincial

---

27. These cities are Beijing, Changchun, Changsha, Chengdu, Chongqing, Dalian, Fuzhou, Guangzhou, Guiyang, Haerbin, Haikou, Hangzhou, Hefei, Huerhaote, Jinan, Kunming,

capitals, as well as sub-provincial level cities.[28] These cities are among the most politically important in China, and because of their status, their policies and strategies are often referenced and copied by other localities (Hong 2004).

Data was collected by searching news.baidu.com using the city name and the term Dibao in Chinese, and limiting the search to six-month periods. For example, to compile the data for Beijing, 11 searches were conducted, using the terms "Beijing AND (Minimum Livelihood Guarantee OR Dibao)" (北京 AND [最低生活保障 OR 低保]) from January 1, 2008 to June 30, 2008, "Beijing AND (Minimum Livelihood Guarantee OR Dibao)" from July 1, 2008 to December 31, 2009, and so on for each six-month period until June 30, 2013. For each search, all pages of results were collected.[29] After removing duplicate reports of the same benefit, 3,022 distinct reports related to Dibao were identified.[30] These reports came from a total of 639 online sites, with the largest number of reports coming from online news aggregators news.sina.com.cn (338), news.163.com (190), and news.qq.com (121).

Each report was read by trained research team members to determine whether it related to an ad hoc Dibao benefit, resulting in 2,390 (79%) distinct reports of ad hoc benefits. Reports not included were those that focused on changes in the Dibao line, as well as reports that described or criticized the Dibao program and its outcomes. News related to visits by government officials to Dibao households were included, since visits by officials almost always entail gifts and other material benefits. For the reports of ad hoc benefits, human coders then determined whether the benefit was distributed by the government or by private sources. An example of a private source would be a local Carrefour, a branch of the French grocery chain, donating food to Dibao families. Because private distribution of ad hoc benefits often involves collaboration with local community administrators, both public and private benefits are included in the analysis.[31] Next, human coders identified whether the benefit was a cash transfer, an in-kind transfer (e.g., cooking oil, reduced utilities costs, reduced

---

Lanzhou, Nanchang, Nanjing, Nanning, Ningbo, Qingdao, Shanghai, Shenyang, Shenzhen, Shijiazhuang, Taiyuan, Tianjin, Urumqi, Wuhan, Wuxi, Xiamen, Xian, Xining, Yinchuan, and Zhengzhou.

28. Sub-provincial cities are independently administered cities, distinct from prefectural-level cities governed by the province. There are currently 15 sub-provincial cities, and all are provincial capitals.

29. The rule of collecting the first 100 pages of results was utilized, but among the 396 city-time period searches conducted, none came close to reaching 100 pages.

30. Duplication removal was done through human reading.

31. The exclusion of benefits from private sources does not affect any substantive results.

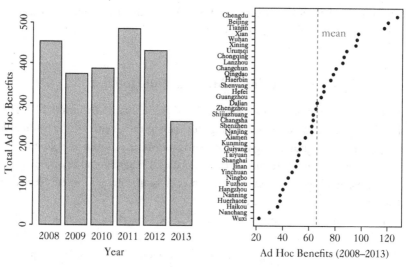

FIGURE A.5 Ad hoc benefits by year and by city

housing costs), or a service (e.g., free cancer screening). Coders also identified the category of the benefit (e.g., housing, food, education), whether anyone with Dibao status could obtain the benefit or whether there was a limit to the number of Dibao households that could receive the benefit, whether the benefit targeted a particular demographic (e.g., elderly over the age of 75, disabled children, pregnant women), and, finally, the date the ad hoc benefit went into effect.[32]

The left panel of Figure A.5 shows the number of ad hoc benefits we collected by year from January 1, 2008 to June 30, 2013. In 2008, 454 unique ad hoc benefits were identified, 374 in 2009, 388 in 2010, 485 in 2011, 432 in 2012, and 257 in the first half of 2013. We do not see a decline in reports of ad hoc benefits going back in time, suggesting that online news sources capture a relatively consistent sample of ad hoc benefits over our time period.

The right panel of Figure A.5 shows the number of ad hoc benefits collected by city for the entire time period. The figure reveals substantial variations in the use of ad hoc benefits among cities. Over the course of four years, only 22 ad hoc benefits were distributed in Wuxi, while 127 were distributed in Chengdu.

Across all cities, the vast majority (89%) of benefits are funded by the government. Of the non-state-funded benefits, nearly 7% come from state-owned

---

32. Also recorded were the date of the news report and the date the benefit was announced. Analysis is based on the date the ad hoc benefit went into effect (i.e., was distributed to Dibao recipients).

enterprises and government-organized NGOs, like the the Women's Federation, and only 4% are funded by private sources.

A.7.1 Political Meetings and Holidays

Because the timing of the Two Meeting or Lianghui varies by locality, I collect the date and duration of these meetings for each of the 36 cities using baidu.com search. Since Lianghui are significant events for politics as well as policy, details of all meetings are easily found for these 36 cities. Lianghui tend to occur toward the beginning of the year and are sometimes close in date to Chinese New Year, which is based on the lunar calendar.

I focus on three national holidays, Chinese New Year, Qingming Festival, and National Day, which represent different motivations for protest and possibly different motives for government distribution of benefits. While protests during Chinese New Year may be motivated by practical concerns for material benefits, protests during Qingming may be more likely motivated by grievances over wrongful deaths, and protests during National Day may be more explicitly motivated by political discontent. In addition, the reasons why local governments would distribute Dibao benefits before these three holidays may differ. In particular, there is a deep tradition of gift giving before Chinese New Year (Qian, Abdur Razzaque, and Kau 2007; Yau 1988). As a result, benefits distributed by local governments before Chinese New Year also may be aimed at shoring up general support for the regime. However, this motivation does not apply for Qingming and National Day.

A.7.2 Social Assistance versus Social Insurance

I analyze announcements related to China's Old Age Insurance program for urban and rural residents (城乡居民社会养老保险) before and after the three major holidays—Chinese New Year, Qingming Festival, and National Day. Old Age Insurance is funded by individual contributions as well as government subsidies rather than employee contributions. This means that among social insurance programs, the Old Age Insurance program for residents is more similar to Dibao programs because it is partially funded by local governments. If any social insurance program were used to prevent collective action, I would expect it to be the Old Age Insurance program.

I gather online reports related to China's Old Age Insurance program as well as Dibao from 2013 to 2017 so the data is comparable. I use Google custom search to search for the names of all provinces and prefecture-level cities, along with search

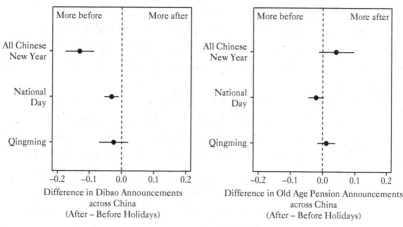

FIGURE A.6 Comparison of Dibao and Old Age Insurance

terms of "Old Age Insurance"[33] and "Dibao."[34] I collect data for time periods surrounding the three main holidays to compare announcements around these politically sensitive time periods for Old Age Insurance and Dibao.[35]

The left panel of Figure A.6 shows the difference in the number of Dibao announcements for all Chinese New Year holidays, for National Day, and for Qingming Festival. This figure shows the point estimate and 95% confidence intervals of the difference in the average number of online reports related to Dibao announced up to 10 days before the start of these holidays, and the average number of online reports related to Dibao announced up to 10 days after the start of these holidays for each location-year.[36] The left panel of Figure A.6 shows that there are more Dibao announcements before the start of Chinese New Year than during or after, before the start of National Day than during and after, and before the start of Qingming Festival than during or after. Based on a t-test, the difference in Dibao announcements is statistically significant at the 5% level for Chinese New Year and for National Day but not for Qingming Festival. It is 13% (9%–17%) more likely

---

33. Search terms include 城乡居民社会养老保险, 城镇居民社会养老保险, 城居保, and 城乡居保.

34. Search terms include 低保 and 最低生活保障.

35. Because the length of these holidays varies, I collect data on Old Age Insurance between January 1 and February 28 or 29 from 2013 to 2017 for Chinese New Year; between March 15 and April 15 from 2013 to 2017 for Qingming Festival; and between September 15 and October 31 for National Day.

36. This represents 347 locations for five years for Chinese New Year and Qingming, and 347 locations for four years for National Day because data collection was conducted in the middle of 2017, before National Day had occurred that year.

that announcements are made before the Chinese New Year holiday than during or after. For National Day, it is 3% (1%–5%) more likely that announcements are made before the holiday than during or after, and for Qingming festival, it is 2.5% (-2%–7%) more likely that announcements are made before the holiday than during or after.

The patterns look very different for Old Age Insurance. The right panel of Figure A.6 shows the difference in the number of Old Age Insurance announcements for all Chinese New Year holidays, for National Day, and for Qingming Festival. This figure shows the point estimate and 95% confidence intervals of the difference between the average number of online reports related to Old Age Insurance announced up to 10 days before the start of these three national holidays and the average number of online reports related to Old Age Insurance announced up to 10 days after the start of these holidays for each location-year. These results show that for Chinese New Year and Qingming Festival, more Old Age Insurance announcements are made *during and after* the holiday than before the holiday. For National Day, more announcements are made before the holiday than during or after. None of the differences in announcements are statistically significant. Based on a t-test, it is 4% (-1%–10%) more likely that Old Age Insurance announcements are made during or after the Chinese New Year holiday than before. It is 2% (-0.3%–4%) more likely that announcements are made before National Day than after, and it is 1% (-2%–4%) more likely that announcements related to Old Age Insurance are made after Qingming Festival than before. While the lack of statistical significance of the results could be due to the relatively small number of announcements, the point estimates of differences in the number of announcements made before and after these three holidays are much smaller for Old Age Insurance than for Dibao, and the point estimate is in the opposite direction (more announcements after than before) for Old Age Insurance announcements made around Chinese New Year and Qingming Festival.

References

Acemoglu, Daron, and James Robinson. 2006. *Economic Origins of Dictatorship and Democracy*. Cambridge: Cambridge University Press.

Ades, Alberto F, and Edward L. Glaeser. 1994. "Trade and circuses: explaining urban giants." Technical report National Bureau of Economic Research.

Ahmad, Ehtisham, and Athar Hussain. 1991. "Social security in China: a historical perspective." In *Social Security in Developing Countries*, ed. Ehtisham Ahmad, Jean Dreze, John Hills, and Amartya Sen. London: Clarendon Press, pp. 247–304.

Aizer, Anna, Shari Eli, Joseph Ferrie, and Adriana Lleras-Muney. 2016. "The long-run impact of cash transfers to poor families." *American Economic Review* 106(4):935–971.

Albertus, Michael, Sofia Fenner, and Dan Slater. 2018. *Coercive Distribution*. Cambridge: Cambridge University Press.

Amnesty International. 2000. "China: the crackdown on falun gong and other so-called 'heretical organizations'." https://www.refworld.org/docid/3b83b6e00.html.

Andrejevic, Mark, and Kelly Gates. 2014. "Big data surveillance: introduction." *Surveillance & Society* 12(2):185–196.

Ang, Yuen Yuen. 2016. *How China Escaped the Poverty Trap*. Ithaca: Cornell University Press.

Arnold, R. Douglas. 1990. *The Logic of Congressional Action*. New Haven: Yale University Press.

AusAID. 2011. *Targeting the Poorest: An Assessment of Proxy Means Test Methodology*. Commonwealth of Australia.

Baird, Sarah, Craig McIntosh, and Berk Özler. 2011. "Cash or condition? Evidence from a cash transfer experiment." *The Quarterly Journal of Economics* 126(4):1709–1753.

Baird, Sarah, Francisco H.G. Ferreira, Berk Özler, and Michael Woolcock. 2014. "Conditional, unconditional and everything in between: a systematic review of the effects of cash transfer programmes on schooling outcomes." *Journal of Development Effectiveness* 6(1):1–43.

Bates, Robert. 1981. *Markets and States in Tropical Africa: The Political Basis of Agricultural Policies*. Berkeley: University of California Press.

Beck, Paul Allen, Russell J. Dalton, Steven Greene, and Robert Huckfeldt. 2002. "The social calculus of voting: interpersonal, media, and organizational influences on presidential choices." *American Political Science Review* 96(1):57–73.

Béland, Daniel. 2007. "Ideas and institutional change in social security: conversion, layering, and policy drift." *Social Science Quarterly* 88(1):20–38.

Benewick, Robert, Irene Tong, and Jude Howell. 2004. "Self-governance and community: a preliminary comparison between villagers' committees and urban community councils." *China Information* 18(1):11–28.

Benney, Jonathan. 2016. "Weiwen at the grassroots: China's stability maintenance apparatus as a means of conflict resolution." *Journal of Contemporary China* 25(99):389–405.

Bialer, Seweryn. 1982. *Stalin's Successors: Leadership, Stability and Change in the Soviet Union*. Cambridge: Cambridge University Press.

Blaydes, Lisa. 2011. *Elections and Distributive Politics in Mubarak's Egypt*. Cambridge: Cambridge University Press.

Blaydes, Lisa. 2018. *State of Repression: Iraq Under Saddam Hussein*. Princeton: Princeton University Press.

Boix, Carles, and Milan Svolik. 2007. "Non-tyrannical autocracies." http://bit.ly/JGdOMe

Bond, Robert M., Christopher J. Fariss, Jason J. Jones, Adam D.I. Kramer, Cameron Marlow, Jaime E. Settle, and James H. Fowler. 2012. "A 61-million-person experiment in social influence and political mobilization." *Nature* 489(7415):295–298.

Bray, David. 2006. "Building 'community': new strategies of governance in urban China." *Economy and Society* 35(4):530–549.

Breslauer, George W. 1978. "On the adaptability of Soviet welfare-state authoritarianism." In *Soviet Society and the Communist Party*, ed. Karl W. Ryavec. Amherst: The University of Massachusetts Press, pp. 3–25.

Broadhurst, Roderic, and Peng Wang. 2014. "After the bo xilai trial: does corruption threaten China's future?" *Survival* 56(3):157–178.

Brook, Timothy. 1998. *Quelling the People: The Military Suppression of the Beijing Democracy Movement*. Stanford: Stanford University Press.

Brown, Philip, Alan de Brauw, and Du Yang. 2009. "Understanding variation in the design of China's new cooperative medical scheme." *China Quarterly* 198:304–329.

Brownlee, Jason. 2007. *Authoritarianism in an Age of Democratization*. Cambridge: Cambridge University Press.

Bruce, Gary S. 2003. "The prelude to nationwide surveillance in East Germany: Stasi operations and threat perceptions, 1945–1953." *Journal of Cold War Studies* 5(2):3–31.

Brunschwig, Henri. 1974. *Enlightenment and Romanticism in Eighteenth Century Prussia*. Chicago: University of Chicago Press.

Bueno de Mesquita, Bruce, Alastair Smith, Randolph M. Siverson, and James D. Morrow. 2004. *The Logic of Political Survival*. Cambridge: MIT Press.

Burns, John P. 1989. *The Chinese Communist Party's Nomenklatura System*. Armonk, NY: M. E. Sharpe.

Cai, Yongshun. 2002. "The resistance of Chinese laid-off workers in the reform period." *The China Quarterly* 170:327–344.

Cai, Yongshun. 2006. *State and Laid-off Workers in Reform China: The Silence and Collective Action of the Retrenched*. London: Routledge.

Cai, Yongshun. 2008. "Local government and the suppression of popular resistance in China." *The China Quarterly* 193:29–42.

Caliskan, Aylin, Joanna J. Bryson, and Arvind Narayanan. 2017. "Semantics derived automatically from language corpora contain human-like biases." *Science* 356(6334):183–186.

Calonico, Sebastian, Matias D. Cattaneo, and Rocio Titiunik. 2014. "Robust nonparametric confidence intervals for regression-discontinuity designs." *Econometrica* 82(6):2295–2326.

Cammett, Melani. 2014. *Compassionate Communalism: Welfare and Sectarianism in Lebanon*. Ithaca: Cornell University Press.

Cammett, Melani, and Lauren M. MacLean. 2014. *The Politics of Non-state Social Welfare*. Ithaca: Cornell University Press.

Cammett, Melani, and Sukriti Issar. 2010. "Bricks and mortar clientelism: sectarianism and the logics of welfare allocation in Lebanon." *World Politics* 62(3):381–421.

Campbell, Andrea Louise. 2012. "Policy makes mass politics." *Annual Review of Political Science* 15:333–351.

Carey, P. B. R. 1997. *From Burma to Myanmar: Military Rule and the Struggle for Democracy.* Research Institute for the Study of Conflict and Terrorism.

Central Propaganda Department. 2009. *Wangluo Yuqing Xinxi Gongzuo Lilun yu Shiwu [Theories and Guidance on Online Public Sentiment].* Beijing: Xuexi Press.

Chang, Maria Hsia. 2008. *Falun Gong: The End of Days.* New Haven: Yale University Press.

Chen, Baifeng. 2012. "Teding zhiye qunti shangfang de fasheng jizhi [Causes of professional petitioning]." *Shehui Kexue [Social Science]* 8:59–68.

Chen, Feng. 2000. "Subsistence crises, managerial corruption and labour protests in China." *The China Journal* (44):41–63.

Chen, Janet Y. 2012. *Guilty of Indigence: The Urban Poor in China, 1900-1953.* Princeton: Princeton University Press.

Chen, Jian, and Changhai Hu. 2013. "Qian xi xin xingshi xia zhongdian renyuan dongtai guan kong duice [Analysis of countermeasure for the dynamic control of target populations under new conditions]." *Henan Jingcha Xueyuan Xuebao [Journal of Henan Police College]* 22(4):57–60.

Chen, Jidong, Jennifer Pan, and Yiqing Xu. 2016. "Sources of authoritarian responsiveness: a field experiment in China." *American Journal of Political Science* 60(2):383–400.

Chen, Jidong, and Yiqing Xu. 2017. "Information manipulation and reform in authoritarian regimes." *Political Science Research and Methods* 5(1):163–178.

Chen, Shaohua, Martin Ravallion, and Youjuan Wang. 2006. "Di bao: a guaranteed minimum income in China's Cities?" *World Bank Policy Research Working Paper 3805.* http://bit.ly/1gLzUrl.

Chen, Xi. 2009. "Power of troublemaking: Chinese petitioners' tactics and their efficacy." *Comparative Politics* 41(4):451–471.

Chen, Ye, Hongbin Li, and Li-An Zhou. 2005. "Relative performance evaluation and the turnover of provincial leaders in China." *Economic Letters* 88(3):421–425.

Cheng, Tiejun, and Mark Selden. 1994. "The origins and social consequences of China's Hukou system." *The China Quarterly* 139:644–668.

Chestnut Greitens, Sheena. 2016. *Dictators and their Secret Police: Coercive Institutions and State Violence.* Cambridge: Cambridge University Press.

China Administrative Management Association Issue Committee. 2009. *Zhongguo Quntixing Tufa Shijian Chengyin ji Duice [Unexpected Mass Incidents in China: Causes and Countermeasures].* Beijing: Chinese Academy of Governance Press.

China Daily. 2015. "New anti-corruption app sparks instant flood of public reports." http://bit.ly/1GhcZQl (accessed Dec. 13, 2016).

Chwe, Michael Suk-Young. 2013. *Rational Ritual: Culture, Coordination, and Common Knowledge.* Princeton: Princeton University Press.

Cowgill, Donald O. 1974. "The aging of populations and societies." *The Annals of the American Academy of Political and Social Science* 415(1):1–18.

Crawford, Vincent P., and Joel Sobel. 1982. "Strategic information transmission." *Econometrica: Journal of the Econometric Society* 50(6):1431–1451.

Cyberspace Administration of China. 2017. "Hulianwang xinwen xinxi fuwu guanli guiding [internet news and information service management regulations]."

Dabla-Norris, Ms Era. 2005. *Issues in Intergovernmental Fiscal Relations in China.* International Monetary Fund.

Davenport, Christian. 2007. "State repression and political order." *Annual Review of Political Science* 10:1–23.

Davenport, Christian. 2015. *How Social Movements Die.* Cambridge: Cambridge University Press.

Davenport, Christian, Dave Armstrong, and Thomas Zeitzoff. 2019. "Acceptable or Out of Bounds? Scaling Perceptions of Challenger and Government Tactics as well as Understanding Contentious Interaction." *Workshop on Human Rights and Repression: Latin America in Comparative Perspective*. Working paper.

Davenport, Christian, and Molly Inman. 2012. "The state of state repression research since the 1990s." *Terrorism and Political Violence* 24(4):619–634.

Davis, Elizabeth Van Wie. 2008. "Uyghur muslim ethnic separatism in Xinjiang, China." *Asian Affairs: An American Review* 35(1):15–30.

Davis-Friedmann, Deborah. 1983. *Long Lives: Chinese Elderly and the Communist Revolution*. Stanford: Stanford University Press.

Dawson, Richard E, and James A. Robinson. 1963. "Inter-party competition, economic variables, and welfare policies in the American states." *The Journal of Politics* 25(2):265–289.

De La O, Ana. 2013. "Do conditional cash transfers affect electoral behavior? Evidence from a randomized experiment in Mexico." *American Journal of Political Science* 57(1):1–14.

Deng, Yanhua, and Kevin J. O'Brien. 2013. "Relational repression in China: using social ties to demobilize protesters." *The China Quarterly* 215:533–552.

Derleth, James, and Daniel R. Koldyk. 2004. "The Shequ experiment: grassroots political reform in urban China." *Journal of Contemporary China* 13(41):747–777.

Desposato, Scott. 2018. "Subjects and scholars' views on the ethics of political science field experiments." *Perspectives on Politics* 16(3):739–750.

Diamond, Larry. 2010. "Liberation technology." *Journal of Democracy* 21(3):69–83.

Dickson, Bruce J., Pierre F. Landry, Mingming Shen, and Jie Yan. 2016. "Public goods and regime support in urban China." *The China Quarterly* 228:859–880.

Dimitrov, Martin K. 2014a. "Internal government assessments of the quality of governance in China." *Studies in Comparative International Development* 50(1):50–72.

Dimitrov, Martin K. 2014b. "Tracking public opinion under authoritarianism." *Russian History* 41(3):329–353.

Dimitrov, Martin K. 2014c. "What the party wanted to know: citizen complaints as a 'barometer of public opinion' in communist bulgaria." *East European Politics & Societies* 28(2):271–295.

Distelhorst, Greg, and Yue Hou. 2017. "Constituency service under nondemocratic rule: evidence from China." *Journal of Politics* 79(3):1024–1040.

Dutton, Michael. 1992. *Policing and Punishment in China: From Patriarchy to "the People"*. Cambridge: Cambridge University Press.

Dutton, Michael. 2005. *Policing Chinese Politics: A History*. Durham: Duke University Press.

Dutton, Michael Robert, Stacy Hsiu-ju Lo, and Dong Dong Wu. 2008. *Beijing Time*. Cambridge: Harvard University Press.

Earl, Jennifer. 2003. "Tanks, tear gas, and taxes: toward a theory of movement repression." *Sociological Theory* 21(1):44–68.

Earl, Jennifer, and Katrina Kimport. 2011. *Digitally Enabled Social Change: Activism in the Internet Age*. Cambridge: MIT Press.

Earl, Jennifer, and Sarah A. Soule. 2010. "The impacts of repression: The effect of police presence and action on subsequent protest rates." *Research in Social Movements, Conflicts and Change*. 30:75–113.

Economist. 2017. "Chinese officials use hotlines to take the public's pulse." http://whr.tn/1imqqlx (accessed August 30, 2017).

Edgerton-Tarpley, Kathryn. 2008. *Tears from Iron: Cultural Responses to Famine in Nineteenth-Century China*. Berkeley: University of California Press.

Edin, Maria. 2003. "State capacity and local agent control in China: CPP cadre management from a township perspective." *China Quarterly* 173:35–52.

Edmond, Chris. 2013. "Information manipulation, coordination, and regime change." *The Review of Economic Studies* 80:1422–1458.

Egorov, Georgy, and Konstantin Sonin. 2011. "Dictators and their viziers: endogenizing the loyalty–competence trade-off." *Journal of the European Economic Association* 9(5):903–930.

Egorov, Georgy, Sergei Guriev, and Konstantin Sonin. 2009. "Why resource-poor dictators allow freer media: a theory and evidence from panel data." *American Political Science Review* 103(4):645–668.

Estevez-Abe, Margarita, Torben Iversen, and David Soskice. 1999. Social Protection and the Formation of Skills: A Reinterpretation of the Welfare State. *American Political Science Association Annual Meeting*. Atlanta, GA.

Ferdinand, Peter. 2000. "The internet, democracy and democratization." *Democratization* 7(1):1–17.

Fewsmith, Joseph. 2012. "Social management as a way of coping with heightened social tensions." *China Leadership Monitor* 36(6).

Fijnaut, Cyrille J. C. F., and Gary Trade Marx. 1995. *Undercover: Police Surveillance in Comparative Perspective*. New York: Springer.

Florini, Ann M., Hairong Lai, and Yeling Tan. 2012. *China Experiments: From Local Innovations to National Reform*. Washington DC.: Brookings Institution Press.

Forrat, Natalia. 2012. "The authoritarian welfare state: a marginalized concept." *Comparative Historical Social Science Working Paper Series* No. 12-005.

Frantz, Erica, and Andrea Kendall-Taylor. 2014. "A dictator's toolkit: understanding how co-optation affects repression in autocracies." *Journal of Peace Research* 51(3):332–346.

Frazier, Mark. 2002. *The Making of the Chinese Industrial Workplace*. Cambridge: Cambridge University Press.

Frazier, Mark. 2004. "After pension reform: navigating the 'third rail' in China." *Studies in Comparative International Development* 39(2):45–70.

Frazier, Mark. 2010. *Socialist Insecurity: Pensions and the Politics of Uneven Development in China*. Ithaca: Cornell University Press.

Freeman, Will. 2010. "The accuracy of China's 'mass incidents'." *Financial Times* March 1.

Fu, Diana. 2017. "Disguised collective action in China." *Comparative Political Studies* 50(4):499–527.

Fu, Hualing. 2005. "Re-education through labour in historical perspective." *The China Quarterly* 184:811–830.

Fukuyama, Francis. 2014. *Political Order and Political Decay : From the Industrial Revolution to the Globalisation of Democracy*. New York: Farrar, Straus and Giroux.

Gallagher, Mary E. 2017. *Authoritarian Legality in China: Law, Workers, and the State*. Cambridge: Cambridge University Press.

Gandhi, Jennifer. 2008. "Dictatorial institutions and their impact on economic growth." *European Journal of Sociology* 49:3–30.

Gandhi, Jennifer. 2009. *Political Institutions under Dictatorship*. New York: Cambridge University Press.

Gandhi, Jennifer, and Adam Przeworski. 2006. "Cooperation, cooptation, and rebellion under dictatorships." *Economics and Politics* 18(1):1–26.

Gandhi, Jennifer, and Adam Przeworski. 2007. "Authoritarian institutions and the survival of autocrats." *Comparative Political Studies* 40(11):1279–1301.

Gao, Jie. 2016. "'Bypass the lying mouths': how does the CCP tackle information distortion at local levels?" *The China Quarterly* 228:950–969.

Gao, Qin. 2017. *Welfare, Work, and Poverty: Social Assistance in China*. New York: Oxford University Press.

Gao, Qin, and Carl Riskin. 2009. Market versus social benefits: Explaining China's changing income inequality. In *Creating Wealth and Poverty in Postsocialist China*, ed. Deborah Davis, and Feng Wang. Stanford: Stanford University Press, pp. 20–36.

Gerschewski, Johannes. 2013. "The three pillars of stability: legitimation, repression, and co-optation in autocratic regimes." *Democratization* 20(1):13–38.

Goldstein, Melvyn C. 1997. *The Snow Lion and the Dragon: China, Tibet, and the Dalai Lama*. Berkeley: University of California Press.

Goldstone, Jack A., and Charles Tilly. 2001. "Threat (and opportunity): popular action and state response in the dynamics of contentious action." In *Silence and Voice in the Study of Contentious Politics* eds. Ronald R. Aminzade, Jack A. Goldstone, Doug McAdam, Elizabeth J. Perry, William H. Sewell, Sidney Tarrow, and Charles Tilly. Cambridge: Cambridge University Press, pp. 179–94.

Gordon, Colin. 1994. *New Deals: Business, Labor, and Politics in America, 1920-1935*. Cambridge: Cambridge University Press.

Greenhalgh, Susan, and Edwin A. Winckler. 2005. *Governing China's Population: From Leninist to Neoliberal Biopolitics*. Stanford: Stanford University Press.

Gunitsky, Seva. 2015. "Corrupting the cyber-commons: social media as a tool of autocratic stability." *Perspectives on Politics* 13(01):42–54.

Gustafsson, Bjorn A., Li Shi, and Terry Sicular, eds. 2008. *Inequality and Public Policy in China*. Cambridge: Cambridge University Press.

Haber, Stephen. 2007. "Authoritarian government." In *Oxford Handbook of Political Economy*, eds. Barry Weingast, and Donald Wittman. New York: Oxford University Press, pp. 693–707.

Hacker, Jacob S. 2004. "Privatizing risk without privatizing the welfare state: the hidden politics of social policy retrenchment in the United States." *American Political Science Review* 98(2):243–260.

Hacker, Jacob S., and Paul Pierson. 2002. "Business power and social policy: employers and the formation of the American welfare state." *Politics & Society* 30(2):277–325.

Hacker, Jacob S., Paul Pierson, and Kathleen Thelen. 2015. "Drift and conversion: hidden faces of institutional change." In *Advances in Comparative-Historical Analysis*, eds. James Mahoney and Kathleen Thelen. Cambridge: Cambridge University Press, pp. 180–208.

Hall, Peter A. 1993. "Policy paradigms, social learning, and the state: the case of economic policymaking in Britain." *Comparative Politics* 25(3):275–296.

Han, Keqing. 2012. *Zhongguo Chengshi Dibao Fangtanlu [Interviews with Urban Dibao Recipients in China]*. Jinan: Shandong Renmin Press.

Han, Keqing. 2014. *Research on the Urban Minimum Livelihood Guarantee Scheme [Chengshi Zuidi Shenghuo Baozhang Zhidu Yanjiu]*. Beijing: China Social Science Press.

Han, Keqing, and Guo Yu. 2012. "'Welfare dependency': does it exist? ['Fuli yilai': shifou cunzai?]." *Shehui Xue Yanjiu [Sociology Research]* 2:149–167.

Harris, Kevan. 2017. *A Social Revolution: Politics and the Welfare State in Iran*. Berkeley: University of California Press.

Haushofer, Johannes, and Jeremy Shapiro. 2016. "The short-term impact of unconditional cash transfers to the poor: experimental evidence from Kenya." *The Quarterly Journal of Economics* 131(4):1973–2042.

Hauslohner, Peter. 1987. "Gorbachev's social contract." *Soviet Economy* 3(1):54–89.

He, Baogang, and Mark Warren. 2011. "Authoritarian deliberation: the deliberative turn in Chinese political development." *Perspectives on Politics* 9(2):269–289.

He, Baogang, and Stig Thogersen. 2011. "Giving the people a voice? experiments with consultative authoritarian institutions in China." *Journal of Contemporary China* 19(66):675–692.

Heberer, Thomas, and Christian Göbel. 2011. *The Politics of Community Building in Urban China*. London: Routledge.

Heilmann, Sebastian, and Sarah Kirchberger. 2000. "The Chinese nomenklatura in transition." *Leadership* 15:24–917.

Helmke, Gretchen, and Steven Levitsky. 2004. "Informal institutions and comparative politics: a research agenda." *Perspectives on Politics* 2(4):725–740.

Heurlin, Christopher. 2016. *Responsive Authoritarianism in China*. Cambridge: Cambridge University Press.

Ho, Peter. 2001. "Greening without conflict? Environmentalism, NGOs and civil society in China." *Development and Change* 32(5):893–921.

Hobsbawm, Eric. 1973. *Revolutionaries: Contemporary Essays*. New York: Pantheon Books.

Hong, Dayong. 2004. *Zhuanxing Shiqi Zhongguo Shehui Jiuzhu Zhidu [China's Social Assistance System during the Transition Period]*. Liaoning Jiaoyu Press.

Hou, Yue. 2019. *The Private Sector in Public Office*. Cambridge: Cambridge University Press.

Howard, Marc Morjé, and Philip G. Roessler. 2006. "Liberalizing electoral outcomes in competitive authoritarian regimes." *American Journal of Political Science* 50(2):365–381.

Howard, Philip N., Aiden Duffy, Deen Freelon, Muzammil M. Hussain, Will Mari, and Marwa Mazaid. 2011. "Opening closed regimes: what was the role of social media during the arab spring?". Project on Information Technology & Political Islam, Working Paper 2011.1.

Hsiao, William. 1995. "The Chinese health care system: lessons for other nations." *Social Science and Medicine* 41(8):1047–1055.

Huang, Xian. 2014. "Expansion of Chinese social health insurance: who gets what, when and how?" *Journal of Contemporary China* 23(89):923–951.

Huang, Xian. 2015. "Four worlds of welfare: understanding subnational variation in Chinese social health insurance." *The China Quarterly* 222:449–474.

Huang, Xian, and Qin Gao. 2018. "Does social insurance enrollment improve citizen assessment of local government performance? evidence from China." *Social Science Research* 70:28–40.

Huang, Xian, and Qin Gao. 2019. "Alleviating poverty or discontent: The impact of social assistance on Chinese citizens' views of government." *China: An International Journal* 17(1):76–95.

Huang, Yasheng. 1996. "Central-local relations in China during the reform era: the economic and institutional dimensions." *World Development* 24(4):655–672.

Huisman, Mark. 2014. "Imputation of missing network data: some simple procedures." In *Encyclopedia of Social Network Analysis and Mining*, eds. Reda Alhajj and Jon Rokne. New York: Springer, pp. 707–715.

Hulme, David, Joseph Hanlon, and Armando Barrientos. 2012. *Just Give Money to the Poor: The Development Revolution from the Global South*. West Hartford: Kumarian Press.

Human Rights Watch. 2009. "An alleyway in hell: China's abusive "black jails." https://www.hrw.org/report/2009/11/12/alleyway-hell/chinas-abusive-black-jails.

Huntington, Samuel. 1968. *Political Order in Changing Societies*. New Haven: Yale University Press.

Hurst, William. 2004. "Understanding contentious collective action by Chinese laid-off workers: the importance of regional political economy." *Studies in Comparative International Development* 39(2):94–120.

Hurst, William. 2009. *The Chinese Worker after Socialism*. Cambridge: Cambridge University Press.

Hurst, William, and Kevin J. O'Brien. 2002. "China's contentious pensioners." *China Quarterly* 170:345–360.

Irons, Edward A. 2018. "The list: the evolution of China's list of illegal and evil cults." https://cesnur.net/wp-content/uploads/2018/02/tjoc_2_1_3_irons.pdf.

Isaac, Larry, and William R. Kelly. 1981. "Racial insurgency, the state, and welfare expansion: local and national level evidence from the postwar United States." *American Journal of Sociology* 86(6):1348–1386.

Jacobs, Jane. 1961. *The Death and Life of Great American Cities*. New York: Random House.

Jaros, Kyle, and Jennifer Pan. 2018. "China's newsmakers: how media power is shifting in the Xi Jinping era." *The China Quarterly* 233:111–136.

Jennings, Edward T. 1979. "Competition, constituencies, and welfare policies in American states." *American Political Science Review* 73(2):414–429.

Jiang, Junyan, and Dali L. Yang. 2016. "Lying or believing? measuring preference falsification from a political purge in China." *Comparative Political Studies* 49(5):600–634.

Johnson, Ian. 2016. "The Presence of the Past: A Coda." In *The Oxford Illustrated History of Modern China*, ed. Jeffrey N. Wasserstrom. Oxford: Oxford University Press, pp. 301–324.

Kalathil, Shanthi, and Taylor C. Boas. 2010. *Open Networks, Closed Regimes: The Impact of the Internet on Authoritarian Rule*. New York: Carnegie Endowment.

Katznelson, Ira. 1981. *City Trenches: Urban Politics and the Patterning of Class in the United States*. Chicago: University of Chicago Press.

Keohane, Robert O. 1988. "International institutions: two approaches." *International Studies Quarterly* 32(4):379–396.

Keohane, Robert O., and Joseph S. Nye. 1974. "Transgovernmental relations and international organizations." *World Politics* 27(1):39–62.

Kernen, Antoine, and Jean-Louis Rocca. 2000. "Social responses to unemployment and the "new urban poor": case study in Shenyang City and Liaoning Province." *China Perspectives* (27):35–51.

Khan, Azizur Rahman, and Carl Riskin. 2001. *Inequality and Poverty in China in the Age of Globalization*. Oxford: Oxford University Press.

Khawaja, Marwan. 1993. "Repression and popular collective action: evidence from the west bank." *Sociological Forum* 8(1):47–71.

Kim, Myunghwan, and Jure Leskovec. 2011. The network completion problem: inferring missing nodes and edges in networks. In *Proceedings of the 2011 SIAM International Conference on Data Mining*. Mesa: SIAM pp. 47–58.

King, Gary, Jennifer Pan, and Margaret E. Roberts. 2013. "How censorship in China allows government criticism but silences collective expression." *American Political Science Review* 107(2):1–18.

King, Gary, Jennifer Pan, and Margaret E. Roberts. 2014. "Reverse-engineering censorship in China: randomized experimentation and participant observation." *Science* 345(6199):1–10.

King, Gary, Jennifer Pan, and Margaret E. Roberts. 2017. "How the Chinese government fabricates social media posts for strategic distraction, not engaged argument." *American Political Science Review* 111(3):484–501.

Kish, Leslie. 1965. *Survey Sampling*. New York: John Wiley and Sons.

Kojima, Kazuko, and Ryosei Kokubun. 2005. "The 'shequ construction' programme and the Chinese Communist Party." *The Copenhagen Journal of Asian Studies* 16:86–105.

Koselleck, Reinhart. 1969. "Historical criteria of the modern concept of revolution." In R. Koselleck, *Futures Past: On the Semantics of Historical Time*. New York: Columbia University Press, pp. 43–71.

Koss, Daniel. 2015. *Where the Party Rules: The Rank and File of China's Communist State*. New York: Cambridge University Press.

Krasner, Stephen D. 1988. "Sovereignty: an institutional perspective." *Comparative Political Studies* 21(1):66–94.

Kuran, Timur. 1991. "Now out of never: the element of surprise in the East European revolution of 1989." *World Politics* 44(1):7–48.

Kuran, Timur. 1997. *Private Truths, Public Lies: The Social Consequences of Preference Falsification*. Cambridge: Harvard University Press.

Kurzman, Charles. 1996. "Structural opportunity and perceived opportunity in social-movement theory: the Iranian revolution of 1979." *American Sociological Review* 61(1):153–170.

Lampton, David M. 2014. *Following the Leader: Ruling China, from Deng Xiaoping to Xi Jinping*. Berkeley: University of California Press.

Landry, Pierre F., and Mingming Shen. 2005. "Reaching migrants in survey research: the use of the global positioning system to reduce coverage bias in China." *Political Analysis* 13(1):1–22.

Lee, Ching Kwan. 1998. "The labor politics of market socialism: collective inaction and class experiences among state workers in Guangzhou." *Modern China* 24(1):3–33.

Lee, Ching Kwan, and Yonghong Zhang. 2013. "The power of instability: unraveling the microfoundations of bargained authoritarianism in China." *American Journal of Sociology* 118(6):1475–1508.

Lee, Ching Kwan, and Yuan Shen. 2014. "Seeing like the grassroots state: using market and mass line for stability maintenance in China's bargained authoritarianism." In *To Govern China: Evolving Practices of Power*, eds. Vivienne Shue and Patricia M. Thornton. Oxford: Oxford University Press, pp. 177–201.

Lee, Kai-Fu. 2018. *AI Superpowers: China, Silicon Valley, and the New World Order*. New York: Houghton Mifflin Harcourt.

Lee, Peter Nan-Shong, and Chack-Kie Wong. 2001. "The tale of two Chinese cities: rolling back the boundary of the welfare state during the reform era." In *Remaking China's Public Management*, eds. Peter Nan-Shong Lee, and Carlos Wing-Hung Lo. Westport: Quorum Books, pp. 67–96.

Li, Hongbin, and Li-An Zhou. 2005. "Political turnover and economic performance: the incentive role of personnel control in China." *Journal of Public Economics* 89(9):1743–1762.

Li, Lianjiang. 2004. "Political trust in rural China." *Modern China* 30(2):228–258.

Li, Lianjiang. 2010. "Rights consciousness and rules consciousness in contemporary China." *The China Journal* (64):47–68.

Li, Lianjiang, and Kevin J. O'Brien. 2008. "Protest leadership in rural China." *The China Quarterly* 193:1–23.

Li, Lillian. 2007. *Fighting Famine in North China: State, Market, and Enviornmental Decline 1690–1990s*. Stanford: Stanford University Press.

Liang, Fan, Vishnupriya Das, Nadiya Kostyuk, and Muzammil M. Hussain. 2018. "Constructing a data-driven society: China's social credit system as a state surveillance infrastructure." *Policy & Internet* 10(4):415–453.

Lichbach, Mark Irving. 1989. "An evaluation of 'does economic inequality breed political conflict?' studies." *World Politics* 41(4):431–470.

Lifton, Robert Jay. 2012. *Thought Reform and The Psychology of Totalism: A Study of 'Brainwashing' in China*. Chapel Hill: The University of North Carolina Press.

Lin, Wanchuan, Gordon Liu, and Gang Chen. 2009. "The urban resident basic medica insurance: a landmark reform towards universal coverage in China." *Health Economics* 18:S83–96.

Lin, Winston. 2013. "agnostic notes on regression adjustments to experimental data: reexamining freedman's critique." *The Annals of Applied Statistics* 7(1):295–318.

Liu, Mingxing, Juan Wang, Ran Tao, and Rachel Murphy. 2009. "The political economy of earmarked transfers in a state-designated poor county in western China: central policies and local responses." *The China Quarterly* 200:973–994.

Lorentzen, Peter. 2013. "Regularizing rioting: permitting protest in an authoritarian regime." *Quarterly Journal of Political Science* 8(2):127–158.

Los, Maria. 2004. "The technologies of total domination." *Surveillance & Society* 2(1):15–38.

Lust-Okar, Ellen. 2006. "Elections under authoritarianism: preliminary lessons from jordan." *Democratization* 13(3):456–471.

Lyon, David. 2006. *Theorizing Surveillance.* New York: Routledge.

Lyon, David. 2016. Big data surveillance: Snowden, everyday practices and digital futures. In *International Political Sociology*, eds. Tugba Basarn, Didier Bigo, Emmanuel-Pierre Guittet, R. B. J. Walker. New York: Routledge, pp. 268–285.

MacKinnon, Rebecca. 2012. *Consent of the Networked: The Worldwide Struggle For Internet Freedom.* New York: Basic Books.

Magaloni, Beatriz. 2008. "Credible power-sharing and the longevity of authoritarian rule." *Comparative Political Studies* 41(4/5):715–741.

Magaloni, Beatriz, and Ruth Kricheli. 2010. "Political order and one-party rule." *Annual Review of Political Science* 13:123–143.

Mahoney, James. 2000. "Path dependence in historical sociology." *Theory and Society* 29(4):507–548.

Malesky, Edmond J., and Paul Schuler. 2012. "Nodding or needling: analyzing delegate responsiveness in an authoritarian parliament." *American Political Science Review* 104(3):482–502.

Malesky, Edmund, Regina Abrami, and Yu Zheng. 2011. "Accountability and inequality in single-party regimes: a comparative analysis of vietnam and China." *Comparative Politics* 43(4):401–421.

Malloy, James. 1979. *The Politics of Social Security in Brazil.* Pittsburgh: University of Pittsburgh Press.

Manion, Melanie. 1985. "The cadre management system, post-Mao: the appointment, promotion, transfer and removal of party and state leaders." *The China Quarterly* 102:203–233.

Manion, Melanie. 2006. "Democracy, community, trust: the impact of elections in rural China." *Comparative Political Studies* 39(3):301–324.

Manion, Melanie. 2009. *Corruption by Design: Building Clean Government in Mainland China and Hong Kong.* Cambridge: Harvard University Press.

Manion, Melanie. 2016. *Information for Autocrats: Representation in Chinese Local Congresses.* Cambridge: Cambridge University Press.

Mares, Isabela. 2003. *The Politics of Social Risk: Business and Welfare State Development.* Cambridge: Cambridge University Press.

Mares, Isabela, and Matthew Carnes. 2009. "Social policy in developing countries." *Annual Review of Political Science* 12:93–113.

Martin, Cathie Jo, and Duane Swank. 2012. *The Political Construction of Business Interests: Coordination, Growth, and Equality.* Cambridge: Cambridge University Press.

Maskin, Eric, Yingyi Qian, and Chenggang Xu. 2000. "Incentives, information, and organizational form." *Review of Economic Studies* 67(2):359–78.

McAdam, Doug, Sidney Tarrow, and Charles Tilly. 2003. "Dynamics of contention." *Social Movement Studies* 2(1):99–102.

McClurg, Scott D. 2003. "Social networks and political participation: the role of social interaction in explaining political participation." *Political Research Quarterly* 56(4):449–464.

McMillan, John, and Pablo Zoido. 2004. "How to subvert democracy: montesinos in peru." *Journal of Economic Perspectives* 18(4):69–92.

Meissner, Mirjam, and Jost Wübbeke. 2016. "IT-backed authoritarianism: information technology enhances central authority and control capacity under Xi Jinping." In *China's*

Core Executive: Leadership Style, Structure, and Process under Xi Jinping, eds. Sebastian Heilmann and Matthias Stepan. Merics Papers on China, pp. 52–57.

Meng, Tianguang, Jennifer Pan, and Ping Yang. 2017. "Conditional receptivity to citizen participation: evidence from a survey experiment in China." *Comparative Political Studies*, 50(4):399–433.

Mettler, Suzanne. 2011. *The Submerged State: How Invisible Government Policies Undermine American Democracy*. Chicago: University of Chicago Press.

Miller, Blake. 2017. "The limits of commercialized censorship in China." Working Paper.

Milligan, Kevin, and Mark Stabile. 2011. "Do child tax benefits affect the well-being of children? Evidence from Canadian child benefit expansions." *American Economic Journal: Economic Policy* 3(3):175–205.

Min, Wu, and Liu Chong. 2018. "Caizheng fen quan yu chengxiang jumin dibao zhichu [Fiscal decentralization and the expenditure of the urban and rural minimum living standard guarantee program]." *Jingji Kexue [Economic Science]* 5:17–29.

Ministry of Public Security. 2011. *National Sub-county Population Statistics 2010*. Beijing: Qunzhong Publishing House.

Moore, Will H. 1998. "Repression and dissent: substitution, context, and timing." *American Journal of Political Science* 42(3):851–873.

Morozov, Evgeny. 2012. *The Net Delusion: The Dark Side of Internet Freedom*. New York: Public Affairs.

Nathan, Andrew. 2003. "Authoritarian resilience." *Journal of Democracy* 14(1):6–17.

National Grassroots Party Work Key Textbook. 2013. *Zuixin Dang de Xuanchuan Gongzuo Caozuo Fangfa yu Chuangxin Shiwu [Latest Guidelines and Procedures on How to Perform Propaganda Work]*. Beijing: Hongqi Press.

Noakes, Stephen, and Caylan Ford. 2015. "Managing political opposition groups in China: explaining the continuing anti-Falun Gong campaign." *The China Quarterly* 223:658–679.

Noesselt, Nele. 2014. "Microblogs and the adaptation of the Chinese party-state's governance strategy." *Governance* 27(3):449–468.

North, Douglass C., William Summerhill, and Barry Weingast. 2000. "Order, disorder and economic change: latin america vs. north america." In *Governing for Prosperity*, eds. Bruce Bueno de Mesquita and Hilton L. Root. New Haven: Yale University Press, pp. 17–58.

Nozick, Robert. 1969. "Coercion." In *Philosophy, Science, and Method: Essays in Honor of Ernest Nagel*, eds. Sidney Morgenbesser, Patrick Suppes, and Morton White. New York: St. Martin's Press, pp. 440–472.

Oberschall, Anthony. 1973. *Social Conflict and Social Movements*. Upper Saddle River: Prentice Hall.

O'Brien, Kevin. 2008. *Popular Protest in China*. Cambridge: Harvard University Press.

O'Brien, Kevin J. 1996. "Rightful resistance." *World Politics* 49(1):31–55.

O'Brien, Kevin J. 2001. "Villagers, elections, and citizenship in contemporary China." *Modern China* 27(4):407–435.

O'Brien, Kevin J., and Lianjiang Li. 2000. "Accommodating 'democracy' in a one-party state: introducing village elections in China." *The China Quarterly* 162:465–489.

O'Brien, Kevin J., and Lianjiang Li. 2006. *Rightful Resistance in Rural China*. Cambridge: Cambridge University Press.

O'Brien, Kevin, and Lianjiang Li. 1999. "Selective policy implementation in rural China." *Comparative Politics* 31(2):167–86.

O'Brien, Kevin, and Rachel Stern. 2007. "Studying contention in contemporary China." In *Popular Protest in China*, ed. Kevin J. O'Brien. Cambridge: Harvard University Press, pp. 11–25.

OECD. 2013. *OECD e-Government Studies: Egypt 2013*. Paris: OECD Publishing.

Offe, Claus. 1984. *Contradictions of the Welfare State*. Cambridge: MIT Press.

Oi, Jean C. 1999. *Rural China Takes Off: Institutional Foundations of Economic Reform*. Berkeley: University of California Press.

Oi, Jean C., Kim Singer Babiarz, Linxiu Zhang, Renfu Luo, and Scott Rozelle. 2012. "Shifting fiscal control to limit cadre power in China's townships and villages." *The China Quarterly* 211:649–675.

Olivier, Johan L. 1991. "State repression and collective action in South Africa, 1970–84." *South African Journal of Sociology* 22(4):109–117.

Ong, Lynette H. 2015. "'Thugs-for-hire': state coercion and everyday repression in China." In *Workshop on Collective Protest and State Governance in China's Xi Jinping Era*, Cambridge: Harvard-Yenching Institute. Vol. 18, pp. 67–89.

Opp, Karl-Dieter, and Christiane Gern. 1993. "Dissident groups, personal networks, and spontaneous cooperation: the East German revolution of 1989." *American Sociological Review* 58(5):659–680.

Pan, Jennifer. 2020. "Experiments on political activity governments want to keep hidden." In *Advances in Experimental Political Science*, eds. Jamie Druckman and Donald P. Green. New York: Cambridge University Press. Forthcoming.

Pan, Jennifer. 2019. "How Chinese officials use the internet to construct their public image." *Political Science Research and Methods* 7(2):197–213.

Pan, Jennifer, and Alexandra A. Siegel. 2020. "How Saudi crackdowns fail to silence online dissent." *American Political Science Review* 114:109–125.

Pan, Jennifer, and Kaiping Chen. 2018. "Concealing corruption: how Chinese officials distort upward reporting of online grievances." *American Political Science Review* 112(3):602–620.

Parish, William L., and Martin King Whyte. 1978. *Village and Family in Contemporary China*. Chicago: University of Chicago Press.

Park, Albert, Scott Rozelle, Christine Wong, and Changqing Ren. 1996. "Distributional consequences of reforming local public finance in China." *The China Quarterly* 147:751–778.

Perry, Elizabeth. 2002a. *Challenging the Mandate of Heaven: Social Protest and State Power in China*. Armonk: M. E. Sharpe.

Perry, Elizabeth. 2002b. "Moving the masses: emotion work in the Chinese revolution." *Mobilization: An International Quarterly* 7(2):111–128.

Perry, Elizabeth. 2007. "Studying Chinese politics: farewell to revolution?" *The China Journal* 57:1–22.

Perry, Elizabeth. 2008. "Permanent revolution? continuities and discontinuities in Chinese protest." In *Popular Protest in China*, ed. Kevin O'Brien. Cambridge: Harvard University Press, pp. 205–216.

Perry, Elizabeth. 2017. "Cultural governance in contemporary China: 'Re-Orienting' party propaganda." In *To Govern China: Evolving Practices of Power*, eds. Vivienne Shue, and Patricia Thornton. Cambridge: Cambridge University Press, pp. 29–55.

Perry, Elizabeth. 2009. "A new rights consciousness?" *Journal of Democracy* 20(3):17–20.

Persson, Torsten, and Guido Tabellini. 2006. "Democracy and development: the devil in the details." *American Economic Review* 96:319–324.

Peter, Woelert. 2015. "Political rationality vs. technical rationality in China's target-based performance measurement system: the case of social stability maintenance." *Policy and Society* 34(1):37–48.

Petition. 2009. Film.

Pierson, Paul. 1993. "When effect becomes cause: policy feedback and political change." *World Politics* 45(4):595–628.

Pierson, Paul. 1994. *Dismantling the Welfare State?: Reagan, Thatcher and the Politics of Retrenchment*. Cambridge: Cambridge University Press.

Pierson, Paul. 2000. "Three worlds of welfare state research." *Comparative Political Studies* 33(6/7):791–821.

Piketty, Thomas, Li Yang, and Gabriel Zucman. 2017. "Capital accumulation, private property and rising inequality in China, 1978-2015." Washington D.C.: Technical report National Bureau of Economic Research, Working Paper No. 23368.

Piven, Frances, and Richard Cloward. 1971. *Regulating the Poor.* New York: Vintage Press.

Qian, Wang, Mohammed Abdur Razzaque, and Ah Keng Kau. 2007. "Chinese cultural values and gift-giving behavior." *Journal of Consumer Marketing* 24(4):214–228.

Qian, Yingyi, and Chenggang Xu. 1993. "Why China's economic reforms differ: the M-form hierarchy and entry/expansion of the non-state sector." *The Economics of Transition* 1(2):135–170.

Qiang, Xiao. 2011. "The battle for the Chinese internet." *Journal of Democracy* 22(2):47–61.

Qin, Bei, David Stromberg, and Yanhui Wu. 2016. "Why does China allow freer social media? protests versus surveillance and propaganda." *Journal of Economic Perspectives* 31(1):117–140.

Qin, Bei, David Strömberg, and Yanhui Wu. 2018. "Media bias in China." *American Economic Review* 108(9):2442–2476.

Rasler, Karen. 1996. "Concessions, repression, and political protest in the iranian revolution." *American Sociological Review* 61(1):132–152.

Read, Benjamin. 2012. *Roots of the State: Neighborhood Organization and Social Networks in Beijing and Taipei.* Stanford: Stanford University Press.

Repnikova, Maria. 2017. *Media Politics in China: Improvising Power Under Authoritarianism.* Cambridge: Cambridge University Press.

Roberts, Margaret E. 2018. *Censored: Distraction and Diversion Inside China's Great Firewall.* Princeton: Princeton University Press.

Rodan, Garry, and Kanishka Jayasuriya. 2007. "The technocratic politics of administrative participation: case studies of Singapore and Vietnam." *Democratization* 14(5):795–815.

Sabokrou, Mohammad, Mohsen Fayyaz, Mahmood Fathy, Zahra Moayed, and Reinhard Klette. 2018. "Deep-anomaly: fully convolutional neural network for fast anomaly detection in crowded scenes." *Computer Vision and Image Understanding* 172:88–97.

Schickler, Eric. 2001. *Disjointed Pluralism: Institutional innovation and the Development of the US Congress.* Princeton: Princeton University Press.

Schneider, Anne, and Helen Ingram. 1993. "Social construction of target populations: implications for politics and policy." *American Political Science Review* 87(2):334–347.

Schneier, Bruce. 2015. *Data and Goliath: The Hidden Battles to Collect Your Data and Control Your World.* New York: WW Norton.

Schoenhals, Michael. 2013. *Spying for the People: Mao's Secret Agents, 1949–1967.* Cambridge: Cambridge University Press.

Scullard, Howard Hayes. 2010. *From the Gracchi to Nero: A History of Rome 133 BC to AD 68.* New York: Routledge.

Selznick, Philip. 1949. *TVA and the Grass Roots: A Study in the Sociology of Formal Organization.* Berkeley: University of California Press.

Shadmehr, Mehdi. 2014. "Mobilization, repression, and revolution: grievances and opportunities in contentious politics." *The Journal of Politics* 76(3):621–635.

Shao, Y. N. 1988. *Health Care in China.* London: Office of Health Economics.

Shearer, David R. 2014. *Policing Stalin's Socialism: Repression and Social Order in the Soviet Union, 1924-1953.* New Haven: Yale University Press.

Shi, Tianjian. 2001. "Cultural values and political trust: a comparison of the people's republic of China and Taiwan." *Comparative Politics* 33(4):401–419.

Shirk, Susan. 1993. *The Political Logic of Economic Reform in China.* Berkeley: University of California Press.

Shirk, Susan L. 1982. *Competitive Comrades: Career Incentives and Student Strategies in China*. Berkeley: University of California Press.

Sicular, Terry, Ximing Yue, Bjorn A. Gustafsson, and Shi Li. 2010. "How large is China's rural-urban income gap?" In *Paying for Progress in China: Public Finance, Human Welfare, and Changing Patters of Inequality*, ed. Martin King Whyte. Cambridge: Harvard University Press, pp. 85–104.

Skocpol, Theda, and Edwin Amenta. 1986. "States and social policies." *Annual Review of Sociology* 12:131–157.

Slater, Dan, and Sofia Fenner. 2011. "State power and staying power: infrastructural mechanisms and authoritarian durability." *Journal of International Affairs* 65(1):15–29.

Solinger, Dorothy. 2000. "The potential for urban unrest: will the fencers stay on the piste?" In *Is China Unstable*, ed. David Shambaugh. Armonk: M.E. Sharpe, pp. 79–94.

Solinger, Dorothy. 2005. "Path dependency reexamined: Chinese welfare policy in the transition to unemployment." *Comparative Politics* 38(1):83–101.

Solinger, Dorothy. 2008. "The dibao recipients: mollified anti-emblem of urban modernization." *China Perspectives* 4:36–46.

Solinger, Dorothy. 2010. "The urban Dibao: guarantee for Minimum Livelihood Guarantee or for minimal turmoil?" In *Marginalization in Urban China: Comparative Perspectives*, eds. Fulong Wu, and Chris Webster. Houndmills, Basingstoke: Palgrave/Macmillan, pp. 253–77.

Solinger, Dorothy. 2011. "Dibaohu in distress: the meager Minimum Livelihood Guarantee system in Wuhan." In *China's Changing Welfare Mix: Local Perspectives*, eds. Beatriz Carillo, and Jane Duckett. London: Routledge, pp. 36–63.

Solinger, Dorothy J. 2012. "The new urban underclass and its consciousness: is it a class?" *Journal of Contemporary China* 21(78):1011–1028.

Solinger, Dorothy. 2014. "The state, the poor, and the Dibao: three models of the wellsprings of welfare and lessons for China." In *State-Society Relations and Governance in China*, ed. Sujian Guo. Lanham: Lexington Books, pp. 3–13.

Solinger, Dorothy J. 2017. "Manipulating China's 'minimum livelihood guarantee': political shifts in a program for the poor in the period of Xi jinping." *China Perspectives* 2017(2):47–57.

Solinger, Dorothy J., and Ting Jiang. 2016. "When Chinese central orders and promotion criteria conflict: implementation decisions on the destitute in poor versus prosperous cities." *Modern China* 42(6):571–606.

Solinger, Dorothy J., and Yiyang Hu. 2012. "Welfare, wealth and poverty in urban China: the Dibao and its differential disbursement." *The China Quarterly* 211:741–764.

Soss, Joe. 1999. "Lessons of welfare: policy design, political learning, and political action." *American Political Science Review* 93(2):363–380.

Soss, Joe. 2002. *Unwanted Claims: The Politics of Participation in the US Welfare System*. Ann Arbor: University of Michigan Press.

Standing Committee of Guangdong Provincial People's Congress. 1994. "Guangdong sheng anzhi xing mmn shifang he jiechu laodong jiaoyang renyuan de guiding" [Provisions of the people's republic of China on release from prison and release from reeducation through labor work]."

Steinert-Threlkeld, Zachary C. 2017. "Spontaneous collective action: peripheral mobilization during the Arab Spring." *American Political Science Review* 111(2):379–403.

Steinert-Threlkeld, Zachary C., Delia Mocanu, Alessandro Vespignani, and James Fowler. 2015. "Online social networks and offline protest." *EPJ Data Science* 4(1):19.

Steinmetz, George. 1993. *Regulating the Social: The Welfare State and Local Politics in Imperial Germany*. Princeton: Princeton University Press.

Stockdill, Brett C. 2003. *Activism Against AIDS: At the Intersection of Sexuality, Race, Gender, and Class.* Boulder: Lynne Rienner Publishers.

Stockmann, Daniela. 2013. *Media Commercialization and Authoritarian Rule in China.* New York: Cambridge University Press.

Stokes, Susan C. 2005. "Perverse accountability: a formal model of machine politics with evidence from Argentina." *American Political Science Review* 99(03):315–325.

Stokes, Susan C., Thad Dunning, Marcelo Nazareno, and Valeria Brusco. 2013. *Brokers, Voters, and Clientelism: the Puzzle of Distributive Politics.* Cambridge: Cambridge University Press.

Streeck, Wolfgang and Kathleen Ann Thelen. 2005. *Beyond Continuity: Institutional Change in Advanced Political Economies.* Oxford: Oxford University Press.

Sullivan, Christopher Michael, and Christian Davenport. 2017. "The rebel alliance strikes back: understanding the politics of backlash mobilization." *Mobilization* 22(1):39–56.

Svolik, Milan. 2012. *The Politics of Authoritarian Rule.* Cambridge: Cambridge University Press.

Swenson, Peter. 1991. "Bringing capital back in, or social democracy reconsidered: employer power, cross-class alliances, and centralization of industrial relations in Denmark and Sweden." *World Politics* 43(4):513–544.

Tang, Jun. 2003. "Zhongguo chengshi jumin zuidi shenghuo baozhang zhidu de tiaoyueshi fazhan." [The leap forward style of development of Chinese urban residents minimum livelihood guarantee]. In *Shehui Lanpishu: 2003 Nian Zhongguo Shehui Xingshi Fenxi Yu Yuce [Social Blue Book: 2003 Analysis and Predictions of China's Social Situation]*, eds. Xin Ru, Xueyi Lu, and Peilin Li. Beijing: Shehui Kexue Wenxian Press, pp. 243–251.

Tang, Wenfang. 2016. *Populist Authoritarianism: Chinese Political Culture and Regime Sustainability.* New York: Oxford University Press.

Tanner, Harold Miles. 1999. *Strike Hard!: Anti-Crime Campaigns and Chinese Criminal Justice, 1979-1985.* Ithaca: Cornell University Press.

Tanner, Murray Scot. 2000. "State coercion and the balance of Awe: The 1983-1986" 'stern Blows' "anti-crime campaign." *The China Journal* (44):93–125.

Teele, Dawn Langan. 2014. "Reflections on the ethics of field experiments." In *Field Experiments and Their Critics: Essays on the Uses and Abuses of Experimentation in the Social Sciences*, ed. Dawn Langan Teele. New Haven: Yale University Press, pp. 115–140.

Teets, Jessica C. 2013. "Let many civil societies bloom: the rise of consultative authoritarianism in China." *The China Quarterly* 213:19–38.

Teorell, Jan, and Axel Hadenius. 2007. "Pathways from authoritarianism." *Journal of Democracy* 18(1):143–157.

Thaler, Richard. 1985. "Mental accounting and consumer choice." *Marketing Science* 4(3):199–214.

Thelen, Kathleen. 2003. "How institutionalism evolves: insights from comparative historical analysis." In *Comparative Historical Analysis in the Social Sciences*, eds. James Mahoney, and Dietrich Rueschemeyer. Cambridge: Cambridge University Press, pp. 208–240.

Thelen, Kathleen. 2004. *How Institutions Evolve: The Political Economy of Skills in Germany, Britain, the United States, and Japan.* Cambridge: Cambridge University Press.

Thireau, Isabelle, and Hua Linshan. 2003. "The moral universe of aggrieved Chinese workers: workers' appeals to arbitration committees and letters and visits offices." *The China Journal* (50):83–103.

Tilly, Charles. 1978. *From Mobilization to Revolution.* New York: McGraw-Hill.

Tilly, Charles. 2005. *Repression, Mobilization, and Explanation.* Minneapolis: University of Minnesota Press.

Tomba, Luigi. 2014. *The Government Next Door: Neighborhood Politics in Urban China.* Ithaca: Cornell University Press.

Tong, James W. 2009. *Revenge of the Forbidden City: The Suppression of the Falungong in China, 1999-2005*. New York: Oxford University Press.

Truex, Rory. 2016. *Making Autocracy Work*. Cambridge: Cambridge University Press.

Truex, Rory. 2019. "Focal points, dissident calendars, and preemptive repression." *Journal of Conflict Resolution* 63(4):1032–1052.

Tsai, Kellee S. 2006. "Adaptive informal institutions and endogenous institutional change in China." *World Politics* 59(1):116–141.

Tsai, Lily. 2007. *Accountability Without Democracy: Solidary Groups and Public Goods Provision in Rural China*. Cambridge: Cambridge University Press.

Tufekci, Zeynep, and Christopher Wilson. 2012. "Social media and the decision to participate in political protest: observations from tahrir square." *Journal of Communication* 62(2):363–379.

Tullock, Gordon. 1987. *Autocracy*. Dordrecht: Kluwer Academic Publishers.

Tversky, Amos, and Daniel Kahneman. 1992. "Advances in prospect theory: cumulative representation of uncertainty." *Journal of Risk and Uncertainty* 5(4):297–323.

Tyler, Tom R. 1998. "Trust and democratic governance." In *Trust and Governance*, eds. Valerie Braithwaite, Margaret Levi, Karen S. Cook, and Russell Hardin. New York: Russell Sage Foundation.

Wagstaff, Adam, Winnie Yip, Magnus Lindelow, and William Hsiao. 2009. "China's health system and its reform: a review of recent studies." *Health Economics* 18:S7–S23.

Walder, Andrew G. 1988. *Communist Neo-traditionalism: Work and Authority in Chinese Industry*. Berkeley: University of California Press.

Walder, Andrew G. 1989. "The political sociology of the beijing upheaval of 1989." *Problems of Communism* 38:30–40.

Wallace, Jeremy. 2013. "Cities, redistribution, and authoritarian regime survival." *The Journal of Politics* 75(03):632–645.

Wallace, Jeremy. 2014. *Cities and Stability: Urbanization, Redistribution, and Authoritarian Resilience in China*. New York: Oxford University Press.

Wang, Fei-Ling. 2005. *Organizing Through Division and Exclusion: China's Hukou System*. Stanford: Stanford University Press.

Wang, Mingmei. 2016. "Zhongdian renkou guanli shuiping tisheng: Cong xianshi dao tupo [management promotion of monitored population: from the reality to the breakthrough]." *Guizhou Jingguan Zhiye Xueyuan Xue Bao [Journal of the Guizhou Police Officer Vocational College]* 1671-5195:119–123.

Wang, Shaoguang. 2004. "China's health system: from crisis to opportunity." *Yale-China Health Journal* 3:5–49.

Wang, Y. 2016. "A glance at people with disabilities in China." https://www.Chinasource.org/resource-library/articles/a-glance-at-people-with-disabilities-in-China.

Wang, Yuhua, and Carl Minzner. 2015. "The rise of the Chinese security state." *The China Quarterly* 222:339–359.

Wang, Zhanjun. 2018. "Zhongdian renkou dongtai guankong fuwu tixi jiangou yanjiu [study on service system construction of dynamic control of monitored population]." *Zhongguo Xingjing Xueyuan Xuebao [Journal of China's Criminal Police College]* 142(2):55–60.

Wasserstrom, Jeffrey N. 2009. "Middle-class mobilization." *Journal of Democracy* 20(3):29–32.

Way, Lucan A., and Steven Levitsky. 2006. "The dynamics of autocratic coercion after the cold war." *Communist and Post-Communist Studies* 39(3):387–410.

Wedeman, Andrew. 2004. "The intensification of corruption in China." *The China Quarterly* 180:895–921.

Weeks, Jessica. 2008. "Autocratic audience costs: regime type and signaling resolve." *International Organization* 62:354.

Weiner, Amir, and Aigi Rahi-Tamm. 2012. "Getting to know you: the Soviet surveillance system, 1939–57." *Kritika: Explorations in Russian and Eurasian History* 13(1):5–45.

Weyrauch, Walter Otto. 1985. "Gestapo informants: facts and theory of undercover operations." *Columbia Journal of Transnational Law* 24:553.

White, Gordon, and Xiaoyuan Shang. 2003. "State entrepreneurship and community welfare services in urban China." In *Asian Politics in Development: Essays in Honour of Gordon White*, eds. Robert Benewick, Marc Blecher, and Sarah Cook. London: Routledge, pp. 171–193.

Whitfield, Gregory. 2019. "Toward a separate ethics of political field experiments." *Political Research Quarterly* 72(3):527–538.

Whiting, Susan H. 2004. "The cadre evaluation system at the grass roots: the paradox of party rule." In *Holding China Together: Diversity and National Integration in the post-Deng Era*, eds. Dali Yang, and Barry Naughton. Cambridge: Cambridge University Press, pp. 101–119.

Whiting, Susan H. 2006. *Power and Wealth in Rural China: The Political Economy of Institutional Change CC*. Cambridge: Cambridge University Press.

Whyte, Martin, and William Parish. 1984. *Urban Life in Contemporary China*. Chicago: University of Chicago Press.

Will, Pierre-Etienne. 1990. *Bureaucracy and Famine in 18th Century China*. Stanford: Stanford University Press.

Wintrobe, Ronald. 1998. *The Political Economy of Dictatorship*. Cambridge: Cambridge University Press.

Wong, Christine P. W. 1997. *Financing Local Government in the People's Republic of China*. Oxford: Oxford University Press.

Wong, Edward. 2012. "China's Growth Slows, and its political model shows limits." *The New York Times* May 10.

Wong, Linda. 1998. *Marginalization and Social Welfare in China*. London: Routledge.

Wong, Linda, and Bernard Poon. 2005. "From serving neighbors to recontrolling urban society: the transformation of China's community policy." *China Information* 19(3):413–442.

World Bank. 1996. "Poverty reduction and the world bank: progress and challenges in the 1990s." Washington, DC: World Bank.

Wright, Joseph. 2008. "Do authoritarian institutions constrain? how legislatures affect economic growth and investment." *American Journal of Political Science* 52(2):322–343.

Wrong, Dennis. 1988. *Power: Its Forms, Bases and Uses*. Chicago: The University of Chicago Press.

Xinhua. 2012. "China's craze for online anti-corruption." http://bit.ly/2blgIYz.

Xu, Chenggang. 2011. "The fundamental institutions of China's reforms and development." *Journal of Economic Literature* 49(4):1076–1151.

Xu, Kai, and Weiao Li. 2011. "The machinery of stability preservation." *Caijing*, June 6.

Yang, Dali L. 1998. *Calamity and Reform in China: State, Rural Society, and Institutional Change Since the Great Leap Famine*. Stanford: Stanford University Press.

Yang, Dali L. 2017. "China's troubled quest for order: leadership, organization and the contradictions of the stability maintenance regime." *Journal of Contemporary China* 26(103):35–53.

Yang, Guobin. 2009. *The Power of the Internet in China*. New York: Columbia University Press.

Yang, Lu. 2012. "Urban Dibao Program: Targeting and Its Effect." http://iple.cass.cn/upload/2012/03/d20120305153105006.pdf.

Yang, Mayfair Mei-Hui. 1989. "The gift economy and state power in China." *Comparative Studies in Society and History* 31(1):25–54.

Yau, Oliver. 1988. "Chinese cultural values: their dimensions and marketing implications." *European Journal of Marketing* 22(5):44–57.

Yong, Hu. 2005. "Blogs in China. China Media Project Case Study." Beijing: Peking University.

Yörük, Erdem. 2012. "Welfare provision as political containment: the politics of social assistance and the Kurdish conflict in Turkey." *Politics & Society* 40(4):517–547.

Young, Lauren E. 2017. "Mobilization under threat: emotional appeals and dissent in autocracy." Working Paper.

Young, Lauren E. 2019. "The psychology of state repression: fear and dissent decisions in Zimbabwe." *American Political Science Review* 113(1):140–155.

Yu, Keping. 2011. "Civil society in China: concepts, classification and institutional environment." In *State and Civil Society: the Chinese Perspective*, ed. Zhenglai Deng. Singapore: World Scientific Publishing, pp. 88–89.

Yum, June Ock. 1988. "The impact of Confucianism on interpersonal relationships and communication patterns in East Asia." *Communications Monographs* 55(4):374–388.

Zenz, Adrian. 2019. "'Thoroughly reforming them towards a healthy heart attitude': China's political re-education campaign in Xinjiang." *Central Asian Survey* 38(1):102–128.

Zhang, Amei. 1997. *Poverty Alleviation in China: Commitment, Policies and Expenditures*. United Nations Development Programme, Occasional Paper 27.

Zhang, Han, and Jennifer Pan. 2019. "CASM: a deep-learning approach for identifying collective action events with text and image data from social media." *Sociological Methodology* 49(1):1–57.

Zheng, Wang. 2005. "State feminism? gender and socialist state formation in Maoist China." *Feminist Studies* 31(3):519–551.

Zhou, Baogang. 2008. *Shehui Zhuanxingqi Qunti Xing Shijian Yufang, Chuzhi Gongzuo Fanglue [Strategies for Preventing and Managing Mass Incidents During the Reform Period]*. Beijing: People's Public Security University Press.

Zhou, Jingbo, Hongbin Pei, and Haishan Wu. 2018. "Early warning of human crowds based on query data from Baidu maps: analysis based on Shanghai stampede." In *Big Data Support of Urban Planning and Management*, eds. Zhenjiang Shen and Miaoyi Li. New York: Springer, pp. 19–41.

Zipf, George. 1941. *National Unity and Disunity. The Nation As a Bio-Social Organism*. Grand Rapids: Principia Press.

Zuboff, Shoshana. 2015. "Big other: surveillance capitalism and the prospects of an information civilization." *Journal of Information Technology* 30(1):75–89.

Zucco, Cesar. 2013. "When payouts pay off: conditional cash transfers and voting behavior in brazil 2002–10." *American Journal of Political Science* 57(4):810–822.

Zurawski, Nils. 2004. "'I know where you live!'–aspects of watching, surveillance and social control in a conflict zone (Northern Ireland)." *Surveillance & Society* 2(4).

Index

Tables, figures and footnotes are indicated by t, f and n following the page number.